CRITICAL ESSAYS

By the same author:

On Racine
Writing Degree Zero
Elements of Semiology
S/Z
Mythologies

ROLAND BARTHES

CRITICAL ESSAYS

Translated from the French
by Richard Howard

NORTHWESTERN UNIVERSITY PRESS

EVANSTON 1972

Originally published in French
under the title *Essais critiques,*
copyright © 1964 by Editions du Seuil

Roland Barthes is Directeur d'Etudes of the Ecole
Pratique des Hautes Etudes, where he conducts semi-
nars on the sociologies of signs and collective representations. He is a frequent visitor to the United
States, where he has taught in many universities. His
most recent book is a study of Japan.

Poet-critic Richard Howard won the Pulitzer Prize
for *Untitled Subjects,* one of four collections of his
poems; he has translated over 150 French works.

To François Braunschweig

CONTENTS

CONTENTS

TRANSLATOR'S NOTE

The essays in this volume were written during the years that its author's first four books (*Le Degré zéro de l'écriture*, 1953, translated here in 1968; *Michelet*, 1954; *Mythologies*, 1957; *Sur Racine*, 1963, translated here in 1964) were published in France; they chart the course of Barthes's criticism from the vocabularies of existentialism and Marxism (reflections on the social situation of literature and the writer's responsibility before History) to a psychoanalysis of substances (after Bachelard) and a psychoanalytical anthropology (which evidently brought Barthes to his present terms of understanding with Lévi-Strauss and Lacan). Most of the work in *Critical Essays* marks an apparently decisive conversion to structuralism understood in its strictest sense, whereby literature and social life are regarded as "no more than" languages, to be studied not in their content but in their structure, as pure relational systems.

It is not the translator's concern to assess the merit of Barthes's decision; it *is* my concern, of course, to suggest a certain sympathy with the work in English, though I hope my endeavor enforces that sympathy in and of itself. It will be seen, opening this book to any of its thirty-four essays, that Barthes, a writer of great persuasion and power, characteristically "runs" to a very long sentence, a rumination held together by colons and various signs of equivalence ("in other words," "i.e.," "in short"); clearly he is reluctant to let his sentence go until, like Jacob's angel, it turns and blesses him. That blessing is idiosyncratic—one hears the man's voice throughout, intimate but not personal, responsible but not officious, convincing but not accusatory, and at first glance these long chains of colons may seem merely willful. But this is not the case, *as we must read the book through to know.* For despite its circumstantial genesis, *Critical Essays* is what historians used to call a progress, an integral occasion of growth, the account of a mind changing; hence its apprehension of *membership* (it is the colon's literal task: a colonizing of pertinence) is crucial to its goal. To invert Buffon, *l'homme, c'est le style.*

This book, then, is a narrative—heuristic, demonstrative, significant—of the way a discursive writer has become just that: by respecting surfaces as well as depths, by submitting to (and so being exalted by) the responsibility of forms. I claim the stature of a great critic for Roland Barthes on the basis of three achievements, all registered many times over in this book: he recognizes the distinction of the work of his own time; he refreshes the terms by which we come to the work of the past; and he recovers for literature new relations—recognizing what had appeared to be *beyond the pale*—with what is *not* literature: our lives.

RICHARD HOWARD

PREFACE

Collecting here texts published as prefaces or articles during the last decade, their author would gladly elaborate upon the life and times which have produced them, but cannot: he is too certain that the retrospective is never anything but a category of bad faith. Writing must go hand in hand with silence; to write is in a sense to become "still as death," to become someone to whom *the last word* is denied; to write is to offer others, from the start, that last word.

For the meaning of a work (or of a text) cannot be created by the work alone; the author never produces anything but presumptions of meaning, forms, and it is the world which fills them. The texts which follow are like the links of a chain of meaning, but this chain is unattached. Who will fasten it, give it a definitive meaning? Time perhaps: to collect old texts in a new book is an attempt to question time, to solicit time to give its answer to the fragments which come from the past; but time is double—the time of writing and the time of memory—and this duplicity evokes in its turn a subsequent meaning: time itself is a form. Today I may discuss Brechtism or the "new novel" (since these movements occupy the first series of these *Essays*) in semantic terms (since that is where my present language is to be found) and thereby attempt to justify a certain itinerary of my times or of myself, to give it the aspect of an intelligible destiny, but I shall never rule out the possibility that this panoramic language may be apprehended by the word of someone else—who will perhaps be myself. There is an infinite circularity of languages: here is a slender segment of the circle.

By which I mean that even if it is his function to discuss the language of others in such a way that he apparently (and sometimes abusively) seeks to conclude it, the critic, like the writer, never has the last word. Further, that final silence which constitutes their common condition is what reveals the critic's true identity: the critic is a writer. Which is a supposition of being, not of value; the critic does not ask to be conceded a "vision" or a "style," but only to be granted the right to a certain discourse, which is *indirect discourse.*

What is given to a man who rereads himself is not a meaning but an infidelity, or rather: the meaning of an infidelity. This meaning, which we must always come back to, is that writing is never anything but a language, a formal system (whatever truth animates it); at a certain moment (which is perhaps the moment of our deepest crises, whose sole relation to what we say is to change its rhythm), this language can always be spoken by another language; to write (in the course of time) is to seek to discover *the largest language,* the language which is the form of all the others. The writer is a public experimenter: he varies what he recommences; persistent, faithless, he knows only one art: that of theme and variations. On the side of the variations will be found his battles, his values, his ideologies, his times, his desire to live, to know, to participate, to speak, in short his *content;* but on the side of the theme will be found the persistence of *forms,* the great signifying function of the imaginary, which is to say the very intelligence of the world. Only, contrary to what happens in music, each of the writer's variations is itself taken for an authentic theme, whose meaning is immediate and definitive. This mistake is not a slight one; it constitutes literature itself, and more precisely that infinite dialogue between criticism and the work, so that literary time is both the time of authors who advance and the time of criticism which catches up with them—less to give a meaning to the enigmatic work than to destroy those meanings by which it is immediately and forever encumbered.

There is perhaps another reason for the writer's infidelity: writing is an activity; from the point of view of the man writing, it exhausts itself in a succession of practical operations; the writer's time is operative, not historical; it has only an ambiguous relation to the evolutive time of ideas, whose movement it does not share. The tenses of writing are in fact defective: to write is either to project or to terminate, but never to "express"; between beginning and end, a link is missing, which may yet pass for essential, the link of the work itself; one writes perhaps less to materialize an idea than to exhaust a task which bears within itself its own satisfaction. There is a kind of literary vocation in *liquidation*; and though the world always restores his work to him as a motionless object, provided once and for all with a stable meaning, the writer himself cannot experience his work as a basis, but rather as a necessary abandonment: the present of writing is already past, its past always pluperfect; yet it is just when he detaches himself from that past "dogmatically" (by a refusal to inherit, a refusal to be faithful), that the world asks the writer to take responsibility for his work; for social ethics require of him a fidelity to content, whereas he knows only a fidelity to form: what binds him (in his own eyes) is not what he has written but the persistent decision to write it.

The material text (the Book) may therefore have from its author's point of view, an inessential and even to a certain degree an inauthentic character. Hence we often find works which are, by a fundamental ruse, nothing but their own project: the work is written by seeking the work, which begins fictively when it is terminated practically. Is this not the meaning of A *la recherche du temps perdu*—to present the image of a book which is written exclusively by seeking the Book? By an illogical twist of tense, the material work written by Proust thus occupies a strangely intermediary place in the Narrator's activity, situated between an impulse (*I want to write*) and a decision (*I will write*). This is because the writer's time is not a diachronic but an epic time; without present and without past, the writer is entirely given over to a transport, whose goal, if it could be known, would appear as unreal in the eyes of the world as were the romances of chivalry to the eyes of Don Quixote's contemporaries. Which is also why this active time of writing develops well within what is commonly called an *itinerary* (Don Quixote had none, though he was always in pursuit of the same thing). Indeed only epic man, the man of the house and of journeys, of love and of love affairs, can represent for us so faithful an infidelity.

A friend has just lost someone he loves, and I want to express my sympathy. I proceed to write him a letter. Yet the words I find do not satisfy me: they are "phrases": I make up "phrases" out of the most affectionate part of myself; I then realize that the message I want to send this friend, the message which is my sympathy itself, could after all be reduced to a simple word: *condolences.* Yet the very purpose of the communication is opposed to this, for it would be a cold and consequently inverted message, since what I want to communicate is the very warmth of my sympathy. I conclude that in order to correct my message (that is, in order for it to be exact), I must not only vary it, but also that this variation must be original and apparently invented.

This fatal succession of constraints will be recognized as literature itself (that my final message struggles to escape "literature" is merely an ultimate variation, a ruse of literature). Like my condolence note, everything written becomes a work only when it can vary, under certain conditions, an initial message (which, too, is perhaps: *I love, I suffer, I sympathize*). These conditions of variation are the Being of literature (what the Russian formalists called *literaturnost,* "literaturity"), and like my letter, they can finally refer only to the *originality* of the second message. Thus, far from being a vulgar critical notion (one inadmissible today), and provided it is conceived in informational terms (as present language permits), this originality is on the contrary the very basis of literature; for it is only by submitting to its law that I may communicate what I mean with exactitude; in literature as in private communication, to be least "false" I must be most "original," or, if you prefer, most "indirect."

Not that by being original I should be keeping closest to a kind of inspired creation, a kind of grace guaranteeing the truth of my utterance: what is spontaneous is not necessarily authentic. Rather, that first message which was to express my grief immediately, that pure message which would denote just what is in myself, is utopian; the language of others (and what other language could exist?) returns that message to me no less immediately decorated, burdened with an infinity of messages I do not want. My utterance can emerge only from a language: this Saussurean truth has a bearing beyond linguistics. By writing no more than *condolences*, I turn my sympathy into indifference, and the word exposes me as coldly respectful of a certain custom; by beginning a novel, "For a long time I used to go to bed early," however simple the utterance, Proust cannot keep the placement of the adverbial phrase, the use of the first person, the very inauguration of a discourse which will recount, or better still recite, a certain exploration of nocturnal time and space, from developing, already, a second message, which is a certain literature.

Whoever wants to write with exactitude must therefore proceed to the frontiers of language, and it is in this that he actually writes for others (if he spoke only to himself, a kind of spontaneous nomenclature of his feelings would suffice, for feeling is immediately its own name). Since ownership of language is impossible, the writer and the private individual (when he writes) are condemned from the start to *vary* their original messages and, since connotation is inevitable, to choose the best one, the one whose indirectness (however circuitous) least distorts not what they want to say but what they want to make understood; the writer (the friend) is therefore a man for whom speaking is immediately listening to his own language; thus is constituted a received language (though it be a created one), which is the very language of literature. Writing is, then, on every level, the language of others, and we may see in this paradoxical reversal the writer's true "gift"; indeed that is where we must see it, this anticipation of language being the only (and the very fragile) moment when the writer (like the sympathizing friend) can make it understood that he is turning toward others; for no direct message can subsequently communicate that one sympathizes, except by falling back into the signs of compassion: only form permits us to escape the parody of feelings, because form is the very technique whose goal is to understand and to dominate the theater of language.

Originality is therefore the price which must be paid for the hope of being welcomed (and not merely understood) by your reader. As such it is a communication de luxe, many details being necessary to say little enough with any exactitude; but this luxury is a vital one, for once communication is effective (this is literature's profound tendency), banality becomes the heaviest of the threats which weigh upon it. It is because there is a banality anxiety (an anxiety, for literature, with regard to its own death) that literature ceaselessly codifies, by means of its history, its secondary information (its connotation) and inscribes it within certain security margins. Thus we find schools and periods assigning to literary communication a controlled zone, limited on one side by the obligation of a "varied" language and on the other by the closing of that variation, in the form of an acknowledged corpus of figures; this zone, a vital one, is called rhetoric, whose double function is to keep literature from being transformed into the sign of banality (if too direct) and into the sign of originality (if too indirect). The frontiers of rhetoric may widen or narrow, from Gongorism to stenography, but it is certain that rhetoric, which is nothing but the technique of exact information, is linked not only to all literature but even to all communication, once it seeks to make others understand that we acknowledge them: rhetoric is the amorous dimension of writing.

This original message which we must vary in order to make it exact is always what burns within us; there is no other primary *significatum* in literary work than a certain desire: to write is a mode of Eros. But initially this desire has at its disposal no more than a poor and platitudinous language; the affectivity which is at the heart of all literature includes only an absurdly restricted number of functions: *I desire, I suffer, I am angry, I contest, I love, I want to be loved, I am afraid to die*—out of this we must make an infinite literature. Affectivity is banal, or, if you prefer, typical, and this circumstance governs the whole Being of literature; for if the desire to write is merely the constellation of several persistent figures, what is left to the writer is no more than an activity of variation and combination: there are never creators, nothing but combiners, and literature is like the ship Argo whose long history admitted of no creation, nothing but combinations; bracketed with an unchanging function, each piece was nonetheless endlessly renewed, without the whole ever ceasing to be the Argo.

No one, then, can write without passionately taking sides (whatever the apparent detachment of his message) as to all that happens or does not happen in the world; human joys and miseries, what they provoke in us, indignation, judgment, assent, dreams, desires, anxieties—all that is the sole substance of signs; but this power which at first seems inexpressible to us, being so primary, this power is from the start only the named. We are brought back once more to the harsh law of human communication: the original is itself merely the most platitudinous of languages, and it is out of our extreme poverty, not our riches, that we speak of the ineffable. Now it is with this first language, this named, this overnamed language, that literature must do battle: the primary substance of literature is not the unnamable, but on the contrary the named; the man who wants to write must know that he is beginning a long concubinage with a language which is always *previous*. The writer does not "wrest" speech from silence, as we are told in pious literary hagiographies, but inversely, and how much more arduously, more cruelly and less gloriously, detaches a secondary language from the slime of primary languages afforded him by the world, history, his existence, in short by an intelligibility which preexists him, for he comes into a world full of language, and there is no reality not already classified by men: to be born is nothing but to find this code ready-made and to be obliged to accommodate oneself to it. We often hear it said that it is the task of art to *express the inexpressible*; it is the contrary which must be said (with no intention of paradox): the whole task of art is to *unexpress the expressible*, to kidnap from the world's language, which is the poor and powerful language of the passions, another speech, an exact speech.

If this were not the case, if the writer's true function were to give a first voice to something before language, on the one hand he could articulate only an infinite repetition, for the imaginary is poor (it is enriched only if we combine the figures constituting it, rare and meager figures, torrential though they seem to our experience); and on the other, literature would have no need of what has nonetheless always instituted it: a technique; for there cannot be a technique (an art) of creation, but only of variation and of arrangement. Thus we find the techniques of literature, so numerous down through history (though they have been poorly counted and classified), all employed to distance the namable they are doomed to double, to repeat. These techniques are, among others: *rhetoric*, which is the art of varying the banal by recourse to substitutions and displacements of meaning; *articulation*, which makes it possible to give a single message the extent of an infinite peripety (in a novel, for example); *irony*, which is the form the author gives to his own detachment; *fragmentation* or, one might say, *reticence*, which makes it possible to hold back meaning in order to let it spread in the directions open to it. All these techniques, results of the writer's necessity to start from a world and a self which the world and the self have already encumbered with a name, seek to institute an indirect language, in other words a language at once persistent (provided with a goal) and circuitous (accepting infinitely varied stations). This is, as we have seen, an epic situation; but it is also an "Orphic" situation: not because Orpheus "sings," but because the writer and Orpheus are both under the same prohibition, which constitutes their "song": the prohibition from turning back toward what they love.

When Mme Verdurin pointed out to Brichot that he used "I" too much in his war articles, the pedant changed all his "I's" to "one's," "but 'one's' did not prevent the reader from seeing that the writer was speaking about himself, and enabled him never to cease speaking about himself . . . always under the shelter of 'one.'" Grotesque, Brichot is nonetheless the writer;

all the personal categories the writer employs, more numerous than those of grammar, are no more than attempts to give his own person the status of a true sign; the problem, for the writer, is indeed neither to express nor to mask his "I" (Brichot naïvely failed in the attempt, and had moreover no desire to succeed), but to shelter it—that is, at once to caution and to domicile it. Now the instituting of a code generally corresponds to this double necessity: what the writer wants is precisely to transform his "I" into a fragment of a code. Here, once again, we must enter the technique of meaning, and linguistics, once again, will help us do so.

Roman Jakobson, borrowing an expression from Peirce, sees "I" as an indexical symbol; as a symbol, "I" belongs to a particular code, different from one language to the next ("I" becomes *ego, je, ich* according to the codes of Latin, French, German); as an index, it refers to an existential situation, that of the speaker, which is in truth its only meaning, for "I" is entirely and exclusively the person who says "I." In other terms, "I" cannot be defined lexically (except by resorting to expedients such as "the first person singular"), yet it participates in a lexicon (that of English, for example); in it, the message "straddles" the code, it is a shifter, a translator; of all the signs it is the most difficult to use, since the child acquires it last of all and the aphasiac loses it first.

In the second degree, which is always that of literature, the writer, confronted with "I," is in the same situation as the child or the aphasiac, depending on whether he is a novelist or a critic. Like the child who says his own name when speaking of himself, the novelist designates himself through an infinity of third persons; but this designation is in no way a disguise, a projection, or a distance (the child does not disguise himself, dream himself, or alienate himself); it is on the contrary an immediate operation, conducted openly, imperiously (nothing clearer than Brichot's "one's"), an operation the writer requires in order to utter himself through a normal (and no longer "straddling") message, resulting entirely from the code of others, so that to write, far from referring to an "expression" of subjectivity, is on the contrary the very act which converts the indexical symbol into a pure sign. The third person is therefore not a ruse of literature, it is its act of institution previous to every other: to write is to decide to say "he" (and the power to do so). Thus when the writer says "I" (which happens often), this pronoun no longer has anything to do with an indexical symbol, it is a subtly coded mark: *this* "I" is nothing but a "he" to the second degree, a reversed "he" (as the analysis of the Proustian *"je"* would prove). Like the aphasiac, the critic, on the other hand, deprived of any pronoun, can employ only a breached discourse; incapable (or disdainful) of transforming "I" into a sign, there is nothing left for him but to silence it through a kind of zero degree of the person. The critic's "I" is never in what he says, but in what he does not say, or rather in the very discontinuity which marks all critical discourse; perhaps his existence is too strong for him to constitute it as a sign, but perhaps, conversely, it is also too verbal, too steeped in culture, for him to leave it in the state of an indexical symbol. The critic would be the man who cannot produce the "he" of the novel, but who also cannot cast the "I" into pure private life, i.e., renounce writing: he is an aphasiac of "I," while the rest of his language subsists, intact, marked however by the infinite detours imposed upon speech (as in the aphasiac's case) by the constant blockage of a certain sign.

We might even take the comparison further. If the novelist, like the child, decides to codify his "I" in the form of a third person, it is because this "I" does not yet have a history, or because the decision has been made not to give it one. Every novel is a dawn, which is why the novel is, it would seem, the very form of *wanting-to-write*. For just as by speaking of himself in the third person the child experiences that fragile moment when the adult language presents itself to him as a perfect institution which no impure symbol (half-code, half-message) as yet corrupts or disturbs, so it is in order to encounter others that the novelist's "I" takes shelter under "he," that is, under a complete code in which existence does not yet straddle the sign. Conversely, a shadow of the past is invested in the critic's aphasia with regard to "I"; his "I" is too heavy with time for him to be able to renounce it and to bestow it upon the integral code of others (need we point out that the Proustian novel is possible only when time is suspended); unable to abandon this mute face of the symbol, the critic "forgets" the symbol itself in its entirety, like the aphasiac who, also, can destroy his language only insofar as this language has been. Thus, while the novelist is a man who manages to infantilize his "I" until it joins the adult code of others, the critic is a man who ages his "I," who imprisons, preserves, and forgets it, until he withdraws it, intact and incommunicable, from the code of literature.

What marks the critic is therefore a secret practice of the indirect: in order to remain secret, the indirect must here take shelter under the very figures of the direct, of transitivity, of discourse about others. Whence a language which cannot be received as ambiguous, reticent, allusive, or disclaiming. The critic is like a logician who "fills" his functions with true arguments and yet secretly asks us to appreciate only the validity of his equations, not their truth—even while hoping, by a final silent ruse, that this pure validity will function as the very sign of his existence.

There is, then, a certain misapprehension attached by its very structure to the critical work, but this misapprehension cannot be exposed in the critical language itself, for such exposure would constitute a new direct form, in other words an additional mask; in order for the circle to be broken, for the critic to speak of himself with exactitude, he would have to transform himself into a novelist, that is, to substitute for the direct falseness under which he takes shelter, a declared indirectness—declared as the indirectness of all fictions is declared.

This is doubtless why the novel is always the critic's horizon: the critic is the man who is going to write and who, like the Proustian narrator, satisfies this expectation with a supplementary work, who creates himself by seeking himself and whose function is to accomplish his project of writing even while eluding it. The critic is a writer, but a writer postponed; like the writer, he wants to be believed less because of what he writes than because of his decision to write it; but unlike the writer, he cannot *sign* that desire; he remains condemned to error—to truth.

1963

CRITICAL ESSAYS

The World as Object

Hanging in the Dutch museums are works by a minor
master who may be as deserving of literary renown as
Vermeer. Saenredam painted neither faces nor objects,
but chiefly vacant church interiors, reduced to the beige and
innocuous unction of butterscotch ice cream. These churches,
where there is nothing to be seen but expanses of wood and
whitewashed plaster, are irremediably unpeopled, and this negation goes much further than the destruction of idols. Never
has nothingness been so confident. Saenredam's sugary, stubborn surfaces calmly reject the Italian overpopulation of stat-
ues, as well as the horror vacui professed by other Dutch painters. Saenredam is in effect a painter of the absurd; he has
achieved a privative state of the subject, more insidious than
the dislocations of our contemporaries. To paint so lovingly
these meaningless surfaces, and to paint nothing else—that is already a "modern" esthetic of silence.

Saenredam is a paradox: he articulates by antithesis the nature of classical Dutch painting, which has washed away religion only to replace it with man and his empire of things.
Where once the Virgin presided over ranks of angels, man
stands now, his feet upon the thousand objects of everyday

life, triumphantly surrounded by his functions. Behold him, then, at the pinnacle of history, knowing no other fate than a gradual appropriation of matter. No limits to this humanization, and above all, no horizon: in the great Dutch seascapes (Cappelle's or Van de Venne's), the ships are crammed with people or cargo, the water is a ground you could walk on, the sea completely urbanized. A foundering vessel is always close to a shore covered with men and help; the human, here, is a virtue of numbers. As if the destiny of the Dutch landscape is to swarm with men, to be transformed from an elemental infinity to the plenitude of the registry office. This canal, this mill, these trees, these birds (Essaias van de Velde's) are linked by a crowded ferry; the overloaded boat connects the two shores and thus closes the movement of trees and water by the intention of a human movement, reducing these forces of nature to the rank of objects and transforming the Creation into a facility. In the season most contrary to mankind, during one of those savage winters only history describes, Ruysdael still manages to put in a bridge, a house, a man walking down the road; the first warm spring shower is still a long way off, yet this man walking is actually the seed in the earth, for man himself is the seed, stubbornly pushing through this huge ocher sheet.

Here, then, men inscribe themselves upon space, immediately covering it with familiar gestures, memories, customs, and intentions. They establish themselves by means of a path, a mill, a frozen canal, and as soon as they can they arrange their objects in space as in a room; everything in them tends toward the *habitat* pure and simple: it is their heaven. There has been (eloquent) testimony to the domiciliary power of the Dutch canal boat; sturdy, securely decked, concave, it is as full as an egg and produces the egg's felicity: an absence of the void. Consider the Dutch still life: the object is never alone, and never privileged; it is merely there, among many others, painted between one function and another, participating in the disorder of the movements which have picked it up, put it down—in a word, *utilized*. There are objects wherever you look, on the tables, the walls, the floor: pots, pitchers overturned, a clutter of baskets, a bunch of vegetables, a brace of game, milk pans, oyster shells, glasses, cradles. All this is man's space; in it he measures himself and determines his humanity, starting from the memory of his gestures: his *chronos* is covered by functions, there is no other authority in his life but the one he imprints upon the inert by shaping and manipulating it.

This universe of fabrication obviously excludes terror, as it excludes style. The concern of the Dutch painters is not to rid the object of its qualities in order to liberate its essence but, quite the contrary, to accumulate the secondary vibrations of appearance, for what must be incorporated into human space are layers of air, surfaces, and not forms or ideas. The only logical issue of such painting is to coat substance with a kind of glaze against which man may move without impairing the object's usefulness. Still-life painters like Van de Velde or Heda always render matter's most superficial quality: *sheen*. Oysters, lemon pulp, heavy goblets full of dark wine, long clay pipes, gleaming chestnuts, pottery, tarnished metal cups, three grape seeds—what can be the justification of such an assemblage if not to lubricate man's gaze amid his domain, to facilitate his daily business among objects whose riddle is dissolved and which are no longer anything but easy surfaces?

An object's *use* can only help dissipate its essential form and emphasize instead its attributes. Other arts, other ages may have pursued, under the name of style, the essential core of things; here, nothing of the kind: each object is accompanied by its adjectives, substance is buried under its myriad qualities, man never confronts the object, which remains dutifully subjugated to him by precisely what it is assigned to provide. What need have I of the lemon's principial form? What my quite empirical humanity needs is a lemon ready for use, half-peeled, half-sliced, half-lemon, half-juice, caught at the precious moment it exchanges the scandal of its perfect and useless ellipse for the first of its economic qualities, astringency. The object is always open, exposed, accompanied, until it has destroyed itself as closed substance, until it has cashed in all the functional virtues man can derive from stubborn matter. I regard the Dutch "kitchen scenes" (Buelkelaer's, for instance) less as a nation's indulgence of its own appetites (which would be more Belgian than Dutch; patricians like Ruyter and Tromp ate meat only once a week) than as a series of explanations concerning the *instrumentality* of foodstuffs: the units of nourishment are always destroyed as still lifes and restored as moments of a domestic *chronos*; whether it is the crisp green-ness of cucumbers or the pallor of plucked fowls, everywhere the object offers man its *utilized* aspect, not its principial form. Here, in other words, is never a generic state of the object, but only circumstantial states.

Behold then a real transformation of the object, which no longer has an essence but takes refuge entirely within its at-tributes. A more complete subservience of things is unimagi-nable. The entire city of Amsterdam, indeed, seems to have been built with a view to this domestication: few substances here are not annexed to the empire of merchandise. Take the rubble in the corner of a vacant lot or near a railroad siding—what seems more indescribable: not an object, but an element! Yet in Amsterdam, consider this same rubble sifted and loaded onto a barge, led through the canals—you will see objects as clearly defined as cheeses, crates, vats, logs. Add to the vehicu-lar movement of the water the vertical plane of the houses which retain, absorb, interpose, or restore the merchandise: that whole concert of pulleys, chutes, and docks effects a permanent mobilization of the most shapeless substances. Each house—narrow, flat, tilting forward as though to meet the merchandise halfway—suddenly opens at the top: here, push-ing up into the sky, is nothing more than a kind of mystical mouth, the attic, as if each human habitat were merely the rising path of storage, hoarding, that great ancestral gesture of animals and children. As the city is built on water, there are no cellars, everything is taken up to the attic, raised there from outside. Thus objects interrupt every horizon, glide along the water and along the walls. It is objects which articulate space.

The object is by and large constituted by this mobility. Hence the defining power of all these Dutch canals. What we have, clearly, is a water-merchandise complex; it is water which makes the object, giving it all the nuances of a calm, planar mobility, collecting supplies, shifting them without perceptible transition from one exchange to another, making the entire city into a census of agile goods. Take a look at the canals of another minor master, Berckheyde, who has painted virtually nothing but this mild traffic of ownership: everything is, for the object, a means of procession; this bit of wharf is a cynosure of kegs, logs, tarpaulins; man has only to overturn or to hoist; space, obedient creature, does the rest—carries back and forth, selects, distributes, recovers, seems to have no other goal than to complete the projected movement of all these things, separated from matter by the sleek, firm film of *use*; here all objects are prepared for manipulation, all have the detachment and the density of Dutch cheeses: round, waxed, prehensible.

This separation is the extreme limit of the concrete, and I know only one French work which can claim to equal in its itemizing power that of the Dutch canals—our Civil Code. Consider the list of real estate and chattels: "domestic pigeons, wild rabbits, beehives, pond fish, wine presses, stills, ovens, manure and stable litter, wall hangings, mirrors, books and medals, linens, weapons, seeds, wines, hay," etc. Is this not exactly the universe of Dutch painting? Each represents the triumph of an entirely self-sufficient nominalism. Every definition and every manipulation of property produce an art of the catalogue, in other words, of the concrete itself, divided, countable, mobile. The Dutch scenes require a gradual and complete reading; we must begin at one edge and finish at the other, audit the painting like an accountant, not forgetting this corner, that margin, that background, in which is inscribed yet another perfectly rendered object adding its unit to this patient weighing of property or of merchandise.

When applied to social groups regarded by the period as inferior, this enumerative power constitutes certain men as objects. Van Ostade's peasants or Averkamp's skaters are entitled only to the existence of number, and the scenes grouping them must be read not as a repertory of fully human gestures, but rather as an anecdotic catalogue dividing and combining the various elements of a prehumanity; we must decipher the scene the way we read a puzzle. This is because Dutch painting obviously deals with two anthropologies, as distinctly separated as Linnaeus' zoological classes. It is no accident that the word "class" applies to both notions: there is the patrician class (*homo patricius*) and the peasant class (*homo paganicus*), and each encompasses human beings not only of the same social condition but also of the same morphology.

Van Ostade's peasants have abortive, shapeless faces; as if they were unfinished creatures, rough drafts of men, arrested at an earlier stage of human development. Even the children have neither age nor sex; they are identified only by their size. As the ape is separated from man, here the peasant is separated from the burgher precisely insofar as he is deprived of the ultimate characteristics of humanity, those of the *person*. This subclass of men is never represented frontally, an attitude which presupposes at least a gaze: this privilege is reserved for the patrician or the cow, the Dutch totem animal and national provider. From the neck up, these peasants have only a blob which has not yet become a face, its lower part invariably slashed or blurred or somehow twisted askew; it is a shifting prehumanity which reels across space like so many objects endowed with an additional power of drunkenness or hilarity.

Turn now to the young patrician (Verspronck's, for example) frozen into the proposition of an idle god. He is an ultra-person, endowed with the extreme signs of humanity. Just as the peasant face falls short of creation, the patrician face achieves the ultimate degree of identity. This zoological class of rich Dutch burghers possesses, further, its characteristic features: chestnut hair, brown or plum-colored eyes, pinkish skin, prominent nose, soft red lips, and a play of fragile shadows round the salient points of the face. Virtually no portraits of women, except as regents of hospitals, dispensers of public funds, not private fun. Woman is assigned only an instrumental role, as an administrator of charity or a guardian of domestic economy. Man, and man alone, is human. Hence all Dutch painting—still lifes, seascapes, peasant scenes, regents—culminate in a purely masculine iconography whose obsessive expression is the guild portrait.

The guilds or *Doelen* are the subject of so many paintings that we cannot help suspecting the presence of a myth. The *Doelen* are rather like Italian Madonnas, Greek ephebes, Egyptian pharaohs, or German fugues—a classical theme which indicates to the artist the limits of nature. And just as all Madonnas, all ephebes, all pharaohs, and all fugues are somewhat alike, all guild faces are isomorphic. Here, once again, is proof that the face is a social sign, that there is a possible history of faces, and that the most direct product of nature is as subject to process and to signification as the most socialized institutions.

In the guild portraits, one thing is striking: the great size of the heads, the lighting, the excessive truth of the face. The face becomes a kind of hothouse flower, brought to perfection by careful forcing. All these faces are treated as units of one and the same horticultural species, combining generic resemblance and individual identity. There are huge fleshy blooms (Hals) or tawny nebulae (Rembrandt), but this universality has nothing to do with the glabrous neutrality of medieval portraits, which are entirely accessible, ready to receive the signs of the soul, and not those of the person: pain, joy, piety, and pity, a whole fleshless iconography of the passions. The similarity of faces in medieval art is of an ontological order, that of the *Doelen* portraits of a genetic one. A social class unequivocally defined by its economy (identity of commercial function, after all, justifies these guild paintings) is here presented in its anthropological aspect, and this aspect has nothing to do with the secondary characteristics of the physiognomy: it is not because of their seriousness or their confidence that these heads look alike, contrary to socialist-realist portraits, for example, which unify a representation of the workers, say, under a single sign of virility and tension (this is the method of a primitive art). Here the matrix of the human face is not of an ethical order, it is of a carnal order; it consists not of a community of intentions, but of an identity of blood and food; it is formed after a long sedimentation which has accumulated all the characteristics of a social particularity within a class: age, size, morphology, wrinkles, veins, the very order of biology separates the patrician caste from the functional substance (objects, peasants, landscapes) and imprisons it within its own authority.

Entirely identified by their social heredity, these Dutch faces are engaged in none of those visceral adventures which ravage the countenance and expose the body in its momentary destitution. What have they to do with the *chronos* of passion? Theirs is the *chronos* of biology; their flesh has no need, in order to exist, to anticipate or to endure events; it is blood which causes it to be and to command recognition; passion would be pointless, it would add nothing to existence. Consider the exception: Rembrandt's David does not weep, but half veils his head in a curtain; to close the eyes is to close the world, and in all Dutch painting no scene is more aberrant. This is because for once man is endowed with an adjectival quality; he slips from being to having, rejoins a humanity at grips with something else. If we could consider a painting out of the context of its technical or esthetic rules, there would be no difference between a tearful fifteenth-century *Pietà* and some combative Lenin of contemporary Soviet imagery; for in either case, an attribute is provided, not an identity. This is precisely the converse of the little cosmos of Dutch art, where objects exist only by their qualities, whereas man, and man alone, possesses existence-in-itself. A substantive world of man, an adjectival world of things: such is the order of a creation dedicated to contentment.

What is it then which distinguishes these men at the pinnacle of their empire? It is the *numen*. The ancient *numen* was that simple gesture by which divinity signified its decisions, disposing of human destiny by a sort of infralanguage consisting of pure demonstration. Omnipotence does not speak (perhaps because it does not think), it is content with gesture, even with a half-gesture, a hint of a gesture, swiftly absorbed into the slothful serenity of the Divine. The modern prototype of the *numen* might be that circumspect tension, mixed with lassitude and confidence, by which Michelangelo's God draws away from Adam after having created him, and with a suspended gesture assigns him his imminent humanity. Each time the ruling class is represented, it must expose its *numen* or else the painting would be unintelligible. Consider the hagiography of the First Empire: Napoleon is a purely numinous figure, unreal by the very convention of his gesture. At first, this gesture still exists: the emperor is never represented idle; he points or signifies or acts. But there is nothing human about his gesture; it is not the gesture of the workman, *homo faber*, whose functional movement encompasses him in search of its

own effect; it is a gesture immobilized in the least stable moment of its course; it is the idea of power, not its density, which
is thus eternalized. The hand which rises slightly or gently
comes to rest—the very suspension of movement—produces the
phantasmagoria of a power alien to man. The gesture creates,
it does not complete, and consequently its indication matters
more than its course. Consider *The Battle of Eylau* (a painting to remove from its context, if ever there was one): what
a difference in density between the excessive gestures of the
ordinary mortals—shouting, supporting a wounded man, cara-
coling rhetorically—and the waxy impasto of the emperor-God,
surrounded by motionless air, raising a hand huge with every
signification at once, designating everything and nothing,
creating with a terrible languor a future of unknown acts. This
exemplary painting shows us just how the *numen* is constituted: it *signifies* infinite movement yet does not accomplish
it, merely eternalizing the notion of power and not its substance in an embalmed gesture, a gesture arrested at the most
fragile point of its fatigue, imposing on the man who con-
templates and endures it the plenitude of an intelligible power.

Naturally, there is nothing warlike about the *numen* of these
merchants, these Dutch burghers at banquets or grouped
around a table to draw up their accounts, this class at once
social and zoological. How, then, does it impose its unreality?
By looking. It is the gaze which is the *numen* here, the gaze
which disturbs, intimidates, and makes man the ultimate term
of a problem. To be stared at by a portrait is always disconcerting. Nor is this a Dutch specialty. But here the gaze is collective; these men, even these lady regents virilized by age and
function, all these patricians rest upon you the full weight of
their smooth, bare faces. They are gathered together not to
count their money—which they never bother with, despite the
table, the ledger, the pile of gold—not to eat the food—
despite its abundance—but to look at you, thereby signifying
an existence and an authority beyond which you cannot go.
Their gaze is their proof and it is yours. Consider Rembrandt's
cloth merchants—one of them even stands up to get a better
look at you. You become a matter of capital, you are an element of humanity doomed to participate in a *numen* issuing

finally from man and not from God. There is no sadness and no cruelty in that gaze; it is a gaze without adjectives, it is only, completely, a gaze which neither judges you nor appeals to you; it posits you, implicates you, makes you exist. But this creative gesture is endless; you keep on being born, you are sustained, carried to the end of a movement which is one of infinite origin, source, and which appears in an eternal state of suspension. God and the emperor had the power of the hand, man has the gaze. All history reaches the grandeur of its own mystery in an endless look.

It is because the gaze of the *Doelen* institutes a final suspension of history, at the pinnacle of social happiness, that Dutch painting is not satiated, and that its class orientation culminates after all in something which also belongs to other men. What happens when men are, by their own means, content? What is left of man? The *Doelen* answer: a look is left. In this perfectly content patrician world, absolute master of matter and evidently rid of God, the gaze produces a strictly human interrogation and proposes an infinite postponement of history. There is, in these Dutch *Doelen*, the very contrary of a realistic art.

Consider Courbet's *Atelier:* it is a complete allegory. Shut up in a room, the artist is painting a landscape he does not see, turning his back to his (naked) model, who is watching him paint. In other words, the painter establishes himself in a space carefully emptied of any gaze but his own. Now, all art which has only two dimensions, that of the work and that of the spectator, can create only a platitude, since it is no more than the capture of a shopwindow spectacle by a painter-voyeur. Depth is born only at the moment the spectacle itself slowly turns its shadow toward man and begins to look at him.

1953

Objective Literature

On the pediment of the Gare Montparnasse is a huge
neon sign: BONS-KILOMÈTRES, several letters of which
are regularly out of commission. It would be a good
object for Robbe-Grillet, an object after his own heart, this
structure whose malfunctions can mysteriously change places
with each other from one day to the next.

Objects of this kind—extremely complicated, somewhat unstable—are numerous in Robbe-Grillet's work. They are generally objects taken from the urban environment (sidewalk
directories, professional-service signs, post-office notice boards,
electric gates, bridge superstructures) or from ordinary surroundings (light switches, reading glasses, percolators, dressmaker's dummies, packaged sandwiches). "Natural" objects
are rare (trees in the third "Reflected Vision," a bay in *The
Voyeur*), immediately alienated from man and nature, moreover, to become the mainstay of an "optical" reflection.

All these objects are described with an application apparently disproportionate to their, if not insignificant, at least
purely functional character. In Robbe-Grillet, description is
always anthological: it apprehends the object as in a mirror and
constitutes it before us as a spectacle; that is, the object is en-

titled to take up our time regardless of the appeals which the dialectic of the narrative may make to it. The indiscreet object remains *there*; it has the same freedom of exposition as one of Balzac's portraits, though not the same psychological necessity. Another characteristic of this description: it is never allusive, never distills from the sum of lines and substances a certain attribute meant to signify economically the entire nature of the object (Racine: "Dans l'Orient *désert*, quel devint mon ennui,"[1] or Hugo: "Londres, une *rumeur* sous une *fumée*"[2]). Robbe-Grillet's writing has no alibi, no density and no depth: it remains on the surface of the object and inspects it impartially, without favoring any particular quality: it is the exact opposite of poetic writing. Here the word does not explode, nor explore; its function is not to confront the object in order to pluck out of the heart of its substance an ambiguous, summarizing name: language here is not the rape of an abyss, but the rapture of a surface; it is meant to "paint" the object, in other words to caress it, to deposit little by little in the circuit of its space an entire chain of gradual names, none of which will exhaust it.

Yet Robbe-Grillet's scrupulosity of description has nothing in common with the artisanal application of the naturalistic novelist. Traditional realism accumulates qualities as a function of an implicit judgment: its objects have shapes, but also odors, tactile properties, memories, analogies, in short they swarm with significations; they have a thousand modes of being perceived, and never with impunity, since they involve a human movement of disgust or appetite. Instead of this sensorial syncretism, at once anarchic and oriented, Robbe-Grillet imposes a unique order of apprehension: the sense of sight. The object is no longer a center of correspondences, a welter of sensations and symbols: it is merely an optical resistance.

This promotion of the visual involves singular consequences: primarily this, that Robbe-Grillet's object is not composed in depth; it does not protect a heart beneath its surface (and the literary man's traditional role has hitherto been to discern,

1. "In the *empty* East, how great my suffering grew."
2. "London, a *murmur* beneath a *fog*."

beneath the surface, the secret of objects); no, here the object does not exist beyond its phenomenon; it is not double, allegorical; we cannot even say that it is opaque, which would be to recover a dualistic nature. The minuteness with which Robbe-Grillet describes the object has nothing tendentious about it; it completely establishes the object, so that once its appearance is described, it is exhausted; if the author leaves it, he does so not out of submission to a rhetorical propriety, but because the object has no other resistance than that of its surfaces and, once these are "covered," language must withdraw from an encounter which could only be alien to the object, given over to poetry or eloquence. Robbe-Grillet's silence about the romantic heart of things is not an allusive or sacral silence, it is a silence which irremediably establishes the object's limit, not its aura: this slice of tomato in an automat sandwich, described according to Robbe-Grillet's method, constitutes an object without heredity, without associations and without references, a stubborn object rigorously enclosed within the order of its particles, suggestive of nothing but itself, and not involving its reader in a functional or substantial *elsewhere*. "The human condition," Heidegger has said, "is to be *there*." Robbe-Grillet himself quotes this remark apropos of *Waiting for Godot*, and it applies to his own objects as well. The author's entire art is to give the object a *Dasein*, a "being-there," and to strip it of "being-something."

Hence Robbe-Grillet's object has neither function nor substance. Or more precisely, both are absorbed by the object's optical nature. With regard to function, here is an example: So-and-so's dinner was ready—some ham. Such would be at least the adequate sign of the alimentary function. But Robbe-Grillet says: "On the kitchen table, there are three slices of ham laid on a white plate." Here function is cunningly usurped by the very existence of the object: thinness, position, color establish not so much an aliment as a complex space; and if the object is here the function of something, it is not the function of its natural destination (to be eaten) but of a visual itinerary, that of the murderer whose course is a passage from object to object, from surface to surface. As a matter of fact, the object contains a power of mystification: its technological nature, so to speak, is always immediately apparent, the sandwiches are food, the erasers instruments of deletion, the bridges structures for crossing; the object is never unfamiliar, it belongs, by its obvious function, to an urban or everyday setting. But the description persists beyond—just when we expect it to stop, having fulfilled the object's instrumentality, it holds like an inopportune pedal point and transforms the tool into space: its function was only illusory, it is its optical circuit which is real: its humanity begins where its use leaves off.

Substance suffers the same singular distortion. We must recall here that the "coenesthesia" of matter is at the heart of all romantic sensibility (in the broad sense of the word romantic: Jean-Pierre Richard has demonstrated this apropos of Flaubert and other nineteenth-century writers in his *Littérature et sensation*). For the romantic writer, we may establish a thematics of substance precisely to the degree that the object is not optical but tactile, thus involving his reader in a visceral experience of matter (appetite or nausea). In Robbe-Grillet, on the contrary, the promotion of the visual, the sacrifice of all the object's attributes to its "superficial" existence (we must note in passing the discredit traditionally attached to this mode of vision) suppresses any humoral relation to the object. Sight produces existential movements only insofar as it can be reduced to acts of palpation, manducation, or concealment. Now Robbe-Grillet never permits an encroachment upon the optical by the visceral, he pitilessly severs the visual from its extensions.

In Robbe-Grillet's work, I find only one metaphor, that is, a single adjective of substance, applied moreover to the one psychoanalytic object of his collection: the softness of erasers ("I'd like a very soft eraser"). Except for this tactile qualification, designated by the mysterious gratuitousness of the object, which gives the book its title as a scandal or a riddle, there is no thematics in Robbe-Grillet, for optical apprehension, which prevails everywhere else, cannot establish either correspondences or reductions, only symmetries.

By this tyrannical recourse to sight, Robbe-Grillet doubtless intends to assassinate the classical object. The task is an arduous one, for, without realizing it, our intimacy with the world, in literature, is of an organic and not a visual order. The first step of this well-planned murder is to isolate objects, to sever them from their function and from our biology. Robbe-Grillet leaves them only superficial links to situation and space; he removes any possibility of metaphor, cuts them off from that network of analogical forms or states which has always passed for the poet's privileged terrain (and we know how much the myth of poetic "power" has contaminated every order of literary creation).

But what is harder to kill in the classical object is the temptation of the singular and total adjective (the gestaltist adjective, one might say), which manages to bind all the object's metaphysical links (*Dans l'Orient désert* . . .). What Robbe-Grillet seeks to destroy is therefore the adjective: qualification is never, in his writing, anything but spatial, situational, in no case analogical. If we were to transpose this opposition to painting (with all the reservations such comparisons require), we might give, as an example of the classical object, some Dutch still life in which the minuteness of the details is completely subjugated by a dominant quality which transforms all the substances of vision into a single sensation of a visceral order: *sheen*, for example, is the manifest goal of all those compositions of oysters, glasses, wine, and metal, so numerous in Dutch art. Such painting seeks to endow the object with an adjectival skin: it is this half-visual, half-substantial glaze which we ingest by means of a kind of sixth sense, coenesthetic and no longer superficial. It is as if the painter managed to name the object with a warm, dizzying name which catches us up, draws us into its continuity, and implicates us in the homogeneous texture of an ideal substance, consisting of the superlative qualities of all possible substance. This is also the secret of the splendid Baudelairean rhetoric, in which each name, summoned from the most discrepant orders, deposits its tribute of ideal sensations in an ecumenical and somehow radiant perception of matter:

> Mais les bijoux perdus de l'antique Palmyre,
> Les métaux inconnus, les perles de la mer . . .[3]

3. "But the lost jewels of ancient Palmyra, unknown metals, pearls of the sea . . ."

Robbe-Grillet's description has its analogy, on the other hand, to modern painting (in the broad sense of the word modern), insofar as modern painting has abandoned the substantial qualification of space to propose instead a simultaneous reading of figurative planes, and to restore to the object its "essential core." Robbe-Grillet destroys the object's substantial dominance because it hampers his capital intention, which is to insert the object into a dialectics of space. Nor perhaps is this space Euclidean: the care with which the object is located by a kind of proliferation of planes, with which a singularly fragile point of resistance is found in the elasticity of our sight, has nothing to do with the classical concern for naming the directions of the picture.

It must be recalled that in classical description, the picture or scene is always a spectacle, a motionless site, frozen by eternity: the spectator (or the reader) has given the painter power of attorney to circulate around the object, to explore by a shifting gaze its shadows and what Poussin called its "prospect," to restore to it the simultaneity of all possible approaches. Whence the imaginary supremacy of the spectator's "situations" (expressed by the nominalism of the orientations: "on the right . . . on the left . . . in the foreground . . . in the background . . ."). Modern description, on the contrary, at least that of painting, arrests the viewer and releases the spectacle, adjusts it in several tenses to his vision; as we have already remarked, modern canvases leave the wall, they come to the spectator, oppress him with an aggressive space: the painting is no longer a "prospect," it is a "project." This is precisely the effect of Robbe-Grillet's descriptions: they set themselves in motion spatially, the object is released without thereby losing track of its initial positions, it assumes dimension without ceasing to be a plane. We recognize here the same revolution which the cinema has worked upon our visual reflexes.

In *The Erasers*, Robbe-Grillet has had the coquetry to include a scene in which man's relations with the new space are described in an exemplary fashion. Bona is sitting in the center of an empty, bare room, and he describes the spatial field before his eyes: that field (it includes the windowpane behind which appears a horizon of roofs) moves in front of the motionless man, space is "de-Euclidized" then and there. Robbe-Grillet has here reproduced the experimental conditions of cinematographic vision: the cubical room is the theater, its bareness is the darkness necessary for the emergence of the motionless vision, and the windowpane is the screen, flat and yet open to all the dimensions of movement, even to that of time.

Of course all this is not, for the most part, given so directly. Robbe-Grillet's descriptive machinery is in part a mystifying machinery. Witness his apparent application in arranging the elements of the scene according to a classical orientation of the fictive spectator. Like any traditional writer, he throws in a great many of those "on the right's" and "on the left's" whose motor role in classical composition we have just considered. And the fact is that these purely adverbial terms describe nothing: linguistically they are of a gestural order and have no more density than a cybernetic message. This has been, perhaps, the great illusion of classical rhetoric, to believe that the verbal orientation of a scene can have any power of suggestion or representation. In literary terms, which means outside of an operative order, these notions are interchangeable, hence strictly useless: they had no other reason than to justify the spectator's ideal mobility.

If Robbe-Grillet uses them, with the deliberation of a good artisan, it is in order to parody classical space, to disperse the concretion of substance, to dissolve it under the pressure of an overconstructed space. Robbe-Grillet's many specifications, his obsession with topography, his entire demonstrative machinery has the effect of destroying the object's unity by hypersituating it, so that initially substance is drowned under an accumulation of lines and orientations, and subsequently the abuse of planes, though endowed with classical denominations, explodes traditional space and substitutes for it a new space, furnished as we shall see with a temporal depth.

In short, Robbe-Grillet's descriptive operations can be summarized as follows: to destroy Baudelaire by a parodic recourse to Lamartine, and thereby, it goes without saying, to destroy Lamartine. (This comparison is not gratuitous, if we grant that our literary "sensibility" is entirely adjusted, by ancestral reflexes, to a "Lamartinean" vision of space.) Robbe-Grillet's patient analyses, scrupulous to the point of seeming a pastiche of Balzac or Flaubert, by their overprecision ceaselessly corrode the object, attack that adjectival film which classical art deposits on a picture, a scene, in order to induce in its spectator or reader the euphoria of a reconstituted unity. The classical object inevitably secretes its adjective (the Dutch sheen, the Racinean *désert*, the Baudelairean superlative substance): Robbe-Grillet opposes this inevitability, his analysis is an anticoagulant operation: at all costs, the object's carapace must be destroyed, the object must be kept open, available to its new dimension, time.

In order to grasp the object's temporal nature in Robbe-Grillet, we must observe the mutations he makes it undergo, and here again contrast the revolutionary nature of his attempt with the norms of classical description. The latter, certainly, has managed to submit its objects to forces of decay. But precisely: it is as if the object, long since constituted in its space or its substance, thereafter encountered a necessity descended from the empyrean; classical time has no other figure than that of a destroyer of perfection (Chronos and his scythe). In Balzac, in Flaubert, in Baudelaire, even in Proust (but in an inverted mode), the object is the vehicle of a melodrama; it decays, vanishes, or recovers a final glory, participates in short in a veritable eschatology of matter. One might say that the classical object is never anything but the archetype of its own ruin, which means setting against the object's spatial essence a subsequent (hence external) time functioning as a destiny and not as an internal dimension.

Classical time never encounters the object except as its catastrophe or deliquescence. Robbe-Grillet gives his objects an entirely different type of mutability. It is a mutability whose process is invisible: an object, first described at a moment of novelistic continuity, reappears later on, endowed with a scarcely perceptible difference. This difference is of a spatial, situational order (for instance, what was on the right is now on the left). Time dislocates space and constitutes the object as a series of slices which almost completely overlap each other: in that spatial "almost" lies the object's temporal dimension.

Objective Literature

This is a type of variation which we find in a cruder version in the movement of magic-lantern slides or of animated comic strips.

Now we can understand the profound reason why Robbe-Grillet has always reinstated the object in a purely optical fashion: sight is the only sense in which the continuous is an addition of tiny but integral fields: space can tolerate only *completed* variations: man never participates visually in the internal process of decay: however parceled out it may be, he sees only its effects. The object's optical institution is therefore the only kind which can comprehend a forgotten time in the object, grasped by its effect, not by its duration—that is, stripped of its pathos.

Robbe-Grillet's entire endeavor is therefore to invent for the object a space endowed in advance with its points of mutation, so that the object is dislocated rather than decayed. To return to my initial example, the neon sign on the Gare Montparnasse would be a good object for Robbe-Grillet insofar as the proposed complex is here of a purely optical order, consisting of a certain number of *emplacements* which have no freedom except to abolish themselves or to change places with each other. We may, on the other hand, readily imagine objects antipathetic to Robbe-Grillet's method: for example, a lump of sugar dipped in water and gradually dissolving (furnishing geographers their image of karst erosion): here the very continuity of decay would be intolerable to Robbe-Grillet's intention, since it reinstates a comminatory time and a contagious matter. On the contrary, Robbe-Grillet's objects never decay, they mystify or disappear: their time is never degradation or cataclysm: it is only change of place or concealment of elements.

As Robbe-Grillet has indicated in his "Reflected Visions," it is the accidents of reflexiveness which best account for this kind of break: it is enough to imagine that the motionless changes of orientation produced by mirror reflection are decomposed and dispersed throughout duration, in order to obtain the art of Robbe-Grillet itself. But of course the potential insertion of time into the vision of the object is ambiguous: Robbe-Grillet's objects have a temporal dimension, but it is not classical time they possess: it is an unfamiliar time, a time for nothing. One might say that Robbe-Grillet has restored time to the object; but it would be much better to say that he has restored a litotic time; or, more paradoxically but still more accurately: movement minus time.

I have no intention of attempting a plot analysis of *The Erasers* here; yet we must recall that this book is the story of a circular time which in a sense annihilates itself after having involved men and objects in an itinerary at whose end they are left *almost the same* as at the start. It is precisely as if the whole story were reflected in a mirror which puts on the left what is on the right and conversely, so that the "plot's" mutation is nothing more than a mirror reflection disposed over a twenty-four hour interval. Of course, for the return to be significant, the point of departure must be singular. Hence a kind of murder-mystery plot, in which the mirror vision's *almost-the-same* is a corpse's change of identity.

Evidently, the very plot of *The Erasers* merely writes large that same elliptical (or forgotten) time which Robbe-Grillet has introduced into his objects. We might call it mirror time. The demonstration is even more flagrant in *The Voyeur*, in which sidereal time, that of the tide, by modifying the land around a bay, represents the very gesture which causes the direct object to be succeeded by its reflected vision and joins the one to the other. The tide modifies the walker's visual field exactly as reflection reverses the orientation of a space. Except that while the tide is rising, the walker is on the island, absent from the actual duration of the mutation, and time is put between parentheses. This intermittent retreat is in fact the central act of Robbe-Grillet's experiments: to withdraw man from the fabrication or the becoming of objects, and to alienate finally the world from its surface.

Robbe-Grillet's endeavor is decisive insofar as it attacks the raw material of literature which still enjoyed a complete classical privilege: the object. Not that contemporary writers have not already dealt with it, and very effectively—one thinks of Cayrol and Ponge. But Robbe-Grillet's method has something more experimental about it; it aspires to an exhaustive interrogation of the object, from which any lyrical diversion is excluded. In order to encounter an analogous plenitude of treatment, we must turn to modern painting, must observe there the torment of a rational destruction of the classical object. Robbe-Grillet's importance is that he has attacked the last bastion of our traditional art of writing: the organization of literary space. His endeavor is equal in importance to that of surrealism against rationality, or of the *avant-garde* theater (Beckett, Ionesco, Adamov) against the bourgeois stage.

Only, his solution borrows nothing from these corresponding combats: his destruction of classical space is neither oneiric nor irrational; it is based instead on the idea of a new structure of matter and movement: its analogical basis is neither the Freudian nor the Newtonian universe; we must rather think of a mental complex derived from contemporary arts and sciences such as the new physics and the cinema. This can be only roughly indicated, for here as elsewhere what we lack is a history of forms.

And since we also lack an esthetic of the novel (that is, a history of its institution by the writer), we can only roughly indicate Robbe-Grillet's place in the novel's development. Here too we must recall the traditional background against which Robbe-Grillet's endeavor occurs: the novel long established as the experience of a depth: a social depth with Balzac and Zola, a "psychological" depth with Flaubert, a memorial depth with Proust—the novel has always determined its terrain as *interior* to man or society; and there has always been, in the novelist, a corresponding mission to excavate, to mine out. This endoscopic function, sustained by the concomitant myth of a human essence, has always been so natural to the novel that we are tempted to define its exercise (creation or consumption) as a delectation of the abyss.

Robbe-Grillet's endeavor (and that of some of his contemporaries: Cayrol and Pinget, for instance, though in altogether different modes) seeks to establish the novel on the surface: interiority is put in parentheses; objects, spaces, and man's circulation among them are promoted to the rank of subjects. The novel becomes a direct experience of man's surroundings, without this man's being able to fall back on a psychology, a metaphysic, or a psychoanalysis in order to approach the objective milieu he discovers. The novel, here, is no longer of a chthonic, infernal order, it is terrestrial: it teaches us to look at the world no longer with the eyes of a confessor, a physician, or of God—all significant hypostases of the classical novelist—but with the eyes of a man walking in his city with no other horizon but the spectacle before him, no other power than that of his own eyes.

1954

Baudelaire's Theater

What is interesting about Baudelaire's plays [1] is not their dramatic content but their embryonic state: the critic's role is therefore not to dissect these sketches for the image of an achieved theater but, on the contrary, to determine in them the vocation of their failure. It would be futile—and probably cruel to Baudelaire's memory —to imagine the plays these germs might have produced; it is not so to seek out the reasons which kept Baudelaire in this state of imperfect creation, so far from the esthetic of *Les Fleurs du mal.* How well Sartre has shown us that nonfulfill-

1. We know of four projects: the first, *Ideolus* (or *Manoel*) is an unfinished drama in alexandrines written about 1843 (Baudelaire was 22), in collaboration with Ernest Praron. The other three are scenarios: *La Fin de Don Juan* is little more than a plot outline; *Le Marquis du Ier Houzards* is a kind of historical drama in which Baudelaire planned to study the case of an *émigré's* son, Wolfgang de Cadolles, torn between the ideas of his parents and his enthusiasm for the emperor. *L'Ivrogne,* the most Baudelairean of these scenarios, is the story of a crime: a drunk and lazy workman pushes his wife down a well he then fills with cobblestones; the play was to develop the situation indicated in a poem from *Les Fleurs du mal, Le Vin de l'assassin.*

ment itself is a choice, and that to have projected a dramatic *oeuvre* without writing it was for Baudelaire a significant form of his fate.

One notion is essential to the understanding of Baudelairean theater: theatricality. What is theatricality? It is theater-minus-text, it is a density of signs and sensations built up on stage starting from the written argument; it is that ecumenical perception of sensuous artifice—gesture, tone, distance, substance, light—which submerges the text beneath the profusion of its external language. Of course theatricality must be present in the first written germ of a work, it is a datum of creation not of production. There is no great theater without a devouring theatricality—in Aeschylus, in Shakespeare, in Brecht, the written text is from the first carried along by the externality of bodies, of objects, of situations; the utterance immediately explodes into substances. One thing strikes us on the contrary in the three scenarios by Baudelaire (I set no store by *Ideolus*): these are purely narrative scenarios whose theatricality, even potentially, is very weak.

We must not let Baudelaire deceive us by such naïve indications as "very active, bustling production, great military pomp, settings of a poetic effect, fantastic statue, costumes of various nations," etc. This concern for externals, manifested intermittently, like a sudden remorse, affords no profound theatricality. Quite the contrary, it is the very generality of the Baudelairean impression which is alien to the theater: here, as elsewhere, Baudelaire is too intelligent; he substitutes concept for object, replaces the tavern of *L'Ivrogne* by the idea, the "atmosphere" of the tavern, offers the pure concept of military pomp instead of the materiality of flags or uniforms. Paradoxically, nothing attests better to impotence in the theater than this *total* character, somehow romantic, at least exotic, of vision. Each time Baudelaire refers to "production values," he sees them, naïvely, with a spectator's eye—in other words, fulfilled, static, ready-made, precooked and offering a seamless deception which has had time to do away with all traces of its own artifice. The "color of crime" necessary, for example, in the last act of *L'Ivrogne* is a critic's truth, not a dramatist's. In its initial movement, the production can be based only on the plurality and the literalness of objects. Baudelaire, on the other hand, conceives things in the theater only as accompanied by their dreamed-of doubles, endowed with a spirituality vaporous enough to unify them, to alienate them all the more. Now, nothing is more contrary to dramaturgy than the dream. The germs of true theater are always elementary movements of prehension or distancing: the surreality of theater objects is of a sensorial, not an oneiric order.

It is therefore not when Baudelaire speaks of production, of staging, that he is closest to a concrete theater. His authentic theatricality is the sentiment, indeed one might say the torment, of the actor's disturbing corporeality. In one scenario he proposes that Don Juan's son be played by a girl, in another that the hero be surrounded by lovely women each assigned a domestic function, and in a third that the drunkard's wife offer in her very body that appearance of modesty and fragility which call down rape and murder upon her. This is because for Baudelaire the actor's condition is a prostitution ("In a spectacle, in a dance, each takes his pleasure from all the participants"); his charm is therefore not experienced as an episodic and decorative character (contrary to the "bustling" staging, the movements of gypsies or the atmosphere of taverns), it is necessary to the theater as the manifestation of a primary category of the Baudelairean universe: artificiality.

The actor's body is artificial, but its duplicity is much more profound than that of the painted sets or the fake furniture of the stage; the grease paint, the imitation of gestures or intonations, the accessibility of an exposed body—all this is artificial but not factitious, and thereby a part of that delicate transcendence, of an exquisite, essential savor, by which Baudelaire has defined the power of the artificial paradise: the actor bears in himself the very overprecision of an excessive world, like that of hashish, where nothing is invented, but where everything exists in a multiplied intensity. This suggests that Baudelaire had an acute sense of the most secret and also the most disturbing theatricality, the kind which puts the actor at the center of the theatrical prodigy and constitutes the theater as the site of an ultraincarnation, in which the body is double, at once a living body deriving from a trivial nature, and an emphatic, formal body, frozen by its function as an artificial object.

However, this powerful theatricality is merely vestigial in Baudelaire's projects for plays, whereas it flows powerfully through the rest of his work. It would seem that Baudelaire put his theater everywhere except, precisely, in his projects for plays. It is, moreover, a general fact of creation, this kind of marginal development of the elements of a genre—drama, novel, or poetry—within works which nominally are not made to receive them. For instance, France has put her historical drama everywhere in her literature except on stage. Baudelaire's theatricality is animated by the same power of evasion: wherever we do not expect it, it explodes; first and foremost in *Les Paradis artificiels:* here Baudelaire describes a sensory transmutation which is of the same nature as theatrical perception, since in both cases reality is assigned an emphatic accent, which is the stress of an ideality of things. Then in his poetry, at least wherever objects are united by the poet in a kind of radiant perception of matter, amassed, condensed as though on a stage, glowing with colors, lights, and cosmetics, touched here and there by the grace of the artificial; in every description of scenes, finally, for here the preference for a space deeper and stabilized by the painter's theocratic gesture is satisfied in the same manner as in the theater (conversely, "scenes" abound in the scenario of *Le Marquis du Ier Houzards,* which seems to come all of a piece out of Gros or Delacroix, just as *La Fin de Don Juan* or *L'Ivrogne* seem to come from a poetic rather than a strictly theatrical intention).

Thus Baudelaire's theatricality evades his theater in order to spread through the rest of his work. By a converse process, though one just as revealing, elements deriving from extra-dramatic orders abound in these scenarios, as if this theater were striving to destroy itself by a double movement of evasion and intoxication. As soon as it is conceived, the Baudelairean scenario is immediately steeped in novelistic categories: *La Fin de Don Juan,* at least the opening fragment we have of it, ends curiously with a pastiche of Stendhal; Don Juan speaks almost like Mosca: the few words he exchanges with his servant suggest the dialogue of the novel, in which the language of the characters, direct as it may be, retains that precious glaze, that chastened transparency we know Baudelaire applied to all the objects of his creation. Of course the text is no more than a sketch, and Baudelaire might have given his dialogue that absolute literality which is the fundamental status of language in the theater. But we are analyzing here the vocation of a failure and not the potentiality of a project: it is significant that in its nascent state, this ghost of a scenario should have the very tonality of a written literature, frozen by the page, without voice, without viscera.

Time and place, each time they are indicated, testify to the same horror of the theater, at least of the theater as we can imagine it in Baudelaire's day: act and scene are units which immediately hamper Baudelaire, which he repeatedly over-flows and whose regulation he always postpones: sometimes he feels that the act is too short, sometimes too long: in Act III of *Le Marquis du I*er *Houzards* he inserts a flashback which even today only the cinema could manage; in *La Fin de Don Juan*, the scene gradually shifts from city to country, as in some abstract theater (*Faust*); in a general manner, even in its germ, this theater explodes, turns like an unstable chemical mixture, divides into "scenes" (in the pictorial sense of the term) or narratives. This is because, contrary to any true man of the theater, Baudelaire imagines a story entirely narrated, instead of starting from the stage; genetically, the theater is the subsequent creation of a fiction around an initial datum, which is always of a gestural order (liturgy in Aeschylus, actors' intrigues in Molière); Baudelaire evidently conceives the theater as a purely formal avatar, imposed after the fact upon a creative principle of a symbolic order (*Le Marquis du I*er *Houzards*) or an existential one (*L'Ivrogne*). "I confess I have not given a thought to the staging," Baudelaire says at one point; impossible naïveté in any playwright, however minor.

Not that Baudelaire's scenarios are absolutely alien to an esthetic of performance; but precisely insofar as they belong to a generally novelistic order, it is not theater but cinema which might best articulate them, for it is from the novel that cinema derives and not from the theater. The shifting locales, the flashbacks, the exoticism of the scenes, the temporal disproportion of the episodes, in short that torment of laying out the narration, to which Baudelaire's pretheater testifies, might nourish a pure cinema. From this point of view, *Le Marquis du Ier Houzards* is a complete scenario: even the actors in this drama suggest the classical typology of cinema roles. This is because the actor, deriving from a novelistic character and not from a corporeal dream (as is still the case for Don Juan's son, played by a woman, or the drunkard's wife, object of sadism), has no need of the stage's dimension in order to exist: he belongs to a sentimental or social typology, not a morphological one: he is a pure narrative sign, as in the novel and as in the cinema.

What remains, then, which is strictly theatrical in Baudelaire's projects? Nothing, except precisely a pure recourse to the theater. It is as if the mere intention of someday writing plays had sufficed for Baudelaire and had exempted him from sustaining these projects with a strictly theatrical substance, suggested throughout his work but rejected in just those places where it might have been fulfilled. For to this theater which Baudelaire momentarily sought out, he eagerly lent the features most likely to eliminate it at once: a certain triviality, a certain puerility (surprising in relation to Baudelairean dandyism), deriving visibly from the supposed pleasures of the crowd, the "Odeonic" imagination of spectacular scenes (a battle, the emperor reviewing troops, a country dance hall, a gypsy camp, a complicated murder), a whole esthetic of crude impressiveness, cut off from its dramatic motives or, one might say, a formalism of the theatrical act conceived in its effects most flattering to *petit bourgeois* sensibility.

With such a conception of theater, Baudelaire had to protect theatricality from the theater; fearing the sovereign artifice would be threatened by the collective character of the occasion, he hid it far from the stage, gave it refuge in his solitary literature, in his poems, his essays, his *Salons*; so that there is nothing left in this imaginary theater but the prostitution of the actor, the supposed pleasure of the public in the lies (and not in the artifice) of a grandiloquent production. This theater is trivial, but it is a triviality painful precisely insofar as it is pure conduct, mutilated as though deliberately of any poetic or dramatic depth, cut off from any development which might have justified it, crudely indicating that zone in which Baudelaire created himself from project to project, from failure to failure, until he built up that pure murder of literature, which we know since Mallarmé to be the torment and the justification of the modern writer.

It is therefore because the theater, abandoned by a theatricality which seeks refuge everywhere else, then fulfills to perfection a vulgar social nature, that Baudelaire chooses it briefly as the nominal site of an impulse and as the sign of what we would today call a commitment. By this pure gesture (pure because it transmits only his intention, and because this theater exists only as a project), Baudelaire rejoins, but this time on the level of creation, that sociability he pretended to postulate and to flee, according to the dialectic of a choice Sartre has so decisively analyzed. To bring a play to Holstein, the director of the Gaîté, was an action as reassuring as to flatter Sainte-Beuve, to canvas votes for the Academy, or to want the Legion of Honor.

And that is why these theatrical projects touch us so deeply: they belong in Baudelaire to that vast background of negativity against which rises finally the success of *Les Fleurs du mal* like an act which no longer owes anything to talent, that is, to literature. It took General Aupik, Ancelle, Théophile Gautier, Sainte-Beuve, the Academy, the ribbon of the Legion, and this pseudo-Odeonic theater, all these complacencies, accursed or abandoned moreover as soon as they were consented to, for Baudelaire's fulfilled work to be that responsible choice which made, in the end, his life into a great destiny. We would be ungrateful for *Les Fleurs du mal* if we failed to incorporate into its creator's history this agonizing Passion of vulgarity.

1954

Mother Courage Blind

recht's *Mutter Courage*[1] is not for those who, at close range or out of earshot, get rich on war; it would be grotesque, explaining to *them* war's mercantile character! No, it is to those who suffer from wars without profiting by them that *Mutter Courage* is addressed, and that is the primary reason for its greatness: *Mutter Courage* is an entirely popular work, for it is a work whose profound intention can be understood only by the people.

This theater starts from a double vision: of the social evil, and of its remedies. In the case of *Mutter Courage*, the point is to show those who believe in the fatality of war, like Mother Courage, that war is precisely a human phenomenon, not a fatality, and that by attacking its mercantile causes its military consequences can finally be abolished. That is the idea, and this is how Brecht unites his crucial intention to a true theater, so that the proposition's evidence results not from sermon or argument but from the theatrical act itself: Brecht sets before us the whole sweep of the Thirty Years' War; caught up in

1. Performances of Brecht's *Mutter Courage* by the Berliner Emsemble, in Paris (Théâtre des Nations), 1954.

this implacable duration, everything is corrupted (objects, faces, affections), is destroyed (Mother Courage's children, killed one after the next); Mother Courage, a sutler whose trade and life are the wretched fruits of the war, is so much inside the war that she does not see it (merely a glimmer at the end of the first part): she is blind, she submits without understanding; for her, the war is an indisputable fatality.

For her, but no longer for us: because we *see* Mother Courage blind, we *see* what she does not see. Mother Courage is for us a ductile substance: she sees nothing, but we see through her; we understand, in the grip of this dramatic evidence which is the most immediate kind of persuasion, that Mother Courage blind is the victim of what she does not see, which is a remediable evil. This theater creates a decisive split within us: we are at once Mother Courage and we are those who explain her; we participate in the blinding of Mother Courage and we *see* this same blinding; we are passive actors mired in war's fatality and free spectators led to the demystification of this fatality.

For Brecht, the stage narrates, the audience judges; the stage is epic, the audience tragic. This is the very definition of a great popular theater. Take Guignol or Punch, for instance, a theater which has risen out of an ancestral mythology: here too the audience *knows* what the actor does not know; and upon seeing him act so harmfully and so stupidly, the audience is amazed, disturbed, indignant, shouts out the truth, offers the solution: one step more and the spectator will see that the suffering and ignorant actor is himself, will know that when he is plunged into one of those countless Thirty Years' Wars which every age imposes upon him in one form or another, he is in it exactly like Mother Courage, stupidly suffering and unaware of her own power to bring her miseries to an end.

It is therefore crucial that this theater never completely implicate the audience in the spectacle: if the spectator does not keep that slight distance necessary in order to see himself suffering and mystified, all is lost: the spectator must partly identify himself with Mother Courage, and espouse her blindness only to withdraw from it in time and to judge it. The whole of Brecht's dramaturgy is subject to a necessity of *distance*, and the essence of the theater is staked on the perpetuation of this distance: it is not the success of any particular dramatic style which is in question, it is the spectator's consciousness and hence his capacity to make history. Brecht pitilessly excludes as uncivic the dramatic solutions which involve the audience in the spectacle, and by heartfelt pity or knowing winks favors a shameless complicity between history's victim and his new witnesses. Brecht consequently rejects romanticism, rhetoric, naturalism, truculence, estheticism, opera, all the styles of *viscosity* or participation which would lead the spectator to identify himself completely with Mother Courage, to be lost in her, to let himself be swept into her blindness or her futility.

The problem of participation—the delight of our theater estheticians, always ecstatic when they can postulate a diffuse religiosity of the spectacle—is here altogether reconceived; nor have we seen the last of the beneficial consequences of this new principle, which is perhaps a very old principle, moreover, since it rests on the ancestral status of the civic theater, in which the stage is always the object of a tribunal which is in the audience (as it was for the Greek tragedians). We now understand why our traditional dramaturgies are radically false: they congeal the spectator, they are dramaturgies of abdication. Brecht's, on the contrary, possesses a maieutic power; it represents and brings to judgment, it is at once overwhelming and isolating: everything combines to impress without inundating us; it is a theater of solidarity, not of contagion.

Others will describe the concrete—and triumphant—efforts of this dramaturgy to achieve a revolutionary idea, which can alone justify the theater today. In conclusion, let us merely reaffirm the intensity of our response to the Berliner Ensemble's *Mutter Courage*: like every great work, Brecht's is a radical criticism of the evil which precedes it: we are therefore profoundly *edified* by *Mutter Courage*. But this edification is matched by delight: the performance proved to us that this profound criticism has created that theater without alienation which we had dreamed of and which has been discovered before our eyes in a single day, in its adult and already perfected form.

1955

The Brechtian Revolution

For twenty-four centuries, in Europe, the theater has been Aristotelian: even today, in 1955, each time we go to the theater, whether to see Shakespeare or Montherlant, Racine or Roussin, Maria Casarès or Pierre Fresnay, whatever our tastes and whatever our politics, we determine pleasure and boredom, good and bad, as a function of an age-old morality whose credo is this: the more the public is moved, the more it identifies with the hero; the more the stage imitates action, the more the actor incarnates his role, then the more magical the theater and the better the spectacle.[1]

Now comes a man whose work and thought radically contest this art so ancestral that we had the best reasons in the world for believing it to be "natural"; who tells us, despite all tradition, that the public must be only half-committed to the spectacle so as to "know" what is shown, instead of submitting to it; that the actor must create this consciousness by exposing not by incarnating his role; that the spectator must

1. Editorial for the Brecht issue of *Théâtre populaire* (January–February 1955).

never identify completely with the hero but remain free to judge the causes and then the remedies of his suffering; that the action must not be imitated but narrated; that the theater must cease to be magical in order to become critical, which will still be its best way of being passionate.

And precisely to the degree that Brecht's theatrical revolution challenges our habits, our tastes, our reflexes, the very "laws" of the theater in which we live, we must renounce our silence or our irony and face up to Brecht. This magazine has too often condemned the mediocrity or the meanness of our theater, the rarity of its rebellions and the sclerosis of its techniques, to postpone a consideration of a great contemporary dramatist who offers not only a body of work but also a strong, coherent, stable system, one difficult to apply perhaps, but which possesses at least an indisputable and salutary virtue of "scandal" and astonishment.

Whatever our final evaluation of Brecht, we must at least indicate the coincidence of his thought with the great progressive themes of our time: that the evils men suffer are in their own hands—in other words, that the world can be changed; that art can and must intervene in history; that it must contribute to the same goal as the sciences, with which it is united; that we must have an art of explanation and no longer merely an art of expression; that the theater must participate in history by revealing its movement; that the techniques of the stage are themselves "committed"; that, finally, there is no such thing as an "essence" of eternal art, but that each society must invent the art which will be responsible for its own deliverance.

Naturally Brecht's ideas raise problems and provoke resistances, particularly in a country like France, which at present forms a historical complex quite different from East Germany. The issue *Théâtre populaire* is devoting to Brecht does not claim to solve these problems or to triumph over these resistances. Our sole purpose, for the moment, is to afford a wider knowledge of Brecht.

We are opening a dossier, we are far from considering it closed. We invite our readers to add their testimony. This would compensate, in our eyes, for the ignorance or indifference of so many intellectuals and men of the theater with regard to a man whom we regard as, in every sense, a "crucial contemporary."

1955

The Diseases of Costume

I should like to sketch here not a history or an esthetic, but rather a pathology or, if you prefer, an ethic of costume. I shall propose a few very simple rules which may permit us to judge whether a costume is good or bad, healthy or sick.

I must first define the basis I assign to this ethic, to this health. In the name of what shall we decide to judge the costumes for a play? One might answer (as whole epochs have done): historical truth or good taste, faithfulness of detail or pleasure of the eye. For my part, I propose another ideal for our ethic: that of the play itself. Every dramatic work can and must reduce itself to what Brecht calls its social *gestus*, the external, material expression of the social conflicts to which it bears witness. It is obviously up to the director to discover and to manifest this *gestus*, this particular historical scheme which is at the core of every spectacle: at his disposal, in order to do so, he has the ensemble of theatrical techniques: the actor's performance, movement, and location, the setting, lighting, and, specifically, *costume*.

It is therefore on the necessity of manifesting, each time, the social *gestus* of the play that we shall base our ethic of costume. This means that we shall assign to costume a purely functional role, and that this function will be of an intellectual rather than a plastic or emotional order. The costume is nothing more than the second term of a relation which must constantly link the work's meaning to its "exteriority." Hence everything in the costume that blurs the clarity of this relation, that contradicts, obscures, or falsifies the social *gestus* of the spectacle, is bad; on the contrary, everything in the forms, the colors, the substances, and their articulation that helps us to read this *gestus* is good.

So, as in every ethic, let us begin by the negative rules; let us see first what a costume must not be (granted, of course, that the premises of our ethic are accepted).

In a general way, the costume must on no account be an *alibi*, i.e., a justification; the costume must not constitute a dense and brilliant visual locus to which the attention may escape, fleeing the essential reality of the spectacle, what we might call its responsibility; then too, the costume must not be a kind of excuse, a compensatory element whose success redeems, for example, the silence or the indigence of the work. The costume must always keep its value as a pure function, it must neither smother nor swell the play; it must avoid substituting independent values for the signification of the staged action. Hence it is when the costume becomes an end in itself that it becomes condemnable. The costume owes the play a certain number of *prestations:* if one of these services is exaggeratedly developed, if the servant becomes more important than the master, then the costume is sick, it suffers from hypertrophy.

The diseases, errors, or alibis of costume, whatever we call them, I divide into three categories, all very common in our theater.

The basic disease is the hypertrophy of the historical function, what we shall call an archeological verism. It should be recalled that there are two kinds of history: an intelligent history which rediscovers the profound tensions, the specific conflicts of the past; and a superficial history which mechanically reconstructs certain anecdotic details; costume has long been a favorite realm for the exercise of this latter history;

we know the epidemic ravages of the veristic malady in bourgeois art: costume, conceived as an accumulation of true details, absorbs, then atomizes the spectator's entire attention, which is dispersed far from the spectacle, in the region of the infinitely small. The good costume, even when it is historical, is on the contrary a total visual fact; there is a certain scale of truth, beneath which one must not proceed, or else one destroys this fact. The veristic costume, still to be seen in certain operatic productions, achieves the climax of absurdity: the truth of the whole is effaced by the exactitude of the part; the actor disappears beneath the scruple of his buttons, his drapery, and his false hair. The veristic costume infallibly produces the following effect: we see perfectly well that it is true, and yet we don't believe it.

In recent productions, I should give as the example of a good victory over verism Leon Gischia's costumes for *The Prince of Hamburg* (Vilar's TNP production). The play's social *gestus* rests on a certain conception of *the military*, and it is to this argumentative datum that Gischia has subjected his costumes: all their attributes have been made to sustain a semantics of the soldier rather than a semantics of the seventeenth century: the clear forms, the severe yet bold colors, above all the substances—an element much more important than the rest (here, the sensation of leather and broadcloth)—the entire optical surface of the spectacle has assimilated the argument of the work. Similarly, in the Berliner Ensemble's *Mutter Courage*, it is not at all a history-as-dates which has dictated the truth of the costumes: it is the notion of war, of an overland, interminable war, which is sustained and constantly made explicit not by the archeological veracity of a certain shape, a certain object, but by a dusty and plastery gray, by the threadbare state of the fabrics, the dense, stubborn poverty of wicker, rope, and wood.

It is, moreover, always by substances (and not by shapes or colors) that we are finally assured of rediscovering the profoundest version of history. A good costumer must be able to give the public the tactile sense of what it sees, even from a great distance. I never expect much from an artist who elaborates forms and colors without proposing a really thought-out choice of the materials to be used: for it is in the very substance of objects (and not in their planar representation) that the true history of men is to be found.

A second disease, also frequent, is the esthetic one, the hypertrophy of a formal beauty without relation to the play. Naturally, it would be pointless to neglect the strictly plastic values in costume: taste, felicity, balance, the absence of vulgarity, even the search for originality. But too often these necessary values become an end in themselves; the spectator's attention is distracted from the theater, artificially concentrated on a parasitical function: we may then have an admirable esthete's theater, but we no longer have quite a human theater. With a certain excess of puritanism, I should say that I regard as a disturbing sign the phenomenon of applauding the costumes (this is quite frequent in Paris). The curtain goes up, the eye is bewitched, we applaud: but what do we really know, then, except that this red is beautiful or that drapery clever? Do we know if this splendor, these refinements, these discoveries will suit the play, will serve it, will concur in expressing its meaning?

The very type of this deviation is the Bérard esthetic, employed today without rhyme or reason. Sustained by snobbery and worldliness, the esthetic avatar of costume supposes the condemnable independence of each of the elements of the spectacle: to applaud the costumes within the performance itself is to accentuate the divorce of the creators, is to reduce the work to a blind conjunction of virtuosities. It is not the duty of costume to seduce the eye, but to convince it.

The costumer must therefore avoid being either a painter or a couturier; he will mistrust the flat values of painting, will avoid the relations of space proper to this art, precisely because the very definition of painting is that these relations are necessary and sufficient; their wealth, their density, the very tension of their existence, would greatly exceed the argumentative function of the costume; and if the costumer is by profession a painter, he must forget his condition as soon as he becomes a creator of costumes; it is an understatement to say that he must subject his art to the play: he must destroy it, forget pictorial space, and reinvent all over again the woolly or silky space of human bodies. He must also abstain from the *grand couturier* style which today prevails in our boulevard theaters. The *chic* of costume, the studied casualness of an antique drapery one might suppose came straight from Dior, the fashionable distortion of a crinoline, are disastrous alibis which blur the clarity of the argument, make the costume an eternal form, and one "eternally young," divested of the contingencies of history, and, evidently, this is contrary to the rules we posited at the beginning.

There is moreover a modern feature which summarizes this hypertrophy of the esthetic: it is the fetishism of the designer's sketch or model (exhibitions, reproductions). The sketch usually teaches nothing about the costume because it fails to afford the essential experience, that of the material. To see on stage these sketches-as-costumes cannot be a good sign. I am not saying that the sketch is unnecessary; but it is an entirely preparatory operation which should concern only the designer and the dressmaker, the sketch should be entirely destroyed on the stage except for some very rare spectacles in which the art of the fresco is to be deliberately striven for. The sketch or model must remain an instrument, and not become a style.

Lastly, the third disease of costume is money, the hypertrophy of sumptuosity or at least its appearance. This is a very frequent disease in our society, in which the theater is always the object of a contract between the spectator who pays his money and the manager who returns it to him in the most visible form possible; now it is quite obvious that in this case, the illusory sumptuosity of the costumes constitutes a spectacular and reassuring restitution; vulgarly speaking, costume *pays* better than emotion or intellection, always uncertain and without manifest relations to their condition as merchandise. Hence once a theater becomes vulgarized, we see it constantly heightening the luxury of its costumes, visited for themselves and soon becoming the decisive attraction of the spectacle (*Les Indes galantes* at the Opéra, *Les Amants magnifiques* at the Comédie-Française). Where is the theater in all this? Nowhere, of course: the horrible cancer of wealth has completely devoured it.

By a diabolic mechanism, the luxurious costume adds mendacity to what is already base: ours is no longer an age (as Shakespeare's was, for example) when actors wear rich but authentic costumes from seigneurial wardrobes; today, wealth costs too much, we content ourselves with an ersatz—that is, with lies. Thus it is not even luxury but fakes that happen to be hypertrophied today. Sombart has suggested the bourgeois origin of the imitation substance; certainly in France it is particularly the *petit bourgeois* theaters (Folies-Bergère, Comédie-Française, Opéra-Comique) which indulge in such pseudo substances most determinedly. This supposes an infantile condition in the spectator, who is denied simultaneously any critical spirit and any creative imagination. Naturally we cannot entirely banish *imitation wealth* from our costumes; but if we resort to it, we should at least *signify* as much, should refuse to accredit the lie. In the theater, nothing must be hidden. This notion derives from a very simple ethical principle, which has always produced, I believe, a great theater: one must have confidence in the spectator, must resolutely grant him the power of creating wealth himself, of transforming rayon into silk and lies into illusion.

And now, let us consider what a good costume would be; and since we have acknowledged its functional nature, let us attempt to define the kind of prestations to which it is committed. For myself, I see at least two, which are essential:

First of all, *the costume must be an argument*. This intellectual function of costume is generally buried today under the parasitical functions we have just reviewed (verism, estheticism, money). Yet in all the great periods of theater, costume had a powerful semantic value; it was not there only to be seen, it was also there to be *read*, it communicated ideas, information, or sentiments.

The intellectual or cognitive cell of the costume, its basic element, is the *sign*. We have, in a tale from the *Thousand and One Nights*, a magnificent example of the vestimentary sign: we are told that whenever he was angry, the Caliph Haroun al-Rashid put on a red gown. Here the caliph's red gown is a sign, the spectacular *sign* of his anger; it is em-

The Diseases of Costume

powered to transmit visually to the caliph's subjects a datum of the cognitive order: the sovereign's state of mind and all the consequences it implies.

Powerful, popular, and civic theaters have always utilized a precise vestimentary code; they have broadly practiced what we might call a politics of the sign: I shall merely recall that among the Greeks, his mask and the color of his ornaments proclaimed in advance a character's social or emotional condition; that on the medieval church porch and the Elizabethan stage, the colors of the costumes, in certain symbolic cases, permitted a diacritical reading, so to speak, of the state of the actors; and that finally in the *commedia dell'arte*, each psychological type possessed its own conventional clothing. It is bourgeois romanticism which, diminishing its confidence in the public's intellective power, has dissolved the sign in a sort of archeological truth of costume: the sign has deteriorated into a detail, we have taken to producing veridical costumes and no longer significant ones. This debauch of imitation achieved its culminating point in the baroque of the 1900s—a veritable pandemonium of costume.

Since we have just sketched a pathology of costume, we must now indicate some of the diseases which may affect the vestimentary *sign*. These are, in a sense, the maladies of nutrition: the sign is sick whenever it is over- or underfed on meaning. I shall cite only the most common diseases: indigence of the sign (Wagnerian heroines in nightgowns), literalness of the sign (bacchantes signified by bunches of grapes), over-indication of the sign (Chantecler's feathers juxtaposed one by one; total for the play, some hundreds of pounds of feathers); inadequacy of the sign ("historical" costumes applied without differentiation to vague epochs); and lastly, multiplication and internal disequilibrium of the sign (for example, the Folies-Bergère costumes, remarkable for the audacity and clarity of their historical stylization, are complicated, blurred by accessory signs such as those of fantasy or sumptuosity—here all signs are put on the same level).

Can we define a *health* of the sign? At this point we must be wary of formalism: the sign has succeeded when it is functional; we cannot give it an abstract definition; everything depends on the real content of the spectacle; here again, health is above all an absence of disease; the costume is healthy when it leaves the work free to transmit its profound significance, when it does not encumber the play and in a sense permits the actor to go about his essential business without bearing a parasitical burden. What we *can* say, at least, is that a good vestimentary code, an effective servant of the play's *gestus*, excludes naturalism. Brecht has given a remarkable explanation of this, apropos of the costumes for *The Mother*; scenically one does not *signify* the frayed condition of a piece of clothing by putting on stage a threadbare garment. To manifest itself, the frayed condition must be raised to a higher power (this is the very definition of what in the cinema is called the photogenic), provided with a kind of epic dimension: the good sign must always be the fruit of a choice and of an accentuation. Brecht has given all the details of the operations necessary to the construction of the *sign* of wear-and-tear: the intelligence, scruple, and patience involved are remarkable (treatment of the fabric with chlorine, burning the dyestuffs, scraping with a razor blade, maculation by waxes, lacquers, and acids, holes made or else darned and patched); in our theaters, hypnotized by the esthetic finality of our costumes, we are still far from radically submitting the vestimentary *sign* to such detailed treatments and especially to such "thought-out" ones (in France, of course, an art is suspect if it thinks); one does not see Léonor Fini applying a blowtorch to one of those lovely red gowns that sets *le Tout-Paris* on fire.

Another positive function of the costume: *it must create a humanity*, it must favor the actor's human stature, must make his bodily nature perceptible, distinct, and if possible affecting. The costume must serve the human proportions and somehow sculpture the actor, make his silhouette natural, allowing us to imagine that the form of the garment, however eccentric in relation to ourselves, is perfectly consubstantial with his flesh, with his daily life; we must never feel the human body flouted by the disguise.

This humanity of the costume is largely a tributary of its surroundings, of the material milieu in which the actor performs. The concerted agreement between costume and background is perhaps the first law of the theater: we know all too well, for example, from certain opera productions, that the jumble of painted drops, the incessant and futile parade of motley choristers, all these excessively loaded surfaces, make man into a grotesque silhouette, without emotion and without clarity. Now the theater openly demands of its actors a certain corporeal exemplarity; whatever ethic we attribute to it, the theater is in a sense a celebration of the human body, and costume and background must respect this body by expressing its entire human quality. The more organic the link between the costume and the surround, the more justified the costume. It is an infallible test to juxtapose a costume with natural substances like stone, darkness, foliage. If the costume harbors some of the viruses we have indicated, it will be seen at once that it corrupts the landscape, appears mean, seedy, absurd (this was the case, in the cinema, with Guitry's costumes in *Si Versailles m'était conté*, their limited artifice belying the stones and perspectives of the chateau); conversely, if the costume is healthy, the open air must be able to assimilate, even to exalt it.

Another agreement difficult to achieve and yet indispensable is that of the costume and the face. On this point, how many morphological anachronisms! How many modern faces naïvely set on false ruffs, false tunics! We know that this is one of the acutest problems of the historical film (Roman senators with the faces of sheriffs, to which we must offer the comparison of Dreyer's *Passion of Joan of Arc*). In the theater, the same problem: the costume must be able to *absorb* the face; we must feel that a single historical epithelium, invisible but necessary, covers them both.

In short, the good costume must be material enough to signify and transparent enough not to turn its signs into parasites. The costume is a kind of writing and has the ambiguity of writing, which is an instrument in the service of a purpose which transcends it; but if the writing is either too poor or too rich, too beautiful or too ugly, it can no longer be read and fails in its function. The costume, too, must find that kind of rare equilibrium which permits it to help us *read* the theatrical act without encumbering it by any parasitical value: it must renounce every egotism, every excess of good intentions; it must pass unnoticed in itself yet it must also exist: the actors cannot, in every case, appear on stage naked. It must be both material and transparent: we must see it but not look at it. This is perhaps only an apparent paradox: Brecht's recent example suggests that it is in the very accentuation of its materiality that costume has the greatest chances of achieving its necessary submission to the critical goals of the spectacle.

1955

Literal Literature

We don't read a novel by Robbe-Grillet the way—at once total and discontinuous—we "devour" a traditional novel, intellection leaping from paragraph to paragraph, from crisis to crisis, our eyes absorbing the typography only intermittently, as if the act of reading, in its most material gesture, reproduced the very hierarchy of the classical universe, endowed with moments alternately pathetic and insignificant. No, in Robbe-Grillet, narrative itself imposes the necessity of an exhaustive ingestion of the material; the reader is subjected to a kind of relentless education, he has the sense of being held fast to the very continuity of objects and of actions. His capture results not from a rape or a fascination but from a gradual and inevitable investiture. The narrative's pressure is quite steady, appropriate to a literature of evidence.

This new quality of reading is linked, here, to the strictly optical nature of the novelistic substance. As we know, Robbe-Grillet's intention is to accord objects a narrative privilege hitherto granted only to human relations. Whence a profound renewal of the art of description, since in this "objective" universe substance is presented no longer as a function of the human heart (memory, instrumentality), but as an implacable space which man can frequent only by movement, never by use or subjection.

This is a great literary exploration, whose initial reconnaissance was made in *The Erasers*. *The Voyeur* constitutes a second stage, attained quite deliberately, for Robbe-Grillet gives the impression that his creation follows a methodically predetermined path; indeed we may assume that his *oeuvre* will have a demonstration value and that, like every authentic literary act, this value will not be so much literature as the very institution of literature: certainly in the last fifty years, all significant writing possesses this same problematic virtue.

What is interesting about *The Voyeur* is the relation the author establishes between objects and story. In *The Erasers*, the objective world was sustained by elements of a murder mystery. In *The Voyeur*, there is no longer any such qualification of the story: *affabulation* tends to zero, to the point where it can scarcely be named, much less summarized (as the embarrassment of our critics testifies). Of course I can say that on an unidentified island a traveling salesman strangles a shepherd girl and returns to the mainland. But am I quite certain about this murder? The act itself is narratively blanked out (a very visible hole in the middle of the narrative); the reader can only induce it from the murderer's patient effort to erase this void (so to speak), to fill it with a "natural" time. Which is to say that the extent of the objective world, the calm assiduity of reconstitution here close in upon an improbable event: the importance of antecedents and consequences, their prolix literality, their insistence upon being spoken, necessarily cast suspicion upon an act which suddenly, and contrary to the analytic vocation of the discourse, no longer has language for its immediate guarantee.

The act's blankness derives primarily, of course, from the objective nature of the description. A story (what we consider, precisely, "novelistic") is a typical product of our civilizations of the soul. Consider Ombredane's ethnological experiment: the film *Underwater Hunt* is shown to black students in the Congo and to Belgian students; the former offer a purely descriptive summary of what they have seen, precise, concrete, without *affabulation;* the latter, on the contrary, betray a great visual indigence, they have difficulty recalling details, they make up a story, seek certain literary effects, try to produce affective states. It is precisely this spontaneous birth of drama which Robbe-Grillet's optical system aborts at each moment; as with the Congolese, the precision of his spectacle absorbs all its potential interiority (a proof *a contrario*: it is our spiritualized critics who have desperately sought a story in *The Voyeur:* they realized that without a pathological or ethical argument the novel escaped that civilization of the soul which it is their responsibility to defend). There is, then, a conflict between the purely optical world of objects and the world of human interiority. By choosing the former, Robbe-Grillet cannot help being entranced by the annihilation of the anecdote.

There is, as a matter of fact, a tendentious destruction of story in *The Voyeur.* The plot recedes, diminishes, dies away under the weight of objects. Objects invest the story in a military sense, participate in it the better to devour it. It is remarkable that we do not know crime, nor motives, nor affects, nor even acts, but only isolated materials whose description, moreover, is denied any explicit intentionality. The story's data are neither psychological nor even pathological (at least in their narrative situation), they are reduced to certain objects gradually looming out of space and time without any avowed causal contiguity: a little girl (at least her archetype, for her name keeps changing), a piece of string, a stake, a pillar, some candy.

It is only the gradual coordination of these objects which delineates if not the crime itself, at least the place and moment of the crime. The materials are associated with each other by a kind of indifferent chance; but the repetition of certain constellations of objects (string, candy, cigarettes, the hand with pointed nails) creates the probability of a murderous application which would unite them all; and these associations of objects (as we might say, associations of ideas) gradually condition the reader to the existence of a probable plot, though without ever naming it, as if, in Robbe-Grillet's world, we had to shift from the order of objects to the order of events by a patient series of pure reflexes, scrupulously avoiding the mediation of a moral consciousness.

This purity can of course be only tendentious, and the whole of The Voyeur is created by an impossible resistance to anecdote. The objects figure as a kind of zero-theme of the plot. The novel keeps within that narrow and difficult zone in which anecdote (the crime) begins to go bad, to "intentionalize" the splendid stubbornness of objects in simply *being there*. Indeed, this silent inflection of a purely objective world toward interiority and pathology derives simply from a vice of space. If we recall that Robbe-Grillet's profound intention is to account for the whole of objective space, as if the novelist's hand closely followed his vision in an exhaustive apprehension of lines and surfaces, we realize that the return of certain objects, of certain fragments of space, privileged by their very repetition, constitutes in itself a flaw, what we might call an initial softening of the novelist's optical system, based essentially on contiguity and extension. We might then say that insofar as the repeated encounter with certain objects breaks the parallelism of vision and objects, there is a crime, i.e., an event: the geometric flaw, the collapse of space, the eruption of a return is the breach by which a whole psychological, pathological, anecdotic order will threaten to invest the novel. It is precisely here, where the objects, by *re-presenting* themselves, seem to deny their vocation as pure existences, that they invoke the anecdote and its retinue of implicit motives; repetition and conjunction strip them of their *Dasein*, of their *being-there*, in order to endow them with a *being-for-something*.

This mode of iteration is quite different from the thematics of classical authors. The repetition of a theme postulates a depth, the theme is a sign, the symptom of an internal coherence. In Robbe-Grillet, on the contrary, the constellations of objects are not expressive but creative; their purpose is not to reveal but to perform; they have a dynamic, not an heuristic role: before they appear, there exists nothing of what they will produce for the reader: they *make* the crime, they do not betray it: in a word, they are literal. Robbe-Grillet's novel remains, then, perfectly external to a psychoanalytic order: no question here of a world of compensation and justification, in which certain tendencies are expressed or counterexpressed by certain acts; the novel deliberately abolishes all past and all depth, it is a novel of extension, not of comprehension. The crime settles nothing (above all, satisfies no desire for a crime), never provides an answer, a solution, an outcome of crisis: this universe knows neither compression nor explosion, nothing but encounters, intersections of itineraries, returns of objects. And if we are tempted to read rape and murder in *The Voyeur* as acts deriving from a pathology, we are abusively inferring content from form: we are once again victims of that prejudice which makes us attribute to the novel an essence, that of the real, of *our* reality; we always conceive the imaginary as a symbol of the real, we want to see art as a litotes of nature. In Robbe-Grillet's case, how many critics have renounced the blinding literalness of the work in order to try to introduce into this universe whose implacable completeness is only too obvious, a dimension of soul, of evil, whereas Robbe-Grillet's technique is precisely a radical protest against the ineffable.

We might express this refusal of psychoanalysis in another way by saying that in Robbe-Grillet, the event is never *focused*. We need merely think of what in painting, in Rembrandt, for example, is a space visibly centered outside the canvas: this is more or less the world of rays and diffusions we meet in our novels of depth. In Robbe-Grillet, nothing of the kind: light is even and steady, it does not traverse, it displays; the act is not the spatial analogy of a secret source. Even if the narrative acknowledges one privileged moment (the blank page in the middle), it is not thereby concentric: the blank (the crime) is not the center of a fascination, it is merely the extreme point of a course, the limit from which the narrative will flow back toward its origin. This absence of focus undermines the pathology of the murder: the murder is developed according to rhetorical, not thematic means; it is revealed by topics, not by radiation.

We have just suggested that the crime was nothing more than a flaw of space and time (which are one and the same, since the site of the murder, the island, is never anything but the plan of a circuit). The murderer's entire effort is therefore (in the second part of the novel) to seal time back together, to regain a continuity which will be innocence (this is of course the very definition of an alibi, but here the resealing of time is not done in the presence of a detective or a policeman; it is done in the presence of a purely intellective consciousness, which seems to be struggling oneirically in the pangs of an incomplete intention). Similarly, in order for the crime to disappear, objects must lose their insistence on being grouped, constellated; they must be made to regain, retrospectively, a pure relation to contiguity. The desperate search for a seamless space (and as a matter of fact, it is only by its annihilation that we know about the crime) is identified with the very effacement of the crime, or more precisely, this effacement exists only as a kind of artificial glaze spread retroactively over the day. All at once, time assumes density, and we *know* that the crime exists. But it is then, just when time is overloaded with variations, that it assumes a new quality, the *natural:* the more *used* time is, the more plausible it appears: Mathias, the murderer, is obliged to pass his consciousness over the flaw of the crime unceasingly, like an insistent brush. Robbe-Grillet utilizes in these movements a special indirect style (in Latin, this style would employ a continuous subjective, which moreover would betray its user).

We are dealing, then, not so much with a voyeur as with a liar. Or rather, the voyeuristic phase of the first part is succeeded by the mendacious phase of the second: the continuous exercise of the lie is the only psychological function we may grant Mathias, as if, in Robbe-Grillet's eyes, psychologism, causality, intentionality could broach the adequacy of objects only in the form of a crime, and in crime, in the form of an alibi. It is by scrupulously sealing his day together again with a thin coat of *nature* (a mixture of temporality and causality) that Mathias reveals his crime to us (and perhaps to himself?), for we never see Mathias except as a re-making consciousness. This is precisely the theme of Oedipus. The difference is that Oedipus acknowledges a crime which has already been before its discovery, his crime belongs to a magical economy of compensation (the Theban plague), whereas Mathias offers an isolated guilt, intellective and not moral, which is never involved in a general relation to the world (causality, psychology, society); if the crime is corruption, it is here only a corruption of time—and not of human interiority: it is designated not by its ravages, but by a vicious arrangement of duration.

Such, then, is the anecdote of *The Voyeur*: desocialized and demoralized, suspended on the surface of objects, arrested in an impossible movement toward its own abolition, for Robbe-Grillet's project is always to cause the novelistic universe to cohere by means of its objects and by them alone. As in those perilous exercises where the aerialist gradually eliminates parasitical points of support, *affabulation* is little by little reduced, rarefied. Ideally, it would be done away with altogether; and if it still exists in *The Voyeur*, it is rather as the *locus* of a possible story (*affabulation's* zero-degree, or what Lévi-Strauss calls *mana*), in order to spare the reader the too-brutal effects of pure negativity.

Naturally, Robbe-Grillet's endeavor proceeds from a radical formalism. But in literature, this is an ambiguous reproach, for literature is by definition formal; there is no middle term between a writer's extinction and his estheticism, and if we consider formal experiment harmful, it is writing and not experiment which we must forbid. One might say on the contrary that the formalization of the novel as Robbe-Grillet pursues it has value only if it is radical, that is, if the novelist has the courage to postulate tendentiously a novel without content, at least for as long as he seeks to raise the mortgages of bourgeois psychologism: a metaphysical or moral interpretation of *The Voyeur* is certainly possible (as our critics have proved), insofar as the zero-state of the anecdote liberates in an overconfident reader all kinds of metaphysical investitures; it is still possible to occupy the letter of the narrative by an implicit spirituality and to transform a literature of pure evidence into a literature of protest or outcry: by definition, the former is accessible to the latter. For my part, I believe that this would be to strip *The Voyeur* of all interest. It is a book which can sustain itself only as an absolute exercise in negation, and as such it can take place in that very narrow zone, in that rare vertigo where literature unavailingly tries to destroy itself, and apprehends itself in one and the same movement, destroying and destroyed. Few works enter this mortal margin, but they are doubtless, today, the only ones which matter: in our present social circumstances, literature cannot be at once granted to the world and in advance of it, as is appropriate to any art of transcendence, except in a state of permanent presuicide; literature can exist only as the figure of its own problem, self-pursuing, self-scourging. Otherwise, whatever the generosity or the exactitude of its content, literature always ends by succumbing under the weight of a traditional form which compromises it insofar as it serves as an alibi for the alienated society which produces, consumes, and justifies it. *The Voyeur* cannot be separated from what is today the constitutively reactionary status of literature, but by trying to asepticize the very form of narrative, it is perhaps preparing, without yet achieving, a deconditioning of the reader in relation to the essentialist art of the bourgeois novel. Such at least is the hypothesis this book allows us to propose.

1955

Putting on
the Greeks

Each time that we, modern men, must stage a Greek tragedy, we find ourselves facing the same problems, and each time we bring to their solution the same good will and the same uncertainty, the same respect and the same confusion. Every Greek play I have seen performed, beginning with the very ones in which I had my share of responsibility as a student, testified to the same irresolution, to the same inability to choose among opposing claims.

The fact of the matter is that conscious or not, we never manage to free ourselves from a dilemma: are the Greek plays to be performed as of their own time or as of ours? Should we reconstruct or transpose? emphasize resemblances or differences? We always vacillate without ever deciding, well-intentioned and blundering, now eager to reinvigorate the spectacle by an inopportune fidelity to some "archeological" requirement, now to sublimate it by modern esthetic effects appropriate, we assume, to the "eternal" quality of this theater. The result of these compromises is always disappointing: we never know what to think of this reconstructed ancient theater. Does it concern us? How? Why? The performance never helps us answer these questions clearly.

Barrault's *Oresteia* testifies once again to the same confusions. Style, design, esthetic, and intention mingle here to an extreme degree, and despite an evidently considerable effort and certain partial successes, we do not really know why Barrault has put on the *Oresteia*: the spectacle is not justified.

Doubtless Barrault has professed (if not achieved) a general idea of his spectacle: a matter of breaking with academic traditions and relocating the *Oresteia* if not in history at least in exoticism. To transform a Greek tragedy into a voodoo rite, to determine how much of an irrational, panic quality it might have contained, even in fifth-century Athens, to strip it of all false classical pomp in order to reinvent its ritual nature, to reveal within it the germs of a theater of trance—all of which derives, moreover, much more from Artaud than from an exact knowledge of the Greek theater—all this could very well be admitted, provided it were really undertaken without concessions. But here is where the promise has not been kept: the voodoo rite is a timid affair.

First of all, the exoticism is far from being continuous: there are only three moments when it is explicit: Cassandra's prophecy, the ritual invocation to Agamemnon, the dance of the Erinyes. All the rest of the tragedy is occupied by a totally rhetorical art: no unity between the panic intention of these three scenes and Marie Bell's veil effects. Such discontinuities are intolerable, for they invariably reduce the dramaturgical intention to the status of a picturesque accessory: the voodoo becomes decorative. The exoticism was probably a poor choice, but at least it could have been rescued by its own effectiveness: its only justification would have been to transform the spectator physically, to upset, to fascinate, to "charm" him. Here, nothing of the kind: we remain cool, a little ironic, incapable of believing in a partial panic, immunized beforehand by the art of the "psychological" actors. A choice had to be made: either the voodoo rite or Marie Bell. By trying to bet on the red and the black at once (Marie Bell for humanist criticism and the voodoo rite for the *avant-garde*), Barrault invariably lost a little on both.

And then, this exoticism is too timid anyway. We realize what the intention was in the "magic" scene when Electra and Orestes invoke their dead father. Yet the effect remains very meager. If you set about to create a theater of participation, you must go all the way. Here the *signs* no longer suffice: what is required is a physical commitment from the actors. Now it is precisely this commitment which our traditional art has taught them to imitate, not to live; and since these signs are used up, compromised in a thousand previous plastic diversions, we do not believe in them: a few twirls, a syncopated rhythm in some choral speeches, a little stamping on the floor are not enough to impose the presence of magic upon us.

Nothing is more painful than a participation which does not "take." Surprising that the fervent partisans of this form of theater should be so vague, so uninventive, so scared, one might say, just when at last they have an occasion to achieve that physical theater, that total theater we have heard about so often. Once Barrault made the decision—contestable but at least rigorous—of the voodoo rite, he had to exploit it utterly: any jazz session, even a performance of *Carmen Jones* would have given him an example of that summatory presence of the actor, that aggression of the spectacle itself, that kind of visceral explosion his *Oresteia* reflects so faintly. Wishing doesn't make the witch doctor.

We find this confusion of styles in the costumes as well. Temporally, the *Oresteia* comprehends three levels: the supposed epoch of the myth, the epoch of Aeschylus, the epoch of the spectator. One of these three levels of reference should have been chosen and kept to, for as we shall see shortly, our only possible relation to Greek tragedy is in the consciousness we can have of its historical situation. Now, Marie-Hélène Dasté's costumes, some of which are plastically very fine, contain all three styles together. Agamemnon and Clytemnestra are dressed *à la barbare*, committing the tragedy to an archaic, Minoan signification which would be perfectly legitimate if the choice were a general one. But here are Orestes, Electra, and Apollo contradicting this choice: they are fifth-century Greeks; they introduce, among the monstrous gigantism of the primitive garments, grace, measure, the simple and sober humanity of classical silhouettes. Finally, as all too often at the Théâtre Marigny, the stage is sometimes invaded by a sumptuous mannerism, the *"grand couturier"* touch of our so-Parisian theaters: Cassandra is swathed in timeless pleats, the lair of the Atrides is draped in upholstery straight from Hermès (the boutique, not the god), and in the final apotheosis, a rice-powdered Pallas looms up out of a baby-blue cloud—just like the Folies-Bergère.

This naïve amalgam of Crete and the Faubourg Saint-Honoré does a great deal to spoil the *Oresteia*'s cause: the spectator no longer knows what he is seeing: he seems to be facing an abstract (because visually composite) tragedy, he is confirmed in a tendency which is only too natural to him: to reject a rigorously historical comprehension of the work performed. Here estheticism functions, once again, as an alibi; it masks an irresponsibility: this happens so consistently in Barrault's productions that we might label any gratuitous beauty of costumes the "Marigny style." It was already apparent in Barrault's *Bérénice*, which had not yet gone so far as to dress Pyrrhus as a Roman, Titus as a Louis XIV marquis, and Bérénice in a Fath gown: though that is the equivalent of the hodgepodge afforded by the *Oresteia*.

The disjunction of styles affects the actors every bit as seriously. One might assume their performance would have at least the unity of error; not even that: each speaks the text his own way, without concern for anyone else's style. Robert Vidalin plays Agamemnon according to the by-now-caricatural tradition of the Théâtre-Français: he really belongs in some parody put on by René Clair. At the opposite extreme, Barrault affects a kind of "naturalness" inherited from the patter roles of classical comedy; but by dint of trying to avoid the traditional rhetoric, his role shrinks, flattens, turns quite frail, insignificant: crushed by the errors of his colleagues, he has not been able to offset them with an elementary tragic hardness.

Beside him, Marie Bell plays Clytemnestra *à la* Racine or *à la* Bernstein (at a distance, more or less the same thing). The weight of this age-old tragedy has not made her abandon one bit of her personal rhetoric; it is a dramatic art of the *intention*, of the gesture and the glance heavy with meaning, of the *signified secret*, an art suitable for any scene of conjugal discord and bourgeois adultery, but which introduces into tragedy a cunning and, in a word, a *vulgarity* utterly anachronistic to it. Here is where the general misjudgment of the interpretation becomes most awkward, for a more subtle error is involved: it is true that the tragic characters manifest "sentiments"; but these "sentiments" (pride, jealousy, rancor, indignation) are not at all psychological in our modern sense of the word. These are not individualist passions, born in the solitude of a romantic heart; pride is not a sin here, a marvelous and complicated disease; it is an offense against the city, it is a political excess; rancor is the expression of an ancient right, that of the vendetta, while indignation is always the oratorical claim of a new right, the accession of the people to the reprobatory judgment of the ancient laws. This political context of the heroic passions governs their entire interpretation. A psychological art is above all an art of secrecy, of the thing at once concealed and confessed, for an essentialist ideology customarily represents the individual as inhabited, unknown to himself, by his passions: whence a traditional dramatic art which shows the spectator a ravaged interiority without the character's appearing to suspect it; this kind of pretense (in the double sense of inadequacy and of cunning) establishes a dramatic art of the nuance, in other words of a specious disjunction between the letter and the spirit of the character, between his language-as-subject and his passion-as-object. Tragic art, on the contrary, is based on an absolutely literal speech: here passion has no interior density, it is entirely extroverted, oriented toward its civic context. No "psychological" character will ever say: "I am proud"; Clytemnestra does, and all the difference is there. Hence nothing is more surprising, nothing more clearly signifies the fundamental error of this interpretation than to hear Marie Bell proclaim in the text a passion which her whole personal manner, trained by the performance of hundreds of "psychological" plays, a scheming and stagy manner, belies, for it betrays the shadowless exteriority of the play. Only Marguerite Jamois (Cassandra) seems to me to approach this art of the evident which should have enveloped the entire tragedy: she sees and speaks, she speaks what she sees, there is no more to it than that.

Yes, tragedy is an art of the evident, and it is, precisely, all that contradicts this "evidencing" which quickly becomes intolerable. Claudel perceived this very clearly and insisted that the tragic chorus maintain a stubborn, almost liturgical immobility. In the preface to his translation of the *Oresteia* he specifies that the chorus should be seated in stalls from one end of the spectacle to the other, and that each member should read his lines from a lectern in front of him. Doubtless such a staging contradicts an "archeological" truth, for we know that the Greek chorus danced. But since we do not know what these dances were, and since, even reconstructed, they would not have the same effect as in the fifth century, we must find equivalences. By restoring to the chorus, by a liturgical analogy, its function as a literal commentator, by expressing the massive nature of its interventions, by giving it quite explicitly the modern attributes of wisdom (seat, lectern), and by rediscovering its profoundly epic character as a narrator, Claudel's solution seems to be the only one which might account for the situation of the tragic chorus. Why has it never been tried?

Barrault has sought for a "dynamic," a "natural" chorus, but this choice testifies to the same uncertainty as the rest of his production. The confusion is even graver here, for the chorus is the hard core of tragedy: its function must be indisputably evident, everything about it—speech, costume, location—must be of a single nature and a single effect; finally, though it is "popular," sententious, and prosaic, there can be no question of a naïveté that would be "natural," psychological, individualized, picturesque. The chorus must remain an unforeseen organism, it must astonish and disconcert. This is hardly the case at the Marigny: here we find two contrary faults, both of which overshoot the true solution: emphasis and "naturalness." Sometimes the members shift position according to vague symmetrical designs, as in a gymnastic exhibition; sometimes they try for familiar or realistic attitudes, a knowing anarchy of movement; sometimes they declaim like preachers from the pulpit, sometimes they assume a conversational tone. This confusion of styles establishes on stage an unforgivable offense: irresponsibility. This erratic state of the chorus appears still more obvious, if not in the nature at least in the arrangement of the musical substratum: the impression is one of countless cuts, of an incessant mutilation which reduces the contribution of the music to a few samples revealed in an aside, illicitly, almost guiltily: it becomes difficult, under these conditions, to judge the quality of the score, but we *can* say that we do not know why it is there, and what the idea is which has governed its composition.

Barrault's *Oresteia* is an ambiguous spectacle, then, in which we encounter, though merely as sketches, contradictory options. It therefore remains to say why such confusion is more serious here than elsewhere: because it contradicts the only relation we can have, today, with ancient tragedy, which is *clarity*. To perform a tragedy by Aeschylus in 1955 has a meaning only if we are determined to answer these two questions clearly: what was the *Oresteia* for Aeschylus' contemporaries? What have we, in the twentieth century, to do with the ancient meaning of the work?

Several texts help us answer the first question: Paul Mazon's excellent introduction to his translation in the Budé Series; then, on the level of a broader sociology, Bachofen's *Mutterrecht* (1861), Engels' *Origin of the Family, Private Property, and the State* (1884), George Thomson's *Aeschylus and Athens* (1941). In the context of its period, and despite the moderate political position of Aeschylus himself, the *Oresteia* was incontestably a "progressive" work; it testifies to the transition from a matriarchal society, represented by the Erinyes, to the patriarchal society represented by Apollo and Athena. This is not the place to develop these theses, which have benefited by a broadly socialized explanation. One need merely be convinced that the *Oresteia* is a profoundly politicized work: it is exemplary of the relation which can unite a precise historical structure and a particular myth. Others may choose to see in it an eternal problematics of Evil and of Judgment; nonetheless the *Oresteia* is above all the work of a specific period, of a definite social condition, and of a contingent moral argument.

And it is precisely this explanation which permits us to answer the second question: our relation to the *Oresteia*, as men of 1955, is the evident nature of its particularity. Nearly twenty-five centuries separate us from this work: the transition from matriarchy to patriarchy, the substitution of new gods for old, and of arbitration for retaliation—none of this belongs to our present history; and it is just because of this flagrant difference that we can judge critically an ideological and social state in which we no longer participate and which henceforth appears to us objectively in all its remoteness. The *Oresteia* tells us what the men of its period sought to transcend, the obscurantism they tried to clarify; but it tells us at the same time that these efforts are anachronistic for us, that the new gods it sought to establish are gods we have conquered in our turn. There is a movement of history, a difficult but incontestable transformation of barbarism, the growing assurance that man possesses, in himself alone, the remedy for his ills—an assurance we must ceaselessly rediscover, for it is by realizing the distance already covered that we gain courage and hope for the distance which remains to be traveled.

It is therefore by giving the *Oresteia* its precise figure, by which I mean not an archeological figure but a historical one, that we shall manifest the link that unites us to this work. Performed in its particularity, in its monolithic aspect, progressive in relation to its own past but barbarous in relation to our present, the ancient tragedy concerns us in that it allows us to understand clearly, by all the means of the theater, that history is plastic, fluid, at the service of men, if only they try to make themselves its master in all lucidity. To grasp the historical specificity of the *Oresteia*, its exact originality, is for us the only way of making a dynamic use of it, a use endowed with responsibility.

It is for this reason that we reject a chaotic production, in which timid and partially honored options, now archeological and now esthetic, now essentialist (an eternal moral debate) and now exotic (the voodoo rite) ultimately manage, by their very vacillation, to rob us of the sentiment of a clear work, defined within and by history, remote as a past which was once ours but which we no longer desire. What we desire is that at every moment, and wherever it comes from, the theater speak Agamemnon's sentence: "The bonds are loosened, the remedy exists."

1955

Whose Theater?
Whose *Avant-Garde*?

O ur dictionaries do not tell us precisely when the term *avant-garde* was first used in a cultural sense. Apparently the notion is quite recent, a product of that moment in history when to certain of its writers the bourgeoisie appeared as an esthetically retrograde force, one to be contested. For the artist, most likely, the *avant-garde* has always been a means of resolving a specific historical contradiction: that of an unmasked bourgeoisie which could no longer proclaim its original universalism except in the form of a violent protest turned against itself: initially by an esthetic violence directed against the Philistines, then, with increasing commitment, by an ethical violence, when it became the duty of a *life style* to contest the bourgeois order (among the surrealists, for example); but never by a political violence.

Why not? Because, in a historical perspective, this protest has never been anything but a proxy: the bourgeoisie delegated some of its creators to tasks of formal subversion, though without actually disinheriting them: is it not the bourgeoisie, after all, which dispenses to *avant-garde* art the parsimonious support of its public, i.e., of its money? The very etymology of the term designates a portion—a somewhat exuberant, somewhat eccentric portion—of the bourgeois army. As if there were a secret and profound equilibrium between the troops of conformist art and its bold outriders. What we have here is a phenomenon well known in sociology, the phenomenon of complementarism, of which Lévi-Strauss has given an excellent description: the *avant-garde* author is somewhat like the witch doctor of so-called primitive societies: he *concentrates* the irregularity, the better to purge it from society as a whole. No doubt the bourgeoisie, in its declining phase, has required these aberrant operations which so noticeably label certain of its temptations. The *avant-garde* is in fact another cathartic phenomenon, a kind of vaccine intended to inject a little subjectivity, a little freedom under the crust of bourgeois values: we feel better for having taken part—a declared but limited part—in the disease.

Of course this *economy* of the *avant-garde* is real only on the scale of history. Subjectively and in the perspective of the creator himself, the *avant-garde* is experienced as a total liberation. However, Man is one thing, men are another. A creative experience can be radical only if it attacks the real, i.e., the political, structure of society. Beyond the personal struggle of the *avant-garde* writer, and whatever its exemplary force, there always comes a moment when Order recalls its vanguard. Significantly, it is never the bourgeoisie which has threatened the *avant-garde*; once the cutting edge of the new language is blunted, the bourgeoisie raises no objection to accommodating it, to appropriating it for its own purposes; Rimbaud annexed by Claudel, Cocteau in the Académie-Française, surrealism infused into the mass cinema—the *avant-garde* rarely pursues its career as a prodigal son *all the way*; sooner or later it returns to the bosom which had given it, with life, a freedom of pure postponement.

No, to tell the truth, the *avant-garde* is threatened by only one force, which is not the bourgeoisie: political consciousness. The surrealist movement was not broken up by bourgeois attacks but by the insistent representation of a political problem, in a word, of the communist problem. It seems that no sooner is the *avant-garde* won over to the necessity of revolutionary tasks than it renounces itself, agrees to die. And not out of a simple concern for clarity (the realistic artist's need to be understood by the people). The incompatibility is deeper. The *avant-garde* is always a way of celebrating the death of the bourgeoisie, for its own death still belongs to the bourgeoisie; but further than this the *avant-garde* cannot go; it cannot conceive the funerary term it expresses as a moment of germination, as the transition from a closed society to an open one; it is impotent by nature to infuse its protest with the hope of a new assent to the world: it wants to die, to say so, and it wants everything to die with it. The often fascinating liberation it imposes on language is actually a sentence without appeal: all sociability is abhorrent to it, and rightly so, since it refuses to perceive sociability on any but the bourgeois model.

As the parasite and property of the bourgeoisie, the *avant-garde* must follow its evolution: today, apparently, we are watching its slow death, either because the bourgeoisie will recuperate it altogether, ultimately putting on splendid evenings of Beckett and Audiberti (and tomorrow Ionesco, already acclimated by humanist criticism), or because the *avant-garde* playwright, acceding to a political consciousness of the theater, will renounce pure ethical protest (indubitably Adamov's case) for a new realism.

In this periodical,[1] where we have always championed the necessity of a political theater, we nevertheless measure all that the *avant-garde* can contribute to such a theater; it can propose new techniques, subvert our complacencies, enrich the dramatic vocabulary, awaken the realistic author to the need for a certain freedom of tone, rouse him from his usual apathy with regard to forms. One of the great dangers of the political theater is its fear of falling into bourgeois formalism; this obsession blinds it until it falls into the opposite excess: the realistic theater too often succumbs to a timidity of structure, a conformism of language; the charge of anarchy makes it easy enough to submit to the exhausted forms of the bourgeois theater without realizing that it is the very materiality of the theater and not just its ideology which must be

1. *Théâtre populaire.*

reconceived. Here the *avant-garde* can help. Especially since so many of its innovations derive from an acute observation of present realities: the "audacities" which sometimes shock academic criticism are, in fact and already, common currency in a collective art like the cinema; a popular, especially a young, public can understand them very well or in any case very quickly. And we are entitled to expect a great deal from a playwright who might give that new political art the deconditioning powers of the old *avant-garde* theater.

1956

The Tasks of
Brechtian Criticism

It is safe to predict that Brecht's work will become increasingly important for us; not only because it is great, but because it is exemplary as well; it shines, today at least, with an exceptional luster amid two deserts: the desert of our contemporary theater, where aside from his there are no great names to cite; and the desert of revolutionary art, sterile since the beginnings of the Zhdanovian impasse. Any reflection on theater and on revolution must come to terms with Brecht, who brought about this situation himself: the entire force of his work opposes the reactionary myth of unconscious genius; its greatness is the kind which best suits our period, the greatness of responsibility; it is a work which is in a state of "complicity" with the world, with our world: a knowledge of Brecht, a reflection on Brecht, in a word, Brechtian criticism is by definition extensive with the problematics of our time. We must tirelessly repeat this truth: knowing Brecht is of a different order of importance from knowing Shakespeare or Gogol; because it is for us, precisely, that Brecht has written his plays, and not for eternity. Brechtian criticism will therefore be written by the spectator, the reader, the consumer, and not the exegete: it is a criticism of a *concerned* man. And if I myself were to write the criticism whose context I am sketching here, I should not fail to suggest, at the risk of appearing indiscreet, how this work touches me and helps me, personally, as an individual. But to confine myself here to the essentials of a program of Brechtian criticism, I shall merely suggest the levels of analysis which such criticism should successively investigate.

(1) *Sociology.* Generally speaking, we do not yet have adequate means of investigation to define the theater's public, or publics. Furthermore, in France at least, Brecht has not yet emerged from the experimental theaters (except for the TNP's *Mother Courage,* a production so misconceived that the case is anything but instructive). For the moment, therefore, we can study only the press reactions.

There are four types to distinguish. By the extreme right, Brecht's work is totally discredited because of its political commitment: Brecht's theater is mediocre *because* it is communist. By the right (a more complicated right, which can extend to the "modernist" bourgeoisie of *L'Express*), Brecht is subjected to the usual political denaturation: the man is dissociated from the work, the former consigned to politics (emphasizing successively and contradictorily his independence and his servility with regard to the Party), and the latter enlisted under the banners of an eternal theater: Brecht's work, we are told, is great in spite of Brecht, against Brecht.

On the left, there is first of all a humanist reading: Brecht is made into one of those giant creative figures committed to a humanitarian promotion of man, like Romain Rolland or Barbusse. This sympathetic view unfortunately disguises an anti-intellectualist prejudice frequent in certain far-left circles: in order to "humanize" Brecht, the theoretical part of his work is discredited or at least minimized: the plays are great *despite* Brecht's systematic views on epic theater, the actor, alienation, etc.: here we encounter one of the basic theorems of *petit-bourgeois* culture, the romantic contrast between heart and head, between intuition and reflection, between the ineffable and the rational—an opposition which ultimately masks a magical conception of art. Finally, the communists themselves express certain reservations (in France, at least) with regard to Brecht's opposition to the positive hero, his epic conception of theater, and the "formalist" orientation of his dramaturgy. Apart from the contestation of Roger Vailland, based on a defense of French tragedy as a dialectical art of crisis, these criticisms proceed from a Zhdanovian conception of art.

I am citing a dossier from memory; it should be examined in detail. The point, moreover, is not to refute Brecht's critics, but rather to approach Brecht by the means our society spontaneously employs to digest him. Brecht reveals whoever speaks about him, and this revelation naturally concerns Brecht to the highest degree.

(2) *Ideology.* Must we oppose the "digestions" of the Brechtian canon by a canonical truth of Brecht? In a sense and within certain limits, yes. There is a specific ideological content, coherent, consistent, and remarkably organized, in Brecht's theater, one which protests against abusive distortions. This content must be described.

In order to do this, we possess two kinds of texts: first of all, the theoretical texts, of an acute intelligence (it is no matter of indifference to encounter a man of the theater who is intelligent), of a great ideological lucidity, and which it would be childish to underrate on the pretext that they are only an intellectual appendage to an essentially *creative* body of work. Of course Brecht's theater is made to be performed. But before performing it or seeing it performed, there is no ban on its being understood: this intelligence is organically linked to its constitutive function, which is to transform a public even as it is being entertained. In a Marxist like Brecht, the relations between theory and practice must not be underestimated or distorted. To separate the Brechtian theater from its theoretical foundations would be as erroneous as to try to understand Marx's action without reading *The Communist Manifesto* or Lenin's politics without reading *The State and the Revolution.* There is no official decree or supernatural intervention which graciously dispenses the theater from the demands of theoretical reflection. Against an entire tendency of our criticism, we must assert the capital importance of Brecht's systematic writings: it does not weaken the creative value of this theater to regard it as a reasoned theater.

Moreover, the plays themselves afford the chief elements of Brechtian ideology. I can indicate here only the principal ones: the historical and not "natural" character of human misfortunes; the spiritual contagion of economic alienation, whose final effect is to blind the very men it oppresses as to the causes of their servitude; the correctible status of Nature, the tractability of the world; the necessary adequation of means and situations (for instance, in a bad society, the law can be re-established only by a reprobate judge); the transformation of ancient psychological "conflicts" into historical contradictions, subject as such to the corrective power of men.

We must note here that these truths are never set forth except as the consequence of concrete situations, and these situations are infinitely plastic. Contrary to the rightist prejudice, Brecht's theater is not a thesis theater, not a propaganda theater. What Brecht takes from Marxism are not slogans, an articulation of arguments, but a general method of explanation. It follows that in Brecht's theater the Marxist elements always seem to be recreated. Basically, Brecht's greatness, and his solitude, is that he keeps inventing Marxism. The ideological theme, in Brecht, could be precisely defined as a dynamic of events which combines observation and explanation, ethics and politics: according to the profoundest Marxist teaching, each theme is at once the expression of what men want to be and of what things are, at once a protest (because it unmasks) and a reconciliation (because it explains).

(3) *Semiology*. Semiology is the study of signs and significations. I do not want to engage here in a discussion of this science, which was postulated some forty years ago by the linguist Saussure and which is generally accused of formalism. Without letting ourselves be intimidated by the words, we might say that Brechtian dramaturgy, the theory of *Episierung*, of alienation, and the entire practice of the Berliner Ensemble with regard to sets and costumes, propose an explicit semiological problem. For what Brechtian dramaturgy postulates is that today at least, the responsibility of a dramatic art is not so much to express reality as to signify it. Hence

there must be a certain distance between signified and signifier: revolutionary art must admit a certain arbitrary nature of signs, it must acknowledge a certain "formalism," in the sense that it must treat form according to an appropriate method, which is the semiological method. All Brechtian art protests against the Zhdanovian confusion between ideology and semiology, which has led to such an esthetic impasse.

We realize, moreover, why this aspect of Brechtian thought is most antipathetic to bourgeois and Zhdanovian criticism: both are attached to an esthetic of the "natural" expression of reality: art for them is a false Nature, a *pseudo-Physis*. For Brecht, on the contrary, art today—i.e., at the heart of a historical conflict whose stake in human disalienation—art today must be an *anti-Physis*. Brecht's formalism is a radical protest against the confusions of the bourgeois and *petit-bourgeois* false Nature: in a still-alienated society, art must be critical, it must cut off all illusions, even that of "Nature": the sign must be partially arbitrary, otherwise we fall back on an art of expression, an art of essentialist illusion.

(4) *Morality.* Brechtian theater is a moral theater, that is, a theater which asks, with the spectator: what is to be done in such a situation? At this point we should classify and describe the archetypical situations of the Brechtian theater; they may be reduced, I think, to a single question: how to be good in a bad society? It seems to me very important to articulate the moral structure of Brecht's theater: granted that Marxism has had other more urgent tasks than to concern itself with problems of individual conduct; nonetheless capitalist society endures, and communism itself is being transformed: revolutionary action must increasingly cohabit, and in an almost institutional fashion, with the norms of bourgeois and *petit-bourgeois* morality: problems of conduct, and no longer of action, arise. Here is where Brecht can have a great cleansing power, a pedagogical power.

Especially since his morality has nothing catechistic about it, being for the most part strictly interrogative. Indeed, some of his plays conclude with a literal interrogation of the public, to whom the author leaves the responsibility of finding its own solution to the problem raised. Brecht's moral role is to infiltrate a question into what seems self-evident (this is the theme of the exception and the rule). For what is involved here is essentially a morality of invention. Brechtian invention is a tactical process to unite with revolutionary correction. In other words, for Brecht the outcome of every moral impasse depends on a more accurate analysis of the concrete situation in which the subject finds himself: the issue is joined by representing in explicit terms the historical particularity of this situation, its artificial, purely conformist nature. Essentially, Brecht's morality consists of a correct reading of history, and the plasticity of the morality (*to change Custom when necessary*) derives from the very plasticity of history.

1956

"*Will* Burns Us..."

> *Will* burns us, and *power* destroys us: but
> *knowledge* leaves our frail organism
> in a perpetual state of calm.

In the production of the greatest writers, Thibaudet remarks, there often exists a *limit work*, a singular, almost
disconcerting text which constitutes at once the secret and
the caricature of their creation, suggesting thereby the aberrant work they have not written and perhaps wanted to
write; examples of such "dreams," wonderfully combining a
creator's positive and negative aspects, are Chateaubriand's
Life of Rancé, Flaubert's *Bouvard and Pécuchet*; perhaps
Balzac's limit work is *Le Faiseur*.[1]

First of all, because *Le Faiseur* is a play—i.e., an untimely
growth in that mature and specialized organism, the Balzacian
novel. What is this supernumerary process doing here (four
plays as opposed to a hundred novels), this theater swarming
with all the ghosts of French comedy from Molière to Labiche?
Testifying no doubt to an absolute *energy* (the word must
be taken in its Balzacian sense of an ultimate creative power),
freed from all the opacity, all the deliberation of novelistic
narrative. *Le Faiseur* may be a farce, but it is a farce which
burns: it is the phosphorus of creation; here speed is no longer

---

1. A TNP production, directed by Jean Vilar.

graceful, lively, insolent, as in classical comedy; it is hard, implacable, electric, eager to sweep on and unconcerned to enlighten: there is an essential haste in the play. The lines twitch restlessly from one actor to the next, as if above the volleys of the plot, in a higher zone of creation, the characters were linked together by a complicity of rhythm: *Le Faiseur* is something of a ballet, and the very abundance of its asides, that dreaded weapon of the theater's old arsenal, adds to the headlong course a kind of intense complication: here the dialogue always has at least two dimensions. The oratorical character of a novelistic style is broken up, reduced to a metallic, admirably *played* language: it is a magnificent theatrical style, the very language of the theater in the theater.

Le Faiseur dates from Balzac's last years. By 1848, the French bourgeoisie was on the brink of collapse: the industrialist or landowner, the thrifty and prudent director of family enterprise, the Louis-Philippe capitalist, hoarder of concrete possessions, was to be replaced by the financial adventurer, the absolute speculator, the pirate of the Bourse, the man who can create everything out of nothing. It has often been remarked that at many points in his *oeuvre*, Balzac painted the society of the Second Empire before the fact. This applies to Mercadet, the capitalist magician, who miraculously detaches money from property.

Mercadet is an alchemist (a Faustian theme dear to Balzac's heart), he labors to produce something out of nothing. Nothing, here, is even more than nothing; it is the positive void of money, the hole which has all the characteristics of existence: it is debt. Debt is a prison (in the peak years of the debtor's prison—that famous Clichy which recurs so obsessively in *Le Faiseur*); Balzac himself was confined in debt all his life, and one might say that the Balzacian *oeuvre* is the concrete trace of a furious struggle to emerge from it: to write was first of all to extinguish debt, to transcend it. Similarly, *Le Faiseur* as a play, as a dramatic duration, is a series of frenzied movements to escape from debt, to break the infernal jail of monetary void. Mercadet is a man who employs every means to escape the strait jacket of his debts.

Not out of moral impulsion, but rather by a kind of Dionysiac exercise of creation: Mercadet does not work to pay his debts, he works in an absolute fashion to create money *ex nihilo*. Speculation is the sublimated, alchemical form of capitalist profit: as a modern man, Mercadet no longer works with concrete goods, but with ideas of goods, with essences of money. However concrete his work (as evidenced by the complications of the plot), it deals with abstract objects. Already, paper money is an initial spiritualization of gold; stocks are its final, impalpable state: the humanity metal (of usurers and misers) will be replaced by humanity stocks (of speculators, *faiseurs* who *do* something with the void). For Mercadet, speculation is a demiurgic operation to discover the modern philosophers' stone: the gold which is not gold.

Le Faiseur's great theme, then, is the void. This void is incarnated in Godeau, the phantom partner whom we always wait for, whom we never see, and who ultimately creates a fortune from his very void. Godeau is a hallucinating invention; Godeau is not a creature, he is an absence, but this absence exists, because Godeau is a *function*: perhaps the whole new world lies in this transition from being to action, from object to function: there is no longer any need for things to exist, it is enough if they function; or rather, they can function without existing. Balzac envisioned the modernity about to dawn, no longer as a world of goods and persons (categories of the Napoleonic Code), but as a world of functions and shares, of "holding actions": what exists is no longer what *is* but what *holds*. In *Le Faiseur*, all the characters are void (except the women), but they exist precisely because their void is contiguous: they hold each other up.

Is this mechanics victorious? Does Mercadet find his philosophers' stone, does he create money out of nothing? As a matter of fact, there are two denouements to *Le Faiseur*. One is moral: Mercadet's alchemy is foiled by his wife's scruples, and Mercadet would be ruined if Godeau did not arrive (though we do not see him) and send his partner off to Touraine to end his days as a stay-at-home gentleman farmer—that is, as the very opposite of a speculator. This is the written denouement, though it may not be the real one. The potential truth is that Mercadet wins: we know that the creation's deeper meaning is that Godeau does not arrive: Mercadet is an absolute creator, he owes nothing except to himself, to his alchemical power.

The group of women (Mme Mercadet and her daughter Julie), to whom we should add the suitor Minard, a young man with noble sentiments, is situated well outside the alchemical circuit; it represents the old order, that world of limited but concrete property, of reliable incomes, paid debts, savings; a world if not abhorred (for there is nothing esthetic or moral about Mercadet's superenergy), at least uninteresting: a world which can flourish (at the play's end) only in the heaviest version of possession, that of land (property in Touraine). We see how polar the oppositions of this theater are: on the one side, weight, sentiment, morality, the object; on the other, lightness, galvanism, the function. This is why *Le Faiseur* is a limit work: the themes are drained of all ambiguity, separated in a blinding, pitiless light.

Further, Balzac has perhaps achieved here his greatest martyrdom as a creator: to delineate in Mercadet the figure of a father inaccessible to paternity. As we know, the father (Goriot is the perfect incarnation) is the cardinal person of Balzacian creation, at once absolute creator and total victim of his creatures. Mercadet, subtilized, etherealized by the vice of speculation, is a false father; he sacrifices his daughter. And the destructive sweep of this work is such that an unheard-of thing happens to this daughter, an audacity very rare in our theaters: this daughter is *ugly*, and her very ugliness is an object of speculation. To speculate on beauty is still to establish an accountancy of being; to speculate on the ugly is to bring nothingness full circle: Mercadet, a satanic figure of "power" and "will" in the pure state, would be completely burnt, destroyed, if a last *coup de théâtre* did not restore to him the weight of the family and of the earth. It is true, moreover, that nothing remains of the *"faiseur"*: devoured, subtilized by the movement of his passion and by the infinite dizziness of his omnipotence, the speculator manifests the glory and the punishment of every Balzacian Prometheus, of all those thieves of the divine fire, of whom Mercadet is in a sense the final algebraic formula, at once grotesque and terrible.

1957

The Last Happy Writer

What have we in common, today, with Voltaire? From a modern point of view, his philosophy is outmoded. It is possible to believe in the fixity of essences and in the chaos of history, but no longer in the same way as Voltaire. In any case, atheists no longer throw themselves at the feet of deists, who moreover no longer exist. Dialectics has killed off Manicheanism, and we rarely discuss the ways of Providence. As for Voltaire's enemies, they have disappeared, or been transformed: there are no more Jansenists, no Socinians, no Leibnizians; the Jesuits are no longer named Nonotte or Patouillet.

I was about to say: there is no longer an Inquisition. This is wrong, of course. What has disappeared is the theater of persecution, not persecution itself: the *auto-da-fé* has been subtilized into a police operation, the stake has become the concentration camp, discreetly ignored by its neighbors. In return for which, the figures have changed: in 1721 nine men and eleven women were burned at Grenada in the four ovens of the scaffold, and in 1723 nine men were burned at Madrid to celebrate the arrival of the French princess: they had doubtless married their cousins or eaten meat on Friday. A horrible repression, whose absurdity sustains Voltaire's entire *oeuvre*. But between 1939 and 1945, six million human beings were killed, among others, because they were Jews—they, or their fathers, or their grandfathers.

We have not had a single pamphlet against that. But perhaps it is precisely because the figures have changed. Simplistic as it may appear, there is a proportion between the lightness of the Voltairean artillery and the sporadic artillery of religious crime in the eighteenth century: quantitatively limited, the stake became a principle, i.e., a target: a tremendous advantage for its opponent: such is the stuff of which triumphant writers are made. For the very enormity of racist crimes, their organization by the State, the ideological justifications with which they are masked—all this involves today's writer in much more than a pamphlet, demands a philosophy rather than an irony, an explanation rather than an astonishment. Since Voltaire, history has been imprisoned in a difficulty which lacerates any committed literature and which Voltaire never knew: *no freedom for the enemies of freedom:* no one can any longer give lessons in tolerance to anyone.

In short, what separates us from Voltaire is that he was a happy writer. Better than anyone else, he gave reason's combat a festive style. Everything is spectacle in his battles: the adversary's name—always ridiculous; the disputed doctrine —reduced to a proposition (Voltairean irony is invariably the exposure of a disproportion); the points scored, exploding in every direction until they seem to be a game, dispensing the onlooker from all respect and all pity; the very mobility of the combatant, here disguised under a thousand transparent pseudonyms, there making his European journeys a kind of feinting farce, a perpetual Scapinade. For the skirmishes between Voltaire and the world are not only a spectacle but a superlative spectacle, proclaiming themselves such in the fashion of those Punchinello shows Voltaire loved so much—he had a puppet theater of his own at Cirey.

Voltaire's first happiness was doubtless that of his times. Let there be no mistake: the times were very harsh, and Voltaire has everywhere described their horrors. Yet no period has helped a writer more, given him more assurance that he was fighting for a just and natural cause. The bourgeoisie, the class from which Voltaire came, already held most of its economic positions; a power in commerce and industry, in the ministries, in culture and the sciences, it knew that its triumph coincided with the nation's prosperity and the happiness of each citizen. On its side, potential power, certainty of method, and the still-pure heritage of taste; against it, all a dying world could display of corruption, stupidity, and ferocity. It was indeed a great happiness, a great peace to combat an enemy so uniformly condemnable. The tragic spirit is severe because it acknowledges, by obligation of nature, its adversary's greatness: Voltaire had no tragic spirit: he had to measure himself against no living force, against no idea or individual that could induce him to reflect (except the past: Pascal, and the future: Rousseau; but he conjured them both away): Jesuits, Jansenists, or parliaments, these were great frozen bodies, drained of all intelligence and filled with no more than a ferocity intolerable to the heart and the mind. Authority, even in its bloodiest manifestations, was no more than a decor; merely subject such machinery to human eyes, and it would collapse. Voltaire had that sly and tender gaze (*Zaïre's very heart*, Mme de Genlis tells us, *was in his eyes*), whose destructive power lay in simply bearing life among those great blind masks which still ruled society.

It was, then, a singular happiness to have to do battle in a world where force and stupidity were continually on the same tack: a privileged situation for the mind. The writer was on history's side, all the happier in that he perceived history as a consummation, not as a transcendence which risked sweeping him along with it.

Voltaire's second happiness was precisely to forget history, at the very moment it was supporting him. In order to be happy, Voltaire suspended time; if he has a philosophy, it is that of immobility. We know what he thought: God created the world as a geometer, not as a father. Which means that He does not bother to accompany His creation and that, once regulated, the world no longer sustains relations with God. An original intelligence established a certain type of causality once and for all: there are no objects without ends, no effects without causes, and the relation between one and the other is immutable. Voltairean metaphysics is therefore never anything but an introduction to physics, and Providence a mechanics. For once God has left the world He created (like the clockmaker his clock), neither God nor man ever moves again. Of course good and evil exist; but we are to translate them as happiness and misery, not sin or innocence; for they are merely the elements of a universal causality; they have a necessity, but this necessity is mechanical, not moral: evil does not punish, good does not reward: they do not signify that God is, that He surveys all, but that He has been, that He has created.

If man should take it upon himself to turn from evil to good by a moral impulse, it is the universal order of causes and effects which he injures; he can produce, by this movement, only a farcical chaos (as Memnon does, the day he decides to be wise). Then what can man do with regard to good and evil? Not much: in this machinery which is the Creation, there is room only for a *game*, that is, the very slight amplitude the constructor allows his pieces in which to move. This game is reason. It is capricious—i.e., it attests to no direction of history: reason appears, disappears, with no other law than the very personal effort of certain minds: among the benefits of history (useful inventions, great works) there is a relation of contiguity, never of function. Voltaire's opposition to any intelligence of time is very intense. For Voltaire, there is no history in the modern sense of the word, nothing but chronologies. Voltaire wrote historical works expressly to say that he did not believe in history: the age of Louis XIV is not an organism, it is a cluster of chance meetings, here the dragonnades, there Racine. Nature itself, of course, is never historical: being essentially art, i.e., God's artifice, it cannot move or have moved: the mountains were not wrought by the earth and the waters, God created them once and for all for the use of His creatures, and the fossil fishes—whose discovery so excited the age—are only the prosaic leavings of picnicking pilgrims: there is no evolution.

The philosophy of time will be the contribution of the nineteenth century (and singularly of Germany). We might assume that the relativist lesson of the past is at least replaced in Voltaire, as in his entire age, by that of space. At first glance, this is what occurs: the eighteenth century is not only a great age of travel, the age in which modern capitalism, then preponderantly British, definitively organizes its world market from China to South America; it is above all the age when travel accedes to literature and engages a philosophy. We know the role of the Jesuits, by their *Edifying and Curious Letters,* in the birth of exoticism. From early in the century, these materials were transformed and soon produced a veritable typology of exotic man: we have the Egyptian Sage, the Mohammedan Arab, the Turk, the Chinese, the Siamese, and most prestigious of all, the Persian. All these Orientals are philosophy teachers; but before saying which philosophy, we must note that just when Voltaire begins writing his Tales, which owe a great deal to Oriental folklore, the century has already elaborated a veritable rhetoric of exoticism, a kind of digest whose figures are so well formed and so well known that they can henceforth be utilized without troubling further over descriptions and astonishments; Voltaire will not fail to utilize them in this fashion, for he never troubled to be "original" (an entirely modern notion, moreover); for him, as indeed for any of his contemporaries, the Oriental is not the object, the term of a genuine consideration, but simply a cipher, a convenient sign of communication.

The result of this conceptualization is that the Voltairean journey has no density; the space Voltaire covers so obsessively (we do nothing but travel in his Tales) is not an explorer's space, it is a surveyor's space, and what Voltaire borrows from the allogeneous humanity of the Chinese and the Persian is a new limit, not a new substance; new habitations are attributed to the human essence, it flourishes from the Seine to the Ganges, and Voltaire's novels are less investigations than inspections of an owner whom we "orient" in no particular order because his estate never varies, and whom we interrupt by incessant stops during which we discuss not what we have seen but what we are. This explains why the Voltairean journey is neither realistic nor baroque (the picaresque vein of the century's first narratives has completely dried up); it is not even an operation of knowledge, but merely of affirmation; it is the element of a logic, the figure of an equation; these Oriental countries, which today have so heavy a weight, so pronounced an individuation in world politics, are for Voltaire so many forms, mobile signs without actual content, humanity at zero degrees (Centigrade), which one nimbly grasps in order to signify . . . oneself.

For such is the paradox of Voltairean travel: to manifest an immobility. There are of course other manners, other laws, other moralities than ours, and this is what the journey teaches; but this diversity belongs to the human essence and consequently finds its point of equilibrium very rapidly; it is enough to acknowledge it in order to be done with it: let man (that is, Occidental man) multiply himself a little, let the European philosopher be doubled by the Chinese Sage, the ingenious Huron, and universal man will be created. To aggrandize oneself in order to confirm, not in order to transform oneself—such is the meaning of the Voltairean voyage.

It was doubtless Voltaire's second happiness to be able to depend upon the world's immobility. The bourgeoisie was so close to power that it could already begin not to believe in history. It could also begin to reject any system, to suspect any organized philosophy, that is, to posit its own thinking, its own good sense as a Nature which any doctrine, any intellectual system would offend. This is what Voltaire did so brilliantly, and it was his third happiness: he ceaselessly dissociated intelligence and intellectuality, asserting that the world is an order if we do not try too much to order it, that it is a system if only we renounce systematizing it: this conduct of mind has had a great career subsequently: today we call it anti-intellectualism.

Notable is the fact that all of Voltaire's enemies could be named, that is, their being derived from their certainty: Jesuits, Jansenists, Socinians, Protestants, atheists, all enemies among themselves, but united under Voltaire's attack by their capacity to be defined by a word. Conversely, on the level of denominative systems, Voltaire escapes. Doctrinally, was he a deist? a Leibnizian? a rationalist? Each time, yes and no. He has no system except the hatred of system (and we know that there is nothing grimmer than this very system); today his enemies would be the doctrinaires of history, of science (*vide* his mockery of pure science in *The Man with Forty Ecus*), or of existence; Marxists, existentialists, leftist intellectuals—Voltaire would have hated them, covered them with incessant *lazzi*, as he did the Jesuits in his own day. By continuously setting intelligence against intellectuality, by using one to undermine the other, by reducing the conflicts of ideas to a kind of Manichean struggle between stupidity and intelligence, by identifying all system with stupidity and all freedom of mind with intelligence, Voltaire grounded liberalism on a contradiction. As system of the nonsystem, anti-intellectualism eludes and gains on both counts, perpetually ricocheting between bad faith and good conscience, between a pessimism of substance and a jig of form, between a proclaimed skepticism and a terrorist doubt.

The Voltairean festivity is constituted by this incessant alibi. Voltaire cudgels and dodges at the same time. The world is simple for a man who ends all his letters with the cordial salutation *Ecrasons l'infâme* (i.e., dogmatism). We know that this simplicity and this happiness were bought at the price of an ablation of history and of an immobilization of the world. Further, it is a happiness which excluded many, despite its dazzling victory over obscurantism. Thus, in accord with the legend, the anti-Voltaire is indeed Rousseau. By forcefully positing the idea of man's corruption by society, Rousseau set history moving again, established the principle of a permanent transcendence of history. But by doing so he bequeathed to literature a poisoned legacy. Henceforth, ceaselessly athirst and wounded by a responsibility he can never again completely honor nor completely elude, the intellectual will be defined by his bad conscience: Voltaire was a happy writer, but doubtless the last.

1958

There Is No
Robbe-Grillet School

It appears that Butor is Robbe-Grillet's disciple, and that the two of them, augmented episodically by several others (Nathalie Sarraute, Marguerite Duras, and Claude Simon; but why not Cayrol, whose novelistic technique is often very audacious?), form a new school of the novel. And if our criticism betrays—understandably—some uncertainty as to the doctrinal or simply empirical link which unites them, why then our criticism plunges them, pell-mell, into the *avant-garde*. For we need an *avant-garde*: nothing is more reassuring than a *named* rebellion. The moment has doubtless come when the arbitrary grouping of novelists like Butor and Robbe-Grillet —to mention only those most commonly associated—begins to be awkward, for one as for the other. Butor does not belong to the Robbe-Grillet school, chiefly because this school does not exist. As for the works themselves, they are antinomical.

Robbe-Grillet's endeavor is not a humanist one, his world is not in accord with the world. What he is seeking is the expression of a negativity, i.e., the squaring of the circle in literature. He is not the first. We know today certain important *oeuvres* —rare, it is true—which have been or which are, deliberately, the glorious residue of the impossible: Mallarmé's, for example,

or Blanchot's. What is new about Robbe-Grillet is that he tries
to maintain the negation at the level of novelistic technique
(in other words, he realizes that there is a responsibility of
form, something utterly unsuspected by our antiformalists).
There is, then, at least tendentially, in Robbe-Grillet's work, a
rejection of the story, the anecdote, the psychology of motivations, and at the same time a rejection of the signification of
objects. Whence the importance of optical description: if
Robbe-Grillet describes objects quasi-geometrically, it is in order
to release them from human signification, to *correct* them of
metaphor and anthropomorphism. Visual rigor in Robbe-Grillet (moreover, it is much more a matter of pathology than of
rigor) is therefore purely negative, it institutes nothing, or
rather it institutes precisely the human nothing of the object;
it is like the frozen cloud which conceals the void and consequently designates it. Sight in Robbe-Grillet is essentially a
purifying conduct, a rift—even a painful one—in the solidarity
between man and things. Sight, here, cannot lead to reflection:
it recuperates nothing of man, of his solitude, of his metaphysics. The notion most alien, most antipathetic to Robbe-
Grillet's art is doubtless the notion of tragedy, for in Robbe-Grillet nothing of man is offered as a spectacle, not even his
abandonment. Now it is this radical rejection of tragedy, I believe, which gives Robbe-Grillet's endeavor a pre-eminent value.
Tragedy is but a means of recovering human misery, of subsum-
ing it, hence of justifying it in the form of a necessity, a wisdom,
or a purification: to reject this recuperation and to seek some
technical means of not succumbing to it (nothing is more insidious than tragedy) is today a singular enterprise and, whatever its "formalist" detours, an important one. Not that Robbe-
Grillet has necessarily succeeded in his intention: first of all,
because failure is inherent in its very nature (there is no zero
degree of form, negativity always turns into positivity); and
secondly, because a work is never *throughout* the belated expression of an initial project (the project is also an inference
from the work).

Butor's latest novel, *La Modification*,[1] seems point by point

1. [Published in America as A *Change of Heart.*]

the contrary of Robbe-Grillet's work. What is *La Modification?* Essentially the counterpoint of several worlds whose very correspondence is destined to make objects and events *signify.* There is the world of the letter: a train trip from Paris to Rome. There is the world of spirit, of meaning: a consciousness modifies its project. Whatever the elegance and the discretion of his procedure, Butor's art is symbolic: the journey signifies something, the spatial itinerary, the temporal itinerary, and the spiritual (or memorial) itinerary exchange their literality, and it is this exchange which is signification. Hence, what Robbe-Grillet wants to eliminate from the novel (*Jealousy* is in this regard the best of his works)—the symbol, i.e., destiny—is just what Butor wants to keep. Further: each of the three novels Robbe-Grillet has written constitutes an explicit mockery of the notion of an itinerary (a very coherent mockery, for the itinerary, the disclosure, is a tragic notion): each of Robbe-Grillet's novels closes over its initial identity: time and place have changed, yet no new consciousness has appeared. For Butor, on the contrary, process itself is creative, and creative of consciousness: a new man is constantly being born: time serves to some purpose.

It seems that this positivity goes very far in the spiritual order. The symbol is an essential means of reconciliation between man and the universe; or more precisely, it postulates the very notion of the universe, i.e., of creation. Now, *La Modification* is not only a symbolic novel, it is also a novel of the creature, in the fully actuated sense of the word. I do not believe for a moment that the second-person narrative Butor employs in *La Modification* is a formal artifice, a shrewd variation on the novel's third-person which we must credit to the *avant-garde;* this vocative seems to me quite literal: it is the creator's address to the creature, named, constituted, *created* in all his acts by a judge and progenitor. This interpellation is crucial, for it institutes the hero's consciousness: it is by dint of finding himself under surveillance, described by another consciousness, that the hero's person is modified and that he abandons the notion of marrying his mistress as he had initially determined to do. Thus in Butor the description of objects has a meaning absolutely antinomic to its meaning in Robbe-Grillet.

Robbe-Grillet describes objects in order to expel man from them. Butor, on the contrary, makes objects into revealing attributes of human consciousness, pieces of space and time to which are stuck particles of the person: the object is given in all its painful intimacy with man; it constitutes a part of a man, enters into a dialogue with him, leads him to conceive his own duration, to produce a lucidity, a disgust, in other words, a redemption. Butor's objects make us say *how true!* they aim at the revelation of an essence, they are analogical. On the contrary, Robbe-Grillet's are literal; they engage in no complicity with the reader: neither eccentric nor familiar, they exist in an unheard-of solitude, since this solitude must never refer to a solitude of man, which would still be a means of recuperating the human: the object must be alone, though without ever raising the problem of human solitude. In Butor, on the contrary, the object posits the solitude of man (we need merely remember the compartment in *La Modification*), but only in order to rescue him from it, for this solitude generates a consciousness, and still more, a consciousness under surveillance— i.e., a moral consciousness. Thus the hero of *La Modification* attains to the superlative form of the character, which is the person: the age-old values of our civilization are invested in him, beginning with the tragic order, which exists wherever suffering is recovered as a spectacle and redeemed by its "modification."

Thus it is difficult to imagine two conceptions of art more opposed than those of Robbe-Grillet and Butor. One seeks to decondition the novel of its traditional reflexes, to make it express a world without qualities; this art is the exercise of an absolute freedom (it being clearly understood that such an exercise is not necessarily a performance); whence its declared formalism. The other, on the contrary, is crammed, one might say, with positivity: it is the visible side of a hidden truth— once again literature defines itself by the illusion that it is more than itself, the work being destined to illustrate a transliterary order.

Naturally, the confusion our critics have established between these two conceptions is not entirely innocent. Butor's appearance in the outer space of vanguard literature has made it possible to reproach Robbe-Grillet for his "dryness," his "formalism," his "lack of humanity," as if these were actual lacunae, whereas this negativity—technical and not moral (though our critics constantly, and with constant prejudice, identify fact and value)—is precisely what Robbe-Grillet seeks most rigorously, it is visibly *why he writes*. And symmetrically, the deceptive pairing with Robbe-Grillet permits our critics to make Butor into a "successful" Robbe-Grillet, who thereby graciously adds to the audacity of his formal experimentation a "classical" stock of human wisdom, sensibility, and spirituality. It is an old trick of our criticism to proclaim its breadth of views, its modernism, by baptizing *avant-garde* what it can assimilate, thereby economically combining the security of tradition with the *frisson* of novelty.

And of course, this confusion can only embarrass our two authors: Butor, whose endeavor is thus unduly formalized, though it is much less formal than is supposed; and Robbe-Grillet, whose very formalism is thus underestimated by being made into an inadequacy and not regarded as a deliberate treatment of reality. Perhaps, instead of drawing up (however casually) arbitrary charts of the vanguard novel, it would be more useful to consider the radical discontinuity of such experiments, the causes of that intense fractionalization which is as prevalent in our letters in particular as in our intellectuality in general, just when everything would seem to suggest the need for a united front.

1958

Literature and Metalanguage

Logic teaches us to distinguish the language object from meta-language. The language object is the very matter subject to logical investigation; metalanguage is the necessarily artificial language in which we conduct this investigation. Thus—and this is the role of logical reflection—I can express in a symbolic language (metalanguage) the relations, the structure of a real language (language object).

For centuries, our writers did not imagine it was possible to consider literature (the word itself is recent) as a language, subject, like any other, to logical distinction: literature never reflected upon itself (sometimes upon its figures, but never upon its being), it never divided itself into an object at once scrutinizing and scrutinized; in short, it spoke but did not speak itself. And then, probably with the first shocks to the good conscience of the bourgeoisie, literature began to regard itself as double: at once object and scrutiny of that object, utterance and utterance of that utterance, literature object and metaliterature. These have been, *grosso modo*, the phases of the development: first an artisanal consciousness of literary fabrication, refined to the point of painful scruple, of the impossible (Flaubert); then, the heroic will to identify, in one and the same written matter, literature and the theory of literature (Mallarmé); then, the hope of somehow eluding literary tautology by ceaselessly postponing literature, by declaring that one is going to write, and by making this declaration into literature itself (Proust); then, the testing of literary good faith by deliberately, systematically multiplying to infinity the meanings of the word object without ever abiding by any one sense of what is signified (surrealism); finally, and inversely, rarefying these meanings to the point of trying to achieve a *Dasein* of literary language, a neutrality (though not an innocence) of writing: I am thinking here of the work of Robbe-Grillet.

All these endeavors may someday permit us to define our century (the last hundred years) as the century of the question *What Is Literature?* (Sartre answered it from outside, which gives him an ambiguous literary position.) And precisely because this interrogation is conducted not from outside but within literature itself, or more exactly at its extreme verge, in that asymptotic zone where literature appears to destroy itself as a language object without destroying itself as a metalanguage, and where the metalanguage's quest is defined at the last possible moment as a new language object, it follows that our literature has been for a hundred years a dangerous game with its own death, in other words a way of experiencing, of living that death: our literature is like that Racinean heroine who dies upon learning who she is but lives by seeking her identity (Eriphile in *Iphigénie*). Now this situation defines a truly tragic status: our society, confined for the moment in a kind of historical impasse, permits its literature only the Oedipal question par excellence: *Who am I?* By the same token it forbids the dialectical question: *What is to be done?* The truth of our literature is not in the practical order, but already it is no longer in the natural order: it is a mask which points to itself.

1959

Tacitus and the
Funerary Baroque

ounted, the murders in the *Annals* are few enough
(some fifty for three principates); but read, their effect
is apocalyptic: from element to mass, a new quality appears, the world is transformed.[1] Perhaps that is what the
baroque is: a growing contradiction between unit and totality,
an art in which extent is not additive but multiplicative, in
short, the density of an acceleration: in Tacitus, from year to
year, death *jells,* and the more divided the moments of this
solidification become, the more inseparable their sum: generic
Death is massive, not conceptual; the idea, here, is not the
product of a reduction, but of a repetition. We know of course
that terrorism is not a quantitative phenomenon; we know that
during our Revolution the number of tortures was laughable;
but we also know that for the next century, from Büchner to
Jouve (I am thinking of his preface to selections from Dan-
ton), we have seen terrorism as a being, not a volume. A stoic
during an enlightened despotism, a creature of the Flavians

1. "In the ninth year of the emperor's reign, Fortune suddenly
deranged everything: Tiberius became a cruel tyrant, as well as an
abettor of cruelty in others" (IV.1).

writing under Trajan the history of the Julio-Claudian tyranny,
Tacitus is in the situation of a liberal living the atrocities of
sans-culottism: for him the past is an hallucination, an obsessional theater, a scene even more than a lesson: death is a protocol.

And first of all, in order to destroy number starting from
number, what must be paradoxically established is the unit.
In Tacitus the great anonymous slaughters scarcely rank as
facts, they are not values: such things are always slave massa-
cres: collective death is not human, death begins only with
the individual, in other words, with the patrician. Tacitean
death always discloses a civil status; the victim holds office,
he is a unit, *one*, enclosing his history, his character, his function, his name. Death itself is not algebraic: death is always a
dying; it is almost never an effect; however rapidly evoked,
death appears as a duration, a process to be relished; we can
tell from certain vibrations of the sentence that each victim
knew he was dying; Tacitus always gives this ultimate consciousness to the victims of torture, which is probably how he establishes these deaths in terrorism: because he cites man at the
purest moment of his end; it is the contradiction between object and subject, between thing and consciousness, it is this
final stoic suspense which makes dying a strictly human act:
we kill like animals, we die like men: all the deaths in Tacitus
are instants, both immobility and catastrophe, both silence and
vision.

The act outshines its cause: there is no distinction between
murder and suicide, it is the same dying, sometimes adminis-
tered, sometimes prescribed: the presentation of death establishes death; whether the centurion delivers a blow or an order,
it suffices that he appear, like an angel, for the irreversible to
occur: the instant is there, the outcome accedes to the present.
All these murders have scarcely any causes: delation is enough
—a kind of death ray which works by remote control: crime is
immediately absorbed into its magical denomination: once
you are called guilty, by anyone, you are already doomed; innocence raises no problem, once you are branded. Moreover, it
is because death is a raw fact, and not the element of a reason,
that it is contagious: the wife follows her husband into suicide

without being obliged to do so, relatives die in clusters as soon as one of them is condemned.[2] For those who fling themselves into it—like Gribouille who leaps into the river to avoid the rain—death is life because it puts an end to the ambiguity of signs, it shifts us from the unnamed to the named. The act yields to its name: if the law forbids killing a virgin, then it suffices to rape her before strangling her: it is the name which is rigid, it is the name which is the order of the world. To accede to the security of the fatal name, the reprieved or pardoned person commits suicide. Not to die is not only an accident but a negative, almost a ridiculous state: it occurs only by inadvertence. Supreme reason of this absurd structure, Coceius Nerva enumerates all his reasons for living (he is neither poor, nor ill, nor under suspicion), and despite the emperor's objurgations, he kills himself. And as a crowning confusion, the *Ratio*, eliminated at the moment of the irreparable, is restored *after the fact*: dead, the victim is paradoxically extracted from the funereal universe, introduced into a trial where death is not certain: Nero would have pardoned him, he says, if he had lived; or again, the victim is given a choice of demise; or yet again, the suicide's corpse is strangled so that his estate may be confiscated.

Since dying is a protocol, the victim is always shown in the decor of life: one dreaming on a promontory, another at table, another in his garden, another in his bath. Once death is presented, it is suspended a moment: we perform our toilet, we visit our pyre, we recite verses, we add a codicil to our will: this is the complimentary interval of last words, the interval in which death utters itself. When the act occurs, it is always absorbed into an object: it is death's object which is there, death is *praxis*, *technē*, its mode is instrumental: dagger, sword, cudgel, noose, razor for opening veins, poisoned feather for tickling the throat, wadding chewed by the man dying of hunger, blankets for smothering, cliff from which the victim is thrown, ceiling which falls in (Agrippina), garbage cart in

2. Vetus, his mother-in-law, and his daughter: "Then, in the same chamber, with the same weapon, they sundered their veins and hurried into a bath, covered each, as delicacy required, with a single garment . . ." (XVI.11).

which escape is vain (Messalina)—death always employs the mild substance of life: wood, metal, cloth, innocent tools. In order to be destroyed, the body makes contact, exposes itself, seeks out the object's murderous function hidden under its instrumental surface: this world of terrorism is a world which has no need of the scaffold: it is the object which momentarily abandons its vocation, lends itself to death, supports it.

To die, in Tacitus, is to perceive life. Whence "the fashionable manner": to open the veins or have them opened, to make death liquid, in other words, to convert it to duration and purification: one sprinkles the gods and the bystanders with blood, death is a libation; it is suspended, procrastinated, and one exerts a capricious freedom over it at the very heart of its final fatality—like Petronius opening and closing his veins at will; like Paulina, Seneca's wife, rescued on Nero's orders and retaining for years, in the pallor of her drained face, the very sign of a communication with the void. For this world of dying signifies that death is both easy and resistant: it is ubiquitous and yet eludes; no one escapes it and yet it must be wrestled with, its means must be accumulated, hemlock added to bloodletting and the steam bath, the act ceaselessly retraced, like a drawing consisting of several lines whose final beauty derives both from the multiplication and the rectitude of the essential outline.

For perhaps that is what the baroque is: the torment of a finality in profusion. Tacitean death is an open system, subject at once to a structure and a contestation, to a repetition and a direction; it seems to proliferate on all sides and yet remains imprisoned in a great moral and existential intention. Here again, it is the vegetable image which substantiates the baroque: the deaths correspond, but their symmetry is false, spread out in time, subject to a movement, like that of sprouts on the same stalk: the regularity is a delusion, life directs the funerary system, terrorism is not bookkeeping but vegetation: everything is reproduced and yet nothing is repeated; such is perhaps the meaning of this Tacitean universe, in which the brilliant description of the phoenix (VI.28) seems to construe death symbolically as the purest moment of life.

1959

La Sorcière

Probably *La Sorcière* [1] is the favorite book of Michelet lovers. Why? Perhaps because it has a special boldness, expresses all of Michelet's temptations in an extravagant mode, deliberately establishes itself in ambiguity, which is to say, in totality. Is *La Sorcière* a work of history? Yes, since its movement is diachronic, since it follows the thread of time from the death of paganism to the dawn of the Revolution. No, since this thread is novelistic, attached to a figure and not to an institution. But it is just this duplicity which is fruitful; at once history and novel, *La Sorcière* generates a new insight into reality, initiates what we might call a historical ethnology, or a historical mythology. As novel, the work solidifies time, keeps historical perception from being dispersed or sublimated in the vision of distinct ideas: a whole connection becomes evident which is precisely the tension of a history made by men themselves. As history, it immediately exorcises the ghost of psychological explanation: witchcraft is no longer a lapse of the soul, but the result of a social alienation. The witch is thus both product and object, apprehended in the double movement

1. [Published in English as *Satanism and Witchcraft*.]

of a causality and a creation: born of the poverty of the serfs, she is nonetheless a force which acts upon this poverty: history perpetually tangles cause and effect. At their intersection, a new reality, which is the very object of the book: myth. Michelet keeps correcting psychology by history, then history by psychology: it is this instability which generates *La Sorcière*.

For Michelet, as we know, history is oriented: it proceeds toward an illumination. Not that its movement is purely progressive; the rise of liberty encounters obstacles, setbacks: according to the metaphor Michelet borrowed from Vico, history is a spiral: time restores anterior states, but these circles are wider and wider, no state exactly reproduces its homologue; history is thus a kind of polyphony of splendors and eclipses which ceaselessly correspond, though swept on toward a still point where time must fulfill itself: the French Revolution.

Michelet starts with the institution of serfdom: here the notion of the witch is formed; isolated in her hovel, the serf's young wife listens to those petty demons of the hearth, vestiges of the old pagan gods the Church has routed: she makes them her confidants, while her husband is away at his work. In the serf's wife, the witch is still merely potential; there is no more than an imagined communication between woman and the supernatural: Satan is not yet conceived. Then times grow hard, poverty and abjection intensify; something appears in history which changes men's relations with each other, transforms property into exploitation, drains all humanity from the link between serf and lord: gold. Itself an abstraction of material goods, gold abstracts the human relation; the lord no longer knows his peasants, but only the impersonal gold in which they must pay their tribute. It is here that Michelet, anticipating all subsequent study of alienation, accurately locates the birth of the witch: when the fundamental human relation is destroyed, the serf's wife turns from the hearth to the heath, makes a pact with Satan, and collects in her wilderness, as a precious trust, the nature excluded from the world; the Church faltering, alienated from the great and cut off from the people, it is the witch who then undertakes the magistracies of consolation, the communication with the dead, the fraternity of the great collective sabbaths, the cure of physical diseases for the three centuries in which she triumphs: the leprous (fourteenth), the epileptic (fifteenth), the syphilitic (sixteenth). In other words, with the world condemned to inhumanity by the terrible collusion of gold and serfdom, it is the witch who, by withdrawing from it, recovers and preserves humanity. Thus, throughout the waning Middle Ages, the witch is a function: virtually useless when social relations involve a certain solidarity in and of themselves, she develops to the degree that these relations become impoverished: when they are null and void, the witch triumphs.

Up to this point, it is clear that as a mythic figure, the witch is identified with the progressive forces of history; just as alchemy was the matrix of chemistry, witchcraft is merely the first medicine. In contrast to the Church's sterility, symbolized by the darkness of its *in-pace*, the witch represents light, the beneficent exploitation of Nature, the bold use of poisons as remedies, magical rites being the one way a technique of liberation could be acknowledged by an entire alienated collectivity. What happens in the sixteenth century (a period all the more significant in that we owe to Michelet the very notion of "Renaissance")? The obscurantist crust splits open: as ideologies, the Church and feudalism recede, the exploration of nature passes into the hands of laymen, scholars, and physicians. Thus the witch is no longer necessary, she enters her decadence; not that she disappears (the numerous witchcraft trials sufficiently attest to her vitality); but, as Michelet says, she becomes a professional; deprived of most of her curative vocation, she now participates only in affairs of pure magic (charms, spells), as the suspect confidante of the lady. And Michelet loses interest in her.

Yet his book does not end here. Because the witch is in eclipse does not mean that nature has triumphed. Disclosed by the subsidence of sorcery, the physician becomes the progressive figure of the next two centuries (seventeenth and eighteenth), but the Church is still there; the conflict continues between darkness and day, between priest and physician. By a series of bold transformations, Michelet reverses the functions: beneficent because he was himself a physician during the Middle Ages, Satan now becomes the physician's enemy, becomes the priest; and woman, at first Satan's bride, becomes, in the monarchical period, his victim. This is the meaning of the four great witchcraft trials Michelet fictionalizes at length in the second half of his book (Gauffridi, Loudun, Louviers, Cadière). On one side, the wretched victims, trusting and delicate, the possessed nuns; on the other, the frivolous or Machiavellian seducer-priest; behind these figures, the Church, which pulls the strings, hands them over to the stake, to the *in-pace*, either for obscurantist motives or because of the internecine war between its clans, monks, and priests; in the background, the physician, the layman, impotent judge of these crimes, whose voice alone, unfortunately stifled, could have restored this demonomania to its physical nature (the sanguineous or nervous plethora of girls doomed to spinsterhood and boredom).

Such is the sequence of forms, or to introduce a more ethnological term, of hypostases taken by the double figure of good and evil. Evil is serfdom and gold, the slave's poverty and abjection, in a word, the alienation which causes man to be excluded from nature, which means, for Michelet, from humanity. Good is the very countercurrent of this alienation, Satan, the witch, the figures which focus the light of a dying world, plunged into the dungeons of the Church. Man's exclusion from nature is set in opposition to the witch's exile from the inhabited world. For the witch is essentially labor, humanity's effort to create the world in spite of the world: it is in order to act more effectively that the witch goes into exile. Faced with the drought of medieval history (from the thirteenth century), defined by Michelet under the rubrics of two great themes of sterility, imitation and boredom, the witch, in her triumphant period, typifies all human *praxis*: she is at one and the same time the consciousness of alienation, the movement to destroy it, the ferment of a frozen history, in short, fecundity of time. *Satan*, Michelet says, *is one of the aspects of God.*

This movement of liberation is a general form of history. But the specific point of Satan, Michelet insists, is that in relation to the original servitude, he effects an exact and indeed proportionate subversion: witchcraft is a *reversal*. We all know that the demoniac rites reverse the Christian liturgy, Satan is the obverse of God. But Michelet has taken this inversion much further, construing it poetically, making it a total form of the medieval world: for example, the alienated serf lives by night, not by day, poisonous plants become remedies, etc. This leads to the heart of the Micheletist vision: every substance is double, to live is to choose one of two contraries, to endow the great duality of forms with signification. The separation of substances sets up an internal hierarchy for each. For example, drought, which is the mark of the waning Middle Ages, is merely a state of sterility; sterility itself is the divided-up, the portioned-out, the disjunct, annihilation of human communication; Michelet will therefore contrast to the dry, all undivided substances as the substances of life: the moist and the warm define nature because nature is homogeneous. Such chemistry obviously assumes a historical signification: as the mythic form of nature, the witch represents an undivided state of human labor—the (more or less ideal) moment when man is happy because he has not yet specialized his tasks and his techniques. It is this communism of functions that the witch expresses: transcending history, she attests the happiness of primitive society and prefigures that of future society; passing through time in the manner of a more or less occult essence, she shines forth only in the theophanic moments of history: in Joan of Arc (sublimated figure of the witch), in the Revolution.

Such are the great historical states of the witch: latent (the serf's wife), triumphant (the priestess), decadent (the professional). After which, Michelet turns to the figure of Satan-as-priest. At this level of analysis, what we have are actually phases of one and the same institution, that is, of history. The novel appears when Michelet "thickens" the historical thread, resolutely transforms it into a biographical warp: Function is incarnated in an actual person, organic maturation is substituted for historical evolution, so that the witch unites in herself the general and the particular, the model and the creature: she is at once *a* witch and *the* witch. This novelistic accommodation is very audacious because it is not in the least metaphorical: Michelet keeps his promise to the letter, he discusses the witches, for three hundred years of their history, as one and the same woman.

Novelistic existence is established the moment the witch is provided with a body, scrupulously situated, abundantly described. Take the witch at her first appearance, when she is merely the serf's wife: she is then a slender, weak, timid creature, assigned the physical quality which most touched Michelet, diminutiveness, i.e., he supposed, fragility: her mode of corporeal existence is a minor slither, a kind of household quarantine which makes her lend an ear to the spirits of the hearth, those exiled pagan gods who have taken refuge in the serf's hovel: she exists only by a certain passivity of the ear: such is her body and her atmosphere. The second witch, nourished on the misery of the times and this misery being enormous, is a full-fledged woman; she has exchanged a humiliated body for a triumphant, expansive one. Even the erotic sites have changed: first came the slender waist, the pale flesh, a passive nervousness, a body reduced to utter vulnerability; now we are arrested by the wicked yellow eyes and their offensive glances, what Michelet calls their *gleam*, always a sinister value for him; above all, there is the hair, snaky and black as some Medea's; in short, everything too immaterial or too elusive to be defeated. The third witch is a combined state of the two previous bodies; the delicacy of the first is corrected by the combativeness of the second: the professional witch is a diminutive but malicious woman, slender and oblique, delicate and cunning; her totem is no longer the frightened doe but the cat, graceful and mischievous (also the totem animal of the sinister Robespierre). With regard to Michelet's general thematics, the third witch derives from the knowing little girl (doll, perverse toy), pernicious in that she is double, divided, contradictory, uniting in equivocation the innocence of her age and the knowledge of an adult. Moreover, the witch's transformation through her three ages is itself contradictory: it is an aging process, yet the witch is always young (see in particular the whole passage concerning the young Basque witches, Murgui and Lisalda, whom Michelet condemns though he is obviously attracted to them).

Thereafter, and this is an important novelistic sign, the

witch is always located, she participates substantially in a physical site, interior (objects) or landscape. This site is first of all
the hearth, spatial substitute for intimacy; the hearth is an
eminently beneficent site insofar as it is the terminal point of
rape, the place where man is weak woman's absolute owner,
thereby regaining the natural state par excellence, the undivided nature of the couple (Michelet specifies that the hearth
constitutes a great advance over the erotic communism of the
primitive *villa*). Further, this hearth, defined by contiguous
objects, bed, chest, table, stool, is the architectural expression
of a privileged value (already noted apropos of the pre-witch's
body): diminutiveness. Altogether different is the habitat of
the adult sorceress: a forest of briars, bristling moors, over-
grown circles of dolmens, the theme here is the ragged, the
tangled, a state of nature which has absorbed the witch, closed
over her. The dreadful partitioning of medieval society (in its
corrupt phases) has this corresponding paradox: the witch is
imprisoned in the open place par excellence: nature. Nature
thereby becomes an impossible site: the human takes refuge in
the inhuman. As for the third witch, of whom, moreover,
Michelet speaks much less—the suspect confidante of the great
lady—her mythical surround (as we know from other books) is
the cabinet, the alcove, the professional locus of the chambermaid (a personage abhorred by Michelet as the husband's
insidious rival), in short the disgraced category of the intimate,
the stifled (which is to be linked with the malefic theme of
monarchic intrigue).

This general witch is therefore an entirely real woman, and
Michelet sustains relations with her which we are obliged to
call erotic. Michelet's eroticism, naïvely exhibited in his so-
called nature books, appears piecemeal in all his history books,
especially those written in the second half of his life, after his
second marriage (to Athénaïs Mialaret). Its central figure is
precisely this Athénaïs, who greatly resembled Michelet's portrait of the first witch. The general quality of an erotic object
is, for Michelet, fragility (here, diminutiveness), which permits man both to ravish and to protect, to possess and to respect: here we have a sublimated eroticism, but whose very
sublimation, by a kind of strictly Micheletist return, becomes

erotic all over again. The witch, especially in her first state, is indeed Michelet's bride, frail and sensitive, nervous and abandoned, the *pâle rose* who provokes a double erotic impulse of concupiscence and elevation. But this is not all. We know (from *La Femme*, from *L'Amour*) that Michelet embellishes this fragile creature with a very particular photogenics: blood. What arouses Michelet, in woman, is what she conceals: not nakedness (which would be a banal theme) but the menstrual function which makes woman rhythmic, like Nature, like the ocean, also subject to the lunar rhythm. The husband's right and joy is to accede to this secret of nature, to possess in woman, by this unheard-of confidence, a mediatrix between man and the universe. Michelet exalted this marital privilege in his books on woman, defending it against the rival who is not the lover but the chambermaid, confidante of the natural secret. This whole theme is present in *La Sorcière*: constitutively, one might say, since the witch is a sibyl, in harmony with nature by her lunar rhythm; then when the witch is replaced by the priest, the theme reappears indiscreetly: the relation between the seducer-priest and the chosen nun is entirely erotic, in Michelet's style, only when it involves the essential confidence, the communication of *those shameful and ridiculous things whose avowal is so cruel for a young girl.*

For what Michelet condemns in the sacerdotal or satanic seduction is also what he has always delighted in describing: insidious possession, gradual habitation within woman's secret. The images, in this very book, are countless: sometimes the elfin spirit *slithers* into the serf's wife, sometimes the spirits enter her *like a tapeworm*, sometimes Satan *impales* the witch with a fiery dart. What prevails throughout is the image, not of a penetration—banal metaphor of ordinary eroticism—but of a passing-through and of an installation. The Micheletist utopia is evidently that man be woman's parasite, it is the oceanic marriage of sharks which for months drift in the sea coupled to one another: idyllic adventure in which the motionless penetration of bodies is doubled by the external slither of waters (Michelet has described these ichthyic nuptials in *La Mer*). Beyond woman, we are obviously concerned here with a whole coenesthesia of man in nature, and we understand why the witch is a major figure of the Micheletist pantheon: everything about her prepares her for a great mediating function: installing himself in her, it is in all of nature that man bathes as in a substantial and vital medium.

We see that Michelet's presence in *La Sorcière* is anything but a simple romantic expansion of subjectivity. What Michelet must do, in fact, is to participate magically in the myth without ceasing to describe it: his text is both narration and experience, its function is to compromise the historian, to keep him on the verge of the magical substance, in the state of a spectator who is on the point of falling into a trance; whence the ambiguity of rational judgment, Michelet both believing and not believing, according to the formula he himself used about the Greeks' religious attitude toward their fables. One very remarkable thing about *La Sorcière*, in fact, is that Michelet never contests the effectiveness of the magical act: he speaks of the witch's rites as successful techniques, rationally performed though irrationally conceived. This contradiction, which has embarrassed so many positivist historians, never troubles Michelet: he speaks of magical effects as real: causality is precisely what his narrative permits him to omit, since in fiction the temporal link is always substituted for the logical link. Consider how he deals, for example, with the transformation of the lady into the she-wolf: in the evening, the witch gives her a potion to drink. A rationalist historian would here present a file of documents, a study of the evidence, an explanation of the illusion. This is not Michelet's method. *The potion was taken,* he says, *and in the morning the lady awakened exhausted, bruised . . . she had hunted, killed, etc.* It is just this disjunction between the real and the rational, this primacy of the event over its material cause (*the potion was taken*) which it is the narrative's function to display; thus nothing could come closer to mythic narrative than the Micheletist novel, the legend (i.e., the continuum of narrative) establishing, in both cases, in and of itself, a new rationality.

Instead of intervening between him and the truth, the novel helped Michelet to understand witchcraft in its objective structure. With regard to magic, it is not the positivist historians that Michelet suggests; it is scholars quite as rigorous but whose work is infinitely better adapted to its object: I am thinking of ethnologists like Mauss (notably in his essay on magic). For example, in writing the history of the witch (and not of witchcraft), Michelet anticipates the fundamental choice of modern ethnology: to start from functions, not from institutions; Mauss takes magic back to the magician, that is, to any person who works magic. This is what Michelet does: he describes the rites very summarily, he never analyzes the content of the beliefs (of the representations): what interests him in witchcraft is a personalized function.

The benefit of this method is very great, and gives *La Sorcière*, despite some outmoded dialogues, a very modern accent. First of all, what Michelet declares of the sibyl, in his maniacal feminism, is what the soberest ethnologist would also say: that there is an affinity between woman and magic. For Michelet, this affinity is physical, woman being in harmony with nature by the rhythm of the blood; for Mauss, it is social, their physical particularity establishing women as a veritable class. Nonetheless, the postulate is the same: this erotic theme, far from being a prurient mania of the lovesick old historian, is an ethnological truth illuminating the status of woman in magical societies.

Another truth: I said that Michelet is not concerned to describe the rites themselves; he deals rather with their destination, their effect (summoning the dead, curing the sick). This suggests that he makes little differentiation between rite and technique, a correspondence ethnology has adopted in its assertion that magical gestures are always sketches of a technology. Michelet never distinguishes the witch from her activity: she exists only insofar as she participates in a *praxis*, which is precisely what makes her a progressive figure, according to Michelet: as opposed to the Church, established in the world as a motionless, eternal essence, she is the world making itself. The paradoxical (but correct) result of this intuition is that Michelet's witch has virtually nothing of the sacred about her. Of course there is a close relation between magic and religion, which Mauss has carefully analyzed and which Michelet himself defines as a *reversal*; but it is precisely a complementary and therefore exclusive relation; magic is marginal to religion; it gives over the being of things for the sake of their transformation: this makes the Micheletist witch much more of a worker than a priestess.

Finally, anticipating the principle of all sociology, Michelet does not treat the witch as "other," does not make her the sacred figure of the singular, as romanticism conceived the poet or the magus. His witch is physically solitary (in the woods, out on the heath), not socially alone: a whole collectivity joins her, expresses itself in her, makes use of her. Far from setting herself in noble opposition to society (as the pure rebel does), the Micheletist witch fundamentally participates in her economy. Michelet takes the paradox which sentimentally opposes the individual to society and resolves it in an altogether modern manner; he has clearly understood that between the witch's singularity and the society from which she is detached, there is a relation not of opposition but of complementarity: it is the entire group which establishes the particularity of the magical function; if men expel the witch, it is because they acknowledge her, project a part of themselves into her, a part which is at once legitimate and intolerable; by means of the witch, they legalize a complex economy, a tension that is useful since, in certain disinherited moments of history, it permits them to live. Carried away by the role's positivity, Michelet doubtless scanted the behavior of "normal" society with regard to the witch; he never says, for instance, that in terms of total structure, the Inquisition had a function, not positive of course but significant—in a word, that it exploited the great witchcraft trials with a view to the society's general economy. At least he indicates that between "normal" society and the witch excluded from it there was a relation of sadism, not just of eviction, and that consequently this society consumed the witch, so to speak, much more than it sought to annul her. Does he not say this surprising thing somewhere, *that witches were put to death because of their beauty?* In a sense this makes all of society participate in that complementary structure Lévi-Strauss has analyzed apropos of shamanic societies, the aberration here being merely a means by which a society works out its contradictions. And in our present

society, what best resumes this complementary role of the
Micheletist witch is probably the mythic figure of the intellectual, "the traitor," sufficiently detached from society to discern its alienation, seeking a correction of reality yet impotent
to effect it: excluded from the world and necessary to the
world, directed toward *praxis* but participating in it only by
the motionless mediation of a language, just as the medieval
witch comforted human misery only through a rite and at the
price of an illusion.

If we thus glimpse in *La Sorcière* a thoroughly modern
description of the magical myth, it is because Michelet has had
the audacity to venture himself altogether, to preserve that
redoubtable ambiguity which makes him at once the narrator
(in the mythical sense) and the analyst (in the rational sense)
of history. His sympathy for the witch is not at all that of
a liberal author striving for comprehension of what is alien
to him: Michelet has participated in the myth of the witch
exactly as the witch herself participated, in his own view, in
the myth of magical *praxis:* both voluntarily and involuntarily.
What he has undertaken once again, in writing *La Sorcière*,
is neither a profession (the historian's) nor a priesthood (the
poet's), it is, as he has said elsewhere, a *magistracy*. He felt
obliged by society to administer its intelligence, to narrate all
its functions, even and especially its aberrant ones, which he
has here anticipated were vital. Seeing his own society torn
between two postulations, Christian and materialist, which
Michelet considered equally impossible, he sketched out a
magical compromise, he made himself a sorceror, a gatherer
of bones, a reviver of the dead; he took it upon himself to say
no to the Church and *no* to science, to replace dogma or brute
fact by myth.

That is why today, when mythological history is much more
important than at the time Michelet published *La Sorcière*
(1862), his book recovers its actuality, once again becomes
serious. Michelet's many enemies, from Sainte-Beuve to
Mathiez, supposed they could be rid of him by confining him
in a poetics of pure intuition; but his subjectivity, as we have
seen, was only the earliest form of that insistence on totality,

of that truth of comparisons, of that attention to the most insignificant detail of the concrete, which today mark the very method of our human sciences. What was disdainfully labeled poetry in his work we are beginning to recognize as the exact outline of a new science of the social: it is because Michelet was a discredited historian (in the scientistic sense of the term) that he turns out to have been at once a sociologist, an ethnologist, a psychoanalyst, a social historian; although his thought and even his form include vast wastelands (a whole part of himself he could not wrest free of his *petit-bourgeois* background), we can say that he truly anticipated the foundation of a general science of man.

1959

Zazie and Literature

Queneau is not the first writer to contend with literature.[1] Ever since "literature" has existed (that is, judging from the word's date, since quite recently), we can say that the writer's function is to oppose it. What distinguishes Queneau is that his opposition is a hand-to-hand combat: his entire *oeuvre* cleaves to the myth of literature, his contestation is alienated, it feeds on its object, always leaving substance enough for new meals: the noble edifice of written form still stands, but worm-eaten, scaling, dilapidated. In this controled destruction, something new, something ambiguous is elaborated, a kind of suspension of formal values: rather like the beauty of ruins. Nothing vengeful in this impulse—Queneau's activity is not, strictly speaking, sarcastic, it does not emanate from a good conscience, but rather from a complicity.

This surprising contiguity (this identity?) of literature and its enemy is very apparent in *Zazie*. From the point of view of literary architecture, *Zazie* is a *well-made* novel. It embodies all the "virtues" criticism likes to inventory and praise: "classi-

1. Apropos of *Zazie dans le métro* [published in English as *Zazie*].

cal" construction, articulating a limited temporal episode (a strike); "epic" duration, accounted for by an itinerary, a series of stations; objectivity (the story is told from Queneau's point of view); a full cast of characters (hero, secondary figures, and walk-ons); a unified social milieu and setting (Paris); variety and equilibrium of fictional methods (narrative and dialogue). In other words, the entire technique of the French novel, from Stendhal to Zola. Whence the work's familiarity, which is perhaps not foreign to its success, for we cannot be certain that all its readers have consumed this good novel in an altogether *distant* fashion: there is, in *Zazie*, a pleasure of cursive reading, and not only of contour.

Yet once the novel's entire positivity is established, Queneau, without directly destroying it, couples it with an insidious void. As soon as each element of the traditional universe solidifies, Queneau dissolves it, undermines the novel's security: literature's solidity curdles; everything is given a double aspect, made unreal, whitened by that lunar light which is an essential theme of deceit and a theme characteristic of Queneau. The event is never denied, i.e., first posited then negated; it is always *divided*, like the moon's disc, mythically endowed with two antagonistic figures.

The moments of deceit are precisely those which once constituted the glory of traditional rhetoric. First of all, the *figures of thought*: here the forms of duplicity are countless: antiphrasis (the title itself, since Zazie never takes the metro); uncertainty (is it the Panthéon or the Gare de Lyon, Sainte-Chapelle or the Chamber of Commerce?); the confusion of contrary roles (Pedro-Surplus is both a satyr and a cop), of ages (Zazie "ages"), of sexes, this last doubled by an additional enigma, since Gabriel's inversion is uncertain; the error which turns out to be right (Marceline finally becomes Marcel); negative definition (the tobacco shop which is not the one at the corner); tautology (the cop arrested by other cops); mockery (the child who brutalizes the adult, the lady who intervenes), etc.

All these figures are inscribed within the texture of the narrative; they are not conspicuous. The *figures of words*, of course, effect a much more spectacular destruction, one familiar to

Queneau's readers. These are first of all *figures of construction*, which attack literary dignity by a running fire of parodies. Every kind of writing is attacked: epic, Homeric, Latin, medieval, psychological, anecdotal, even the grammatical tenses, favorite vehicles of the myth of fiction, the historical present, and the Flaubertian *passé simple*. Such examples indicate that Queneau's parody has a very special structure: it does not parade a knowledge of the model being mocked; there is no trace of that Ecole-Normale complicity with high culture which characterizes Giraudoux's parodies, for instance, and which is merely a deceptively off-hand way of showing a profound respect for classical-national values; here the parodic expression is frivolous, it dislocates *en passant*—a scab picked off the old literary skin. Queneau's is a parody sapped from within, its very structure masking a scandalous incongruity; it is not imitation (however subtle) but malformation, a dangerous equilibrium between verisimilitude and aberration, verbal theme of a culture whose forms are brought to a state of perpetual deceit.

As for the *figures of speech*, they obviously go much farther than a simple naturalization of our orthography. Sparingly distributed, phonetic transcription always has an aggressive character, it appears only when it is assured of a certain baroque effect; above all it is an invasion of the sacred precincts par excellence: the orthographic ritual (whose social origin is the class barrier). But what is shown and mocked here is not the irrationality of our graphic code; almost all Queneau's reductions have the same meaning: to produce, in place of the word pompously draped in its orthographic gown, a new word, indiscreet, natural, i.e., barbarous: here it is the *francité* of the writing which is undermined, the noble Gallic tongue, the *doux parler de France* abruptly dislocated into a series of stateless vocables, so that our Great Literature, after the detonation, might well be no more than a collection of vaguely Russian or Kwakiutl fragments (and if not, only because of Queneau's pure kindness). Which is not to say that Quenalian phoneticism is purely destructive (is there ever, in literature, a univocal destruction?): all of Queneau's labor on our language is inspired by an obsessional impulse, that of *découpage*, of cutting-up: this is a technique in which riddling is a first step, but whose function is to explore structures, for to code and to decode are the two aspects of one and the same act of penetration, as was indicated, long before Queneau, by the entire Rabelaisian philosophy, for example.

All this belongs to a panoply familiar to Queneau's readers. A new form of mockery, which has attracted a good deal of attention, is that vigorous clausule which young Zazie gratuitously (i.e., tyranically) attaches to most of the assertions made by the grown-ups around her (*Napoleon my ass*). But what is here deflated is not *all* of language; rather, conforming to the most learned definitions of symbolic logic, Zazie clearly distinguishes the language object from metalanguage. The language object is that language which dissolves into action itself, which makes things *act*—it is the primary, transitive language, the one about which we can speak but which itself transforms more than it speaks. It is exactly within this language object that Zazie lives, she never distances or destroys this language. What Zazie speaks is the transitive contact of reality: Zazie *wants* her coke, her blue jeans, her metro; she uses only the imperative or the optative, which is why her language is safe from all mockery.

And it is from this language object that Zazie occasionally emerges in order to paralyze, with her murderous clausule, the metalanguage of the grown-ups. This metalanguage speaks not things but *apropos of* things (or *apropos of* the primary language). It is a parasitical, motionless, sentencious language which doubles the act in the same way as the fly accompanies the coach; instead of the language object's imperative and optative, its principial mode is the indicative, a kind of zero degree of the act intended to *represent* reality, not to change it. This metalanguage secretes, around the letter of utterance, a complementary meaning—ethical, plaintive, sentimental, magisterial, etc.; in short, it is a song, an aria: in it we recognize the very being of literature.

The target, therefore, of Zazie's clausule will of course be just this literary metalanguage. For Queneau, literature is a category of speech, hence of existence, which concerns all of humanity. No doubt, as we have seen, a good deal of the novel is the work of a specialist. Yet it is not novelists who are under fire here; the taxi driver, the night-club dancer, the bartender, the shoemaker, the people who form crowds in the street, all this *real* world (the reality of a language involves an exact sociality) immerses its speech in the great literary forms, experiences its relations and its goals by means of literature. It is not "the people," in Queneau's eyes, who possess the utopian literality of language; it is Zazie (whence, probably, the profound meaning of the role), i.e., an unreal, magical, Faustian being, since Zazie is the superhuman contraction of childhood and maturity, the superposition of "I am outside the world of adults" and of "How much I have lived." Zazie's innocence is not a bloom, a fragile virginity, values which could belong only to the romantic or edifying metalanguage: it is rejection of the aria, and a science of the transitive; Zazie circulates in her novel like a household god, her function is hygienic, counter-mythic: she calls to order.

Zazie's clausule summarizes all the methods of the counter-myth, once it disavows direct explanation and perfidiously decides to become literature. It is a kind of final detonation which surprises the mythical sentence ("Zazie, if you really want to see Les Invalides and the actual tomb of the real Napoleon, I'll take you there." "Napoleon my ass"), retroactively strips it, with a twist of the wrist, of its good conscience. It is easy to account for such an operation in semiological terms: the deflated sentence is itself composed of two languages: the literal meaning (to visit Napoleon's tomb) and the mythical meaning (the noble tone); Zazie abruptly dissociates the two languages; she exposes, in the mythic line, an evident connotation. But her weapon is none other than that very dislocation which literature imposes upon the letter it seizes; by her irreverent clausule Zazie merely connotes what was already connotation; she *puts on* literature (in the colloquial sense) just the way literature *puts on* the reality it sings.

This brings us to what we might call the bad faith of mockery, for mockery itself is merely a reply to the bad faith of seriousness: in turn, each immobilizes the other, *puts it on* without there ever being a decisive victory: mockery voids seriousness, but seriousness understands mockery. Confronting this dilemma, *Zazie dans le métro* is really an exemplary work: by vocation, it dismisses both parties, the serious and the comic. Which accounts for the confusion of our critics: some have taken it seriously as a serious work of art, suited to exegetical decipherment; others, judging the first group grotesque, have called the novel absolutely frivolous ("there is nothing to be said about it"); still others, seeing neither comedy nor serious- ness in the work, have declared they did not understand. But this was precisely the work's intention—to wreck any dialogue about it, representing by the absurd the elusive nature of lan- guage. There is, between Queneau and the serious and mockery of the serious, that very movement of control and escape which governs the familiar game, model of all spoken dialectic, in which paper covers stone, stone smashes scissors, scissors cut paper: one always has the advantage over the other—provided both are mobile terms, forms. The antilanguage is never absolute.

Zazie is actually a utopian character, insofar as she represents a triumphant antilanguage: *no one answers her.* But thereby Zazie is outside humanity (the character engenders a certain "discomfort"): she is anything but a "little girl," her youth is rather a form of abstraction which permits her to judge all language without having to mask her own psyche;[2] she is an asymptotic point, the horizon of an antilanguage which might call to order without bad faith; outside the metalanguage, her function is to represent both its danger and its fatality. This abstraction of the character is crucial: the role is unreal, of an uncertain positivity, it is the expression of a reference more than the voice of a wisdom. This means that for Queneau, the contestation of language is always ambiguous, never conclusive, and that he himself is not a judge but a participant: Queneau does not have a good conscience:[3] the point is not to teach

2. Zazie has only one mythic remark: "I have aged." This is the end of the book.

3. Ionesco's comedy raises a problem of the same kind. Up to and including *The Impromptu of Alma*, Ionesco's work is in good faith because the author does not exclude himself from that ter- rorism of language he sets going. *The Killers* marks a regression, the return to a good conscience, i.e., to a bad faith, since the author finds fault with others' language.

Zazie and Literature

literature a lesson, but to live with it in a state of insecurity.

It is here that Queneau is on the side of modernity: his literature is not a literature of possession and fulfillment; he knows that one cannot "demystify" from the outside, in the name of an ownership, but that one must steep oneself in the void one is revealing: yet he also knows that this compromising of himself would lose all its virtue if it were spoken, recuperated by a direct language: literature is the very mode of the impossible, since it alone can speak its void, and by saying it, again establish a plenitude. In his way, Queneau takes a position at the heart of this contradiction, which perhaps defines our literature today: he assumes the literary mask but at the same time points his finger at it. This is a very difficult and enviable operation; it is perhaps because it is a successful one that there is, in *Zazie*, this last and precious paradox: a dazzling comedy yet one purified of all aggression. As if Queneau psychoanalyzes himself at the same time that he psychoanalyzes literature: Queneau's entire *oeuvre* implies a quite terrible imago of literature.

1959

Workers and Pastors

The French are Catholics, and any figure of the Protestant pastor is of little interest to them: the pastor harbors nothing of the sacred in his person; firmly established in his civil status, endowed with ordinary clothes, wife, and children, severed by his very confession from the theological absolute, an advocate more than a witness, since his ministry is of speech not of sacrament, everything about him escapes election and malediction, those two purveyors of literature; incapable of being damned or holy, like the priests of Barbey or Bernanos, he is, from the French point of view, a bad character for fiction: Gide's *Pastoral Symphony* (poor work, moreover) has always remained an exotic novel.[1]

This mythology, about which there is a great deal to say (what might we not discover, were we to draw *all* the worldly consequences of France's Catholicity?)—this mythology changes, no doubt, once we venture into a Protestant country. In France, the pastor fails to interest insofar as he belongs to a doubly insignificant milieu, both sporadic and assimilated,

1. Apropos of *Je* by Yves Velan. [A section of this novel has been translated in *Tri-Quarterly*, No. 20, Winter 1971.]

which is French Protestantism. Elsewhere, the pastor assumes a social role, he participates in a general economy of classes and ideologies; he exists to the degree that he is responsible; accomplice or victim, in any case witness (and active witness) to a certain political laceration, he is thereby a national adult figure: no longer an insipid copy, lacking cassock or chastity, of the French priest.

This is the first thing to say about Yves Velan's book: it is a Swiss novel. Curiously, by insisting on this novel's nationality, which is not ours, we free it of its exoticism. Apparently, the book has had more repercussions in Switzerland than in France: a proof of its realism: if it touches the Swiss (and some, no doubt, quite disagreeably), it is because it concerns them, and if it concerns them, it is precisely to the degree that they are Swiss. And what matters about this realism is that it inheres in the situation, not in the anecdote; here we approach the paradox that constitutes this novel's value: it is not a "socialist" novel whose declared object, in the manner of the great realistic epitomes, would be to describe the historical relations of the Swiss church and the Swiss proletariat; and yet these relations, the reality of these relations, form the structure of the work and even, I believe, its justification, its deepest ethical impulse.

What occurs? All literature knows that like Orpheus, it cannot, on pain of death, turn around to look at what is behind it: it is condemned to mediation—that is, in a sense, to lying. Balzac could not have described the society of his time with that realism Marx so much admired had he not been divided from it by an ideology addicted to the past: it is actually Balzac's faith, and what we might call from the historical viewpoint his mistake, which served him as a mediation: Balzac was a realist not *in spite of* his theocratism but, indeed, *because of* it; conversely, it is because socialist realism, in its very project, rejects any mediation that (at least in our Western countries) it asphyxiates itself and dies: it dies of being immediate, it dies of rejecting that something which hides reality in order to make it more real, and which is literature.

Now in Yves Velan's *Je*, the mediation is precisely *je*, "I," the subjectivity which is both the mask and the exposure of those social relations no novel has ever been able to describe directly, without sinking into what Marx or Engels contemptuously labeled tendency literature: in Yves Velan's *Je*, what we call class conflicts are given, but they are not treated; or if they are, it is at least at the cost of an apparently enormous distortion, since the reality of these conflicts is expressed in the language most antipathetic to any traditional realism, the language of a certain delirium. The entire paradox, the entire truth of the book thus derives from the fact that it is at once (and by its very project) a political novel and the language of a desperate subjectivity; starting from a situation generated by Marxist language and living with it page by page, feeding on it and feeding it as well—i.e., the laceration of a certain society, the collusion of law and order and the pastorate, the ostracism of the worker movement, the good conscience upon which, perhaps more naïvely here than elsewhere, the morality of ownership prides itself—nonetheless the narrator's language is never that of a political analysis; it is precisely because Yves Velan's pastor experiences social laceration in the language of a pastor and not in that of an abstract man, and because his language consists of all the metaphysical hallucinations of his condition, his education, and his faith,[2] that the mediation necessary to all literature is found, and that this book, to my mind, stirs an old problem, motionless for years (actually, since Sartre's novels): how, at the very heart of literature—that is, of an order of action deprived of any practical sanction—how to describe the political phenomenon without bad faith? How to produce a "committed" literature (an outmoded expression, but one we cannot discard so easily) without resorting, so to speak, to the god of commitment? In short, how to experience commitment, how to even acknowledge it, some other way than as evidence or as a duty?

2. The way in which the pastor attaches a capital letter to every spiritual object is, in semiological terms, what we call a *connotation*, a complementary meaning imposed on a literal meaning; but the usual bad faith of capital letters becomes, in literature, a truth, since it exposes the situation of the person employing them.

Yves Velan's discovery—an esthetic discovery, it must be said, since it concerns a certain way of renewing literature by uniting political substance and the Joycean monologue—is to have given to the laceration of *men* (and not of Man) the language of a libido, armed with all its impulses, its resistances, its alibis. Even if there were only this oral flux, at once desperate, constrained, prolix, and incomplete, the book would be dazzling; but it is more: its unruliness is dialectical, it fastens reality and its own language on a frenzied swivel: each "political" datum is here perceived only through a desperate disturbance of the psyche; and conversely, each hallucination is merely the language of a real situation: thus Yves Velan's pastor does not in the least constitute a "case": the situations he describes, the wounds he receives, the sins he believes he commits, his very desires—all this, which is metaphysical in form, nonetheless derives from an expressly socialized reality: the narrator's subjectivity is not set in opposition to other men in some indefinite fashion, it is not diseased because of a universal and unnamed "other": it suffers, reflects, seeks its identity in a scrupulously defined, specified world whose reality is already apprehended, whose inhabitants are distributed and divided up according to political law; and this anguish seems extravagant to us only in proportion to our own bad faith, which is never willing to pose the problems of commitment except in terms of a pacified, intellectualized consciousness, as if political morality were inevitably the fruit of a Reason, as if the proletariat (another word which apparently no longer exists) could interest only a minority of educated intellectuals, but never a mind still disturbed. Yet the world does not inevitably offer itself in neat segments, the proletariat to the intellectuals, the "other" to neurotic consciousness; for too long we have been persuaded that it took one novel to talk about oneself and another to talk about workers, bourgeois, priests, etc.; Velan's pastor receives the world in its entirety, at one and the same time as fear, sin, and social structure; for us, there are "the workers" and then there are "others"; for him, on the contrary, the workers are precisely the others: social alienation is identified with neurotic alienation: this is what makes him singular; it is perhaps also—weak as he is—what makes him exemplary.

For courage is always a distance, the distance separating an act from the original fear against which it pits itself. Fear is the fundamental state of Velan's pastor, and that is why the least of his acts (of assimilation, of complicity with the world) is courageous; in order to measure the plenitude of a commitment, we must know from what disorder it starts; Velan's pastor starts from very far back: his is a disturbed consciousness, unremittingly subject to the pressure of a tremendous guilt which not only God (of course) inflicts upon him, but more particularly the world—or to be more precise, it is the world itself which possesses the divine function par excellence, the function of seeing: the pastor is *seen*, and the vision of which he is the object constitutes him as a disgraced spectacle: he feels himself to be (and becomes) ugly, naked. Sin, being a sin of essence, that of the body itself—sin is countered by an innocence which can only be that of virility, defined less as a sexual power than as a correct domination of reality. The proletarian world is thus apprehended as strong and just, i.e., inaccessible; of course, the hallucinatory character of this projection is never masked; yet it is this very hallucination which gives the impetus to a correct consciousness of social relations; for these workers, these "men of the people" from whom the pastor is excluded by function and by style and who nonetheless fascinate him, form in his eyes a humanity very correctly ambiguous: on the one hand they are judges, since they see him, and ceaselessly affirm a race denied to the narrator; and on the other hand, there is between them and the pastor a profound complicity, no longer of essence but not yet of *praxis*; a complicity of situation: both are seen by the race of law and order, united in the same reprobation, the same exclusion: ethical misery joins political misery; one might say that the value of this book is that it reveals the ethical genesis of a political sentiment; and its rigor is to have dared trace this origin to its most remote point, that quasi-neurotic zone of morality where the meaning of goodness, escaping the burden of bad faith, is as yet only the meaning of release.

This, I believe, is the crux of the book, this is what justifies its technique, its deviations, the profoundly disturbing manner in which it produces, out of neurosis, a political meaning, in which it speaks of the proletariat in a half-metaphysical, half-erotic language certain to irritate Marxists, believers, and realists all at the same time: it deprives its hero of the benefit of any good conscience. For Velan's pastor is by no means a "red" pastor; he does not even postulate such a thing; he himself names the role, which is to say, he demystifies it in advance. In a sense, the book does not end, does not constitute, strictly speaking, an itinerary, i.e., a liberation or a tragedy: it describes a profound contradiction, shot with gleams of light, that is all; its hero is not "positive," does not lead onward; no doubt, the proletariat can be discerned as a value; but its apologist, Victor, the pastor's friend, who possesses all the powers the latter lacks (atheism and the Party, i.e., the absence of fear), remains a peripheral character: he is a function, with no language of his own, precisely as if sin were *in language*. As for the pastor himself, even his language, though it fills and sustains the novel, is not entirely natural: it does not sound like a transposed confession of the author, it does not suggest an identification: something repellent and a little turgid distances the narrator, detaches him from us, as if the truth were somewhere between these two men, one militant and the other excluded, as if only a kind of unresolved tension could unite the man of *praxis* and the man of sin, as if the world could be correctly seen only by being perpetually recommenced, as if all commitment could be no more than incomplete.

That is what, to my sense of it, this book contributes to contemporary literature: an effort to dialecticize commitment itself, to confront the intellectual (of whom the pastor is after all merely a rough draft) at one and the same time with himself and with the world. It is, I think, this coincidence of the two postulations which constitutes the book's novelty. For Velan, a consciousness advancing into the world is not introduced to it in two successive tenses, first experiencing freedom, then seeking to erode it; freedom and complicity[3]

3. In the Brechtian sense of *Einverständnis,* which is to say, knowledge not only *of* but *with* reality.

are created by one and the same movement, even if this movement remains tragically embarrassed. It is this *embarrassment*
which is new; and it is because this book illuminates such
embarrassment, makes it into a new object for the novel, that
Je helps us challenge all our values of the last decade.

1960

Kafka's Answer

In the duel between you and the
world, back the world.

Amoment has passed, the moment of committed literature.
The end of the Sartrean novel, the imperturbable indigence of socialist fiction, the defects of political theater
—all that, like a receding wave, leaves exposed a singular and
singularly resistant object: literature. Already, moreover, an
opposing wave washes over it, the wave of an asserted detachment: revival of the love story, hostility to "ideas," cult of
fine writing, refusal to be concerned with the world's significations: a whole new ethic of art is being proposed, consisting
of a convenient swivel between romanticism and off-handedness, between the (minimal) risks of poetry and the (effective) protection of intelligence.

Is our literature forever doomed to this exhausting oscillation between political realism and art-for-art's-sake, between
an ethic of commitment and an esthetic purism, between compromise and asepsis? Must it always be poor (if it is merely
itself) or embarrassed (if it is anything but itself)? Can it not
have a proper place in *this world?*

This question now receives an exact answer: Marthe Robert's *Kafka.* Is it Kafka who answers? Yes, of course (for it is
hard to imagine a more scrupulous exegesis than this one),

but we must make no mistake: Kafka is not Kafka-ism. For twenty years, Kafka-ism has nourished the most contrary literatures, from Camus to Ionesco. If we are concerned with describing the bureaucratic terror of the modern moment, *The Trial, The Castle, The Penal Colony* constitute overworked models. If we are concerned with exposing the claims of individualism against the invasion of objects, *The Metamorphosis* is a profitable gimmick. Both realistic and subjective, Kafka's *oeuvre* lends itself to everyone but answers no one. It is true that we do not question it much, for writing in the shadow of his themes does not constitute a question; as Marthe Robert says, solitude, alienation, the quest, the familiarity of the absurd, in short the constants of what is called the Kafka-esque universe—don't these belong to all our writers, once they refuse to write in the service of a world of ownership? As a matter of fact, Kafka's answer is addressed to the person who has questioned him least, to *the artist*.

This is what Marthe Robert tells us: that Kafka's meaning is in his *technique*. A brand new argument, not only in relation to Kafka, but in relation to all our literature, so that Marthe Robert's apparently modest commentary (is this not one more book on Kafka, published in a pleasant popularizing series?) forms a profoundly original essay, providing that good, that precious nourishment of the mind which results from the correspondence of an intelligence and an interrogation.

For after all, paradoxical as it seems, we possess virtually nothing on literary technique. When a writer reflects on his art (something for the most part rare and abhorred), it is to tell us how he conceives the world, what relations he entertains with it, his image of Man; in short, each writer says he is a realist, never how. Now literature is only a means, devoid of cause and purpose; in fact, that is what defines it. You can of course attempt a sociology of the literary institution; but you can limit the act of writing by neither a *why* nor a *wherefore*. The writer is like the artisan who diligently fabricates some complicated object, as ignorant of its model as of its use, analogous to Ashby's homeostat. To ask oneself why one writes is already an advance over the blissful unconsciousness of "inspiration," but it is a despairing advance—there is no answer. Apart from demand and apart from success, empirical alibis much more than real motives, the literary act is without cause and without goal precisely because it is devoid of sanction: it proposes itself to the world without any *praxis* establishing or justifying it: it is an absolutely intransitive act, it modifies nothing, nothing *reassures* it.

So then? Well, that is its paradox; this act exhausts itself in its technique, it exists only in the condition of a manner. For the (sterile) old question: *why write?* Marthe Robert's *Kafka* substitutes a new question: *how write?* And this *how* exhausts the *why*: all at once the impasse is cleared, a truth appears. This is Kafka's truth, this is Kafka's answer (to all those who want to write): *the being of literature is nothing but its technique.*

In short, if we transcribe this truth into semantic terms, this means that a work's specialty is not a matter of its concealed *signified* (no more criticism of "sources" and "ideas"), but only a matter of its *significations*. Kafka's truth is not Kafka's world (no more Kafka-ism), but the *signs* of that world. Thus the work is never an answer to the world's mystery; literature is never dogmatic. By imitating the world and its legends (Marthe Robert is right to devote a chapter of her essay to *imitation*, a crucial function of all great literature), the writer can show only the *sign* without the *signified*: the world is a place endlessly open to signification but endlessly dissatisfied by it. For the writer, literature is that utterance which says until death: I shall not begin to live before I know the meaning of life.

But saying that literature is no more than an interrogation of the world matters only if we propose a technique of interrogation, since this interrogation must persist throughout an apparently assertive narrative. Marthe Robert shows that Kafka's narrative is not woven of symbols, as we have been told so often, but is the fruit of an entirely different technique, the technique of allusion. All Kafka is in the difference. The symbol (Christianity's cross, for instance) is a *convinced* sign, it affirms a (partial) analogy between a form and an idea, it implies a certitude. If the figures and events of Kafka's narrative were symbolic, they would refer to a positive (even if it were a despairing) philosophy, to a universal Man: we cannot differ as to the meaning of a symbol, or else the symbol is a failure. Now, Kafka's narrative authorizes a thousand equally plausible keys—which is to say, it validates none.

Allusion is another matter altogether. It refers the fictive event to something besides itself, but to what? Allusion is a defective force, it undoes the analogy as soon as it has posited it. K is arrested on the orders of a tribunal: that is a familiar image of justice. But we learn that this tribunal does not regard crimes as our justice does: the resemblance is delusive, though not effaced. In short, as Marthe Robert explains, everything proceeds from a kind of semantic contraction: K feels he has been arrested, and everything happens *as if* K were really arrested (*The Trial*); Kafka's father treats him as a parasite, and everything happens *as if* Kafka were transformed into a parasite (*The Metamorphosis*). Kafka creates his work by systematically suppressing the *as if*s: but it is the internal event which becomes the obscure term of the allusion.

Thus allusion, which is a pure technique of signification, is actually a commitment to the world, since it expresses the relation of an individual man and a common language: a system (abhorred phantom of every anti-intellectualism) produces one of the most fiery literatures which has ever existed. For example, Marthe Robert reminds us, we have commonplaces such as *like a dog, a dog's life, a Jew dog*; it suffices to make the metaphoric term the entire object of the narrative, shifting subjectivity to the allusive realm, in order for the insulted man to become a dog in fact: a man treated like a dog *is* a dog. Kafka's technique implies first of all an agreement with the world, a submission to ordinary language, but immediately afterwards, a reservation, a doubt, a fear before the letter of the signs the world proposes. As Marthe Robert puts it, Kafka's relations with the world are governed by a perpetual *yes, but* . . . One can fairly say as much of all our modern literature (and it is in this that Kafka has truly created it), since it identifies, in an inimitable fashion, the realistic project (*yes* to the world) and the ethical project (*but* . . .).

The trajectory separating the *yes* from the *but* is the whole uncertainty of signs, and it is because signs are uncertain that there is a literature. Kafka's technique says that the world's meaning is unutterable, that the artist's only task is to explore possible significations, each of which taken by itself will be only a (necessary) lie but whose multiplicity will be the writer's truth itself. That is Kafka's paradox: art depends on truth, but truth, being indivisible, cannot know itself: to *tell* the truth is to lie. Thus the writer *is* the truth, and yet when he speaks he lies: a work's authority is never situated at the level of its esthetic, but only at the level of the moral experience which makes it an assumed lie; or rather, as Kafka says correcting Kierkegaard: *we arrive at the esthetic enjoyment of being only through a moral experience without pride.*

Kafka's allusive system functions as a kind of enormous sign to interrogate other signs. Now, the exercise of a signifying system (mathematics, to take an example quite remote from literature) has only one requirement, which will therefore be the esthetic requirement itself: rigor. Any lapse, any vagueness in the construction of the allusive system would produce, paradoxically, symbols—would substitute an assertive language for the essentially interrogative function of literature. This is also Kafka's answer to all our inquiries into the novel today: that it is finally the precision of his writing (a structural, not a rhetorical precision, of course: it is not a matter of "fine writing") which commits the writer to the world: not in one of his options, but in his very defection: it is because the world is not finished that literature is possible.

1960

On Brecht's *Mother*

The Berliner Ensemble production of *The Mother* has shown how blind our Tout-Paris must be, to see nothing but propaganda in this play: Brecht's Marxist option exhausts his work no more than the Catholic option exhausts Claudel's. Of course Marxism is indissolubly linked to the play; Marxism is its *object*, not its subject; the subject of *The Mother* is, quite simply—as the title says—maternity.

It is precisely Brecht's strength never to present an idea which is not experienced through a genuine human relation and (this is more original) never to create characters outside the "ideas" which make them exist (no one lives without ideology: the absence of ideology is itself an ideology: this is the subject of *Mother Courage*). It was enough for Brecht to unite these two requirements to produce a surprising play which undermines two stock images: that of Marxism and that of the mother. By her mere condition as a revolutionary mother, Pelageya Vlasova fulfills no stereotype: she does not preach Marxism, she does not launch into abstract tirades on man's exploitation by man; on the other hand, she is not the expected figure of maternal instinct, she is not the essential mother: her being is not on the level of her womb.

On the Marxist side, the problem *The Mother* raises is a real one. We can say that it is a general (and crucial) problem, though considered on the scale of the individual, affecting an entire society on the level of its farthest-reaching history: the problem of political consciousness. If Marxism teaches that the corruption of capitalism is implicit in its very nature, the advent of a communist society depends nonetheless on the historical consciousness of men: it is this consciousness which carries the freedom of history, the famous alternative which promises the world socialism *or* barbarism. Political knowledge is therefore the first object of political action.

This principle establishes the goal of Brecht's entire theater: it is neither a critical theater nor a heroic theater, but a theater of consciousness, or better still: of a nascent consciousness. Whence its great "esthetic" richness, capable of reaching, it seems to me, a very broad public (as is confirmed by Brecht's growing success in the West). First of all, because consciousness is an ambiguous reality, at once social and individual; and since there is no theater except a theater of persons, consciousness is precisely what can be apprehended in history through the individual. Next, because unconsciousness is a spectacle, a good show (the comic, for example); or more exactly, the spectacle of unconsciousness is the birth of consciousness. Next, because the wakening of knowledge is by definition a movement, so that the duration of the action can unite with the duration of the spectacle itself. Lastly, because the birth of consciousness is an adult, i.e., a strictly human, subject; to show this birth is to participate in the effort of the great philosophies, in the very history of the mind.

And it is here, moreover, in this spectacular function of awakening, that *The Mother* reveals its true subject—I mean, of structure and not only of opinion—which is maternity.

Which maternity? Ordinarily, we know but one, that of the genetrix. In our culture, not only is the mother a being of pure instinct, but even when her function is socialized, it is always in a single direction: it is she who forms the child; having given birth first to her son, she then gives birth to his mind: she is an educator, she affords the child his consciousness of the moral world. The whole Christian vision of the family thus rests on a unilateral relation which proceeds from mother to child: even if she does not manage to direct the child, the mother is always the one who prays for him, weeps for him, like Monica for her son Augustine.

In Brecht's *Mother,* the relation is inverted: it is the son who gives birth, spiritually, to the mother. This reversal of nature is a great Brechtian theme: reversal and not destruction: Brecht's work is not a lesson in *relativity,* à la Voltaire: Pavel awakens Pelageya Vlasova to social consciousness (moreover, through *praxis* and not through speech: Pavel is essentially silent), but this is a birth which corresponds to the first one only by enlarging it. The old pagan image (as we find it in Homer) of the sons succeeding the parents like the leaves on the tree, the new growth casting out the old—this motionless or certainly mechanical image gives way to the notion that even as they repeat themselves situations change, objects are transformed, the world progresses by qualities: not only, in the inevitable movement of the generations, is the Brechtian mother not abandoned, not only does she receive after having given, but what she receives is different from what she has given: she who has produced life receives consciousness.

In the bourgeois order, the transmission always proceeds from elders to offspring: this is the very definition of *inheritance,* a word whose fortunes greatly exceed the limits of the civil code (we inherit ideas, values, etc.). In the Brechtian order there is no inheritance unless it is inverted: once the son is dead, it is the mother who continues him, as if she were the new growth, the leaf now unfolding. Thus this ancient theme of the changing of the guard, which has nourished so many heroic-bourgeois plays, has nothing anthropological about it here; it does not illustrate an inevitable law of nature: in *The Mother,* freedom circulates at the very heart of the most "natural" human relation, that of a mother and her son.

Yet all the "emotion" is here, without which there is no Brechtian theater. Consider Helene Weigel's performance, which has been called too reticent—as if maternity were nothing but an order of expression: in order to receive the very consciousness of the world from her son, she must first become "different"; initially, she is the traditional mother, the woman

who does not understand, who scolds a little but still serves
the soup, mends the clothes; she is the child-mother, i.e., the
entire affective density of the relation is preserved. Her consciousness truly blooms only when her son is dead: she is never
united with him. Thus, throughout this ripening, a distance
separates mother from son, reminding us that this correct
itinerary is a cruel one: love is not, here, an effusion, it is that
force which transforms fact into consciousness, then into action: it is love which opens our eyes. Must we be "fanatics"
of Brecht to recognize that this is a theater of feeling?

1960

Authors and Writers

ho speaks? Who writes? We still lack a sociology of language. What we know is that language is a power and that, from public body to social class, a group of men is sufficiently defined if it possesses, to various degrees, the national language. Now, for a very long time—probably for the entire classical capitalist period, i.e., from the sixteenth to the nineteenth century, in France—the uncontested owners of the language, and they alone, were authors; if we except preachers and jurists (enclosed moreover in functional languages), no one else spoke, and this "monopoly" of the language produced, paradoxically, a rigid order, an order less of producers than of production: it was not the literary profession which was structured (it has developed greatly in three hundred years, from the domestic poet to the businessman-writer), but the very substance of this literary discourse, subjected to rules of use, genre, and composition, more or less immutable from Marot to Verlaine, from Montaigne to Gide. Contrary to so-called primitive societies, in which there is witchcraft only through the agency of a witch doctor, as Mauss has shown, the literary institution transcended the literary functions, and within this institution, its essential raw material, language. Institutionally, the literature of France is its language, a half-linguistic, half-esthetic system which has not lacked a mythic dimension as well, that of its clarity.

When, in France, did the author cease being the only one to speak? Doubtless at the time of the Revolution, when there first appear men who appropriate the authors' language for political ends. The institution remains in place: it is still a matter of that great French language, whose lexicon and euphony are respectfully preserved throughout the greatest paroxysm of French history; but the functions change, the personnel is increased for the next hundred years; the authors themselves, from Chateaubriand or Maistre to Hugo or Zola, help broaden the literary function, transform this institution-alized language of which they are still the acknowledged owners into the instrument of a new action; and alongside these authors in the strict sense of the word, a new group is constituted and develops, a new custodian of the public language. Intellectuals? The word has a complex resonance;[1] I prefer calling them here *writers*. And since the present may be that fragile moment in history where the two functions coexist, I should like to sketch a comparative typology of the author and the writer with reference to the substance they share: language.

The author performs a function, the writer an activity. Not that the author is a pure essence: he acts, but his action is immanent in its object, it is performed paradoxically on its own instrument: language; the author is the man who *labors*, who works up his utterance (even if he is inspired) and functionally absorbs himself in this labor, this work. His activity involves two kinds of norm: technical (of composition, genre, style) and artisanal (of patience, correctness, perfection). The paradox is that, the raw material becoming in a sense its own end, literature is at bottom a tautological activity, like that of those cybernetic machines constructed for themselves (Ashby's homeostat): the author is a man who radically absorbs the world's *why* in a *how to write*. And the miracle, so to speak, is that this

1. Apparently the word *intellectual,* in the sense we give it today, was born at the time of the Dreyfus affair, obviously applied by the anti-*Dreyfusards* to the *Dreyfusards*.

narcissistic activity has always provoked an interrogation of the world: by enclosing himself in the *how to write,* the author ultimately discovers the open question par excellence: why the world? What is the meaning of things? In short, it is precisely when the author's work becomes its own end that it regains a mediating character: the author conceives of literature as an end, the world restores it to him as a means: and it is in this perpetual inconclusiveness that the author rediscovers the world, an alien world moreover, since literature represents it as a question—never, finally, as an answer.

Language is neither an instrument nor a vehicle: it is a structure, as we increasingly suspect; but the author is the only man, by definition, to lose his own structure and that of the world in the structure of language. Yet this language is an (infinitely) labored substance; it is a little like a superlanguage —reality is never anything but a pretext for it (for the author, *to write* is an intransitive verb); hence it can never explain the world, or at least, when it claims to explain the world, it does so only the better to conceal its ambiguity: once the explanation is fixed in a work, it immediately becomes an ambiguous product of the real, to which it is linked by perspective; in short, literature is always unrealistic, but its very unreality permits it to question the world—though these questions can never be direct: starting from a theocratic explanation of the world, Balzac finally does nothing but interrogate. Thus the author existentially forbids himself two kinds of language, whatever the intelligence or the sincerity of his enterprise: first, *doctrine,* since he converts despite himself, by his very project, every explanation into a spectacle: he is always an inductor of ambiguity;[2] second, *evidence,* since he has consigned himself to language, the author cannot have a naïve consciousness, cannot "work up" a protest without his message finally bearing much more on the working-up than on the protest: by identifying himself with language, the author loses all claim to truth, for language is precisely that structure whose very goal (at least historically, since the Sophists), once it is no longer rigorously transitive, is to neutral-

2. An author can produce a system, but it will never be consumed as such.

ize the true and the false.[3] But what he obviously gains is the power to disturb the world, to afford it the dizzying spectacle of *praxis* without sanction. This is why it is absurd to ask an author for "commitment": a "committed" author claims simultaneous participation in two structures, inevitably a source of deception. What we can ask of an author is that he be responsible; again, let there be no mistake: whether or not an author is responsible for his opinions is unimportant; whether or not an author assumes, more or less intelligently, the ideological implications of his work is also secondary; an author's true responsibility is to support literature as a failed commitment, as a Mosaic glance at the Promised Land of the real (this is Kafka's responsibility, for example).

Naturally, literature is not a grace, it is the body of the projects and decisions which lead a man to fulfill himself (that is, in a sense, to essentialize himself) in language alone: an author is a man who wants to be an author. Naturally too, society, which consumes the author, transforms project into vocation, labor into talent, and technique into art: thus is born the myth of fine writing: the author is a salaried priest, he is the half-respectable, half-ridiculous guardian of the sanctuary of the great French language, a kind of national treasure, a sacred merchandise, produced, taught, consumed, and exported in the context of a sublime economy of values. This sacralization of the author's struggle with form has great consequences, and not merely formal ones: it permits society—or Society—to distance the work's content when it risks becoming an embarrassment, to convert it into pure spectacle, to which it is entitled to apply a liberal (i.e., an indifferent) judgment, to neutralize the revolt of passion, the subversion of criticism (which forces the "committed" author into an incessant and impotent provocation)—in short, to recuperate the author: every author is eventually

---

3. Structure of reality and structure of language: no better indication of the difficulty of a coincidence between the two than the constant failure of dialectic, once it becomes discourse: for language is not dialectic, it can only say "we must be dialectical," but it cannot be so itself: language is a representation without perspective, except precisely for the author's; but the author dialecticizes himself, he does not dialecticize the world.

digested by the literary institution, unless he scuttles himself, i.e., unless he ceases to identify his being with that of language: this is why so few authors renounce writing, for that is literally to kill themselves, to die to the being they have chosen; and if there are such authors, their silence echoes like an inexplicable conversion (Rimbaud).[4]

The *writer*, on the other hand, is a "transitive" man, he posits a goal (to give evidence, to explain, to instruct), of which language is merely a means; for him language supports a *praxis*, it does not constitute one. Thus language is restored to the nature of an instrument of communication, a vehicle of "thought." Even if the writer pays some attention to style, this concern is never ontological. The writer performs no essential technical action upon language; he employs an utterance common to all writers, a *koinē* in which we can of course distinguish certain dialects (Marxist, for example, or Christian, or existentialist), but very rarely styles. For what defines the writer is the fact that his project of communication is *naïve*: he does not admit that his message is reflexive, that it closes over itself, and that we can read in it, diacritically, anything else but what he means: what writer would tolerate a psychoanalysis of his language? He considers that his work resolves an ambiguity, institutes an irreversible explanation (even if he regards himself as a modest instructor); whereas for the author, as we have seen, it is just the other way around: he knows that his language, intransitive by choice and by labor, inaugurates an ambiguity, even if it appears to be peremptory, that it offers itself, paradoxically, as a monumental silence to be deciphered, that it can have no other motto but Jacques Rigaut's profound remark: *and even when I affirm, I am still questioning.*

The author participates in the priest's role, the writer in the clerk's; the author's language is an intransitive act (hence, in a sense, a gesture), the writer's an activity. The paradox is that society consumes a transitive language with many more reserva-

---

4. These are the modern elements of the problem. We know that on the contrary Racine's contemporaries were not at all surprised when he suddenly stopped writing tragedies and became a royal functionary.

tions than an intransitive one: the writer's status, even today when writers abound, is much more problematic than the author's. This is primarily the consequence of a material circumstance: the author's language is a merchandise offered through traditional channels, it is the unique object of an institution created only for literature; the writer's language, on the contrary, can be produced and consumed only in the shadow of institutions which have, originally, an entirely different function than to focus on language: the university, scientific and scholarly research, politics, etc. Then too, the writer's language is dependent in another way: because it is (or considers itself) no more than a simple vehicle, its nature as merchandise is transferred to the project of which it is the instrument: we are presumed to sell "thought" exclusive of any art; now the chief mythic attribute of "pure" thought (it would be better to say "unapplied" thought) is precisely that it is produced outside the channel of money: contrary to form (which costs a lot, as Valéry said), thought costs nothing, but it also does not sell itself, it gives itself—generously. This points up at least two new differences between author and writer. First, the writer's production always has a free but also a somewhat "insistent" character: the writer offers society what society does not always ask of him: situated on the margin of institutions and transactions, his language appears paradoxically more individual, at least in its motifs, than the author's language: *the writer's function is to say at once and on every occasion what he thinks;* [5] and this function suffices, he thinks, to justify him; whence the critical, urgent aspect of the writer's language: it always seems to indicate a conflict between thought's irrepressible character and the inertia of a society reluctant to consume a merchandise which no specific institution normalizes. Thus we see *a contrario* —and this is the second difference—that the social function of literary language (that of the author) is precisely *to transform thought* (or consciousness, or protest) *into merchandise;* society

5. This function of *immediate manifestation* is the very opposite of the author's: (1) the author hoards, he publishes at a rhythm which is not that of his consciousness; (2) he mediatizes what he thinks by a laborious and "regular" form; (3) he permits a free interrogation of his work, he is anything but dogmatic.

wages a kind of vital warfare to appropriate, to acclimatize, to institutionalize the risk of thought, and it is language, that model institution, which affords it the means to do so: the paradox here is that "provocative" *language* is readily accommodated by the literary institution: the scandals of language, from Rimbaud to Ionesco, are rapidly and perfectly integrated; whereas "provocative" *thought*, insofar as it is to be immediate (without mediation), can only exhaust itself in the no man's land of form: the scandal is never total.

I am describing here a contradiction which, in fact, is rarely pure: everyone today moves more or less openly between the two postulations, the author's and the writer's; it is doubtless the responsibility of history which has brought us into the world too late to be complacent authors and too soon (?) to be heeded writers. Today, each member of the intelligentsia harbors both roles in himself, one or the other of which he "retracts" more or less well: authors occasionally have the impulses, the impatiences of writers; writers sometimes gain access to the theater of language. We want *to write something,* and at the same time *we write* (intransitively). In short, our age produces a bastard type: the author-writer. His function is inevitably paradoxical: he provokes and exorcises at the same time; formally, his language is free, screened from the institution of literary language, and yet, enclosed in this very freedom, it secretes its own rules in the form of a common style; having emerged from the club of men-of-letters, the author-writer finds another club, that of the intelligentsia. On the scale of society as a whole, this new group has a complementary function: the intellectual's style functions as the paradoxical sign of a non-language, it permits society to experience the dream of a communication without system (without institution): to write without "style," to communicate "pure thought" without such communication developing any parasitical message—that is the model which the author-writer creates for society. It is a model at once distant and necessary, with which society plays something of a cat-and-mouse game: it acknowledges the author-writer by buying his books (however few), recognizing their public character; and at the same time it keeps him at a distance, obliging him to support himself by means of the subsidiary institutions it controls (the university, for instance), constantly accusing him of intellectualism, i.e., in terms of myth, sterility (a reproach the author never incurs). In short, from an anthropological viewpoint, the author-writer is an excluded figure integrated by his very exclusion, a remote descendant of the accursed: his function in society as a whole is perhaps related to the one Lévi-Strauss attributes to the witch doctor: a function of complementarity, both witch doctor and intellectual in a sense stabilizing a disease which is necessary to the collective economy of health. And naturally it is not surprising that such a conflict (or such a contract, if you prefer) should be joined on the level of language; for language is this paradox: the institutionalization of subjectivity.

1960

Literature Today
Answers to a Questionnaire in *Tel Quel*

I. What are your present preoccupations and to what degree do they relate to literature?

I have always been interested in what might be called the responsibility of forms. But it was only at the end of my book *Mythologies* that I realized this problem must be raised in terms of signification, and since then, signification has been, explicitly, my essential preoccupation. Signification, which is to say: the union of what signifies and of what is signified; which is to say, again: neither form nor content, but the proceedings between them. In other words: ever since the final fifty-page essay of *Mythologies*, ideas and themes interest me less than the way society takes possession of them in order to make them the substance of a certain number of signifying systems. This does not mean that this substance is indifferent; it means that we cannot apprehend it, manipulate it, judge it, make it the basis of philosophical, sociological, or political explanations without first having described and understood the system of signification of which it is merely a term; and since this system is a formal one, I have found myself engaged in a series of structural analyses, all of which aim at defining a certain number of extralinguistic "languages": as many "languages," in fact, as there are cultural objects (whatever their real origin), which society has endowed with a signifying power: for example, food is to be eaten; but it also serves to *signify* (conditions, circumstances, tastes); food is therefore a signifying system, and must one day be described as such. As signifying systems (outside of language, strictly speaking), we may cite: food, clothing, film, fashion, literature.

Naturally, these systems do not have the same structure. We may expect that the most interesting systems, or the most complicated, are those deriving from systems which are themselves already signifying systems: this is true of literature, for instance, which derives from the signifying system par excellence, language. This is also true of fashion, at least as it is spoken by fashion publications; which is why, without directly confronting literature, a system formidable because of its accumulated historical values, I recently undertook to describe the system of signification constituted by women's fashions as they are described by specialized journals. This word *description* makes it sufficiently clear that by locating myself within fashion, I was already in literature; in short, written fashion is merely a special literature, though an exemplary one, since by describing a garment it confers upon it a meaning (of fashion) which is not the literal meaning of the sentence: is this not the very definition of literature? The analogy goes further still: fashion and literature are perhaps what I would call homeostatic systems, that is, systems whose function is not to communicate an objective, exterior *signified* which pre-exists the system, but merely to create an equilibrium of operations, a signification in movement: for fashion is nothing except what it is said to be; and the secondary meaning of a literary text is perhaps evanescent, "empty," although this text does not cease to function as the signifier of this empty meaning. Fashion and literature signify strongly, subtly, with all the complexities of an extreme art, but, if you will, they signify "nothing," their being is in signification, not in what is signified.

If it is true that fashion and literature are signifying systems whose signified is in principle inconclusive, then we must revise our ideas of the history of fashion (but fortunately we have had very few such ideas) and of the history of literature. Both are like the ship Argo: the pieces, the substances, the materials change, to the point where the object is periodically new, and yet the name, i.e., the being of this object, remains always the same; it is therefore a question of systems rather than of objects: their being is in form, not in content or function; there is consequently a formal history of these systems, which perhaps exhausts their history much more than we suppose, insofar as this history is complicated, annulled, or simply dominated by an endogenous becoming of forms; this is obvious in the case of fashion, where the rotation of forms is regular, either annual (on the level of a microdiachrony) or centennial (see the valuable works of Kroeber and Richardson); in the case of literature, the problem is obviously much more complex in that literature is consumed by a society broader and better integrated than the society of fashion; and especially in that literature, purified of the myth of "futility," proper to fashion, is supposed to incarnate a certain consciousness of society as a whole, and hence passes for a value which we might characterize as historically natural. As a matter of fact, the history of literature as a signifying system has never been written; for a long time, we have written the history of *genres* (which has little relation to the history of signifying forms), and it is this history which still prevails in our manuals and even more strictly in our "panoramas" of contemporary literature; then, under the influence either of Taine or of Marx, we have occasionally undertaken a history of the signified in literature; the most remarkable endeavor on this level is doubtless that of Lucien Goldmann: Goldmann has gone very far, since he has attempted to link a form (tragedy) to a content (the vision of a political class); but to my mind, his explanation is incomplete insofar as the link itself, i.e., the signification, is not conceived: between two terms, one historical and the other literary, an analogical relation is postulated (the rejection of tragedy by Pascal and Racine reproduces the political rejection of the rightist wing of Jansenism), so that the signification Goldmann so intuitively cites remains, as I see it, a disguised determinism. What is needed (this is doubtless easier said than done) is to retrace not the history of the signified in literature but the

history of significations, i.e., the history of the semantic techniques by which literature imposes a meaning (even if it is an
"empty" meaning) upon what it says; in short, we must have
the courage to enter the "kitchen of meaning."

*II. You once wrote: "Each new writer reopens, within himself,
the dossier of literature." Isn't there a risk that this incessant,
this necessary resumption of the interrogation will in the future
exercise a dangerous influence on certain writers for whom such
investigation would be no more than a new literary "ritual"—
therefore without any real consequences? And, on the other
hand, isn't your notion of the "failure" necessary to the profound "success" of a work likely to become, too often, intentional?*

There are two kinds of failure: first, the historical failure of a
literature which cannot answer the world's questions without
altering the inconclusive character of the signifying system
which nonetheless constitutes its most adult form: literature,
today, is reduced to putting questions to the world, whereas the
world, being alienated, needs answers; and second, the worldly
failure of the work rejected by a public. The first failure can be
experienced by each author, if he is lucid, as the existential
failure of his project as a writer; there is nothing to be said
about it, it cannot be subjected to a morality, still less to a
simple hygiene: what is there to say about an unhappy consciousness which has, historically, every reason to be unhappy?
This failure belongs to that "interior doctrine which must
never be communicated" (Stendhal). As to the worldly failure,
it can interest (aside from the author himself, of course!) only
sociologists or historians, who will try to read the public's rejection as the index of a social or historical attitude; we may say on
this point that our society rejects very few works and that the
"acculturation" of anathematized, nonconformist, or ascetic
works—in short, of what might be called the *avant-garde*—is
particularly rapid; the cult of failure you speak of is nowhere to
be seen: neither in the public, nor in publishing (of course),
nor among young authors, who seem, for the most part, very
sure of what they are doing; perhaps, moreover, the sentiment

of literature as failure can come only to those who are exterior
to it.

III. In Writing Degree Zero *and at the end of* Mythologies,
*you say that we must seek "a reconciliation of reality and of
men, of description and of explanation, of the object and of
knowledge." Does this reconciliation adopt the position of the
surrealists, for whom the "fracture" between the world and the
human mind is not incurable? How does this opinion relate to
your apology for the (Kafka-esque) "failed commitment" of the
writer? Can you discuss this last notion further?*

For surrealism, despite the political temptations of the movement, the coincidence of reality and the human mind was
possible *immediately,* i.e., exclusive of any mediation, even
revolutionary mediation: surrealism might even be defined as a
technique of immediation. But once you believe society cannot
be disalienated outside of a political or, more broadly, historical
process, this very coincidence (or reconciliation), without ceasing to be credible, shifts to the level of a utopia; then you have
a utopian (and mediate) vision and a realistic (and immediate)
vision of literature; these two visions are not contradictory, but
complementary.

Of course, the realistic and immediate vision, related to an
alienated reality, cannot in any way be an "apology": in an
alienated society, literature is alienated: there is thus no real
literature (even Kafka's) for which one can offer an "apology":
it is not literature which is going to free the world. Yet, in this
"reduced" state in which history places us today, there are
several ways of creating literature: there is a choice, and consequently the writer has if not a morality at least a responsibility.
We can make literature into an *assertive* value—either in reple-
tion, by reconciling it with society's conservative values, or in
tension, by making it the instrument of a struggle for liberation; conversely, we can grant literature an essentially *interrogative* value; literature then becomes the sign (and perhaps the
only possible sign) of that historical opacity in which we live
subjectively; admirably served by that inconclusive signifying
system which, to my mind, constitutes literature, the writer can

then at one and the same time profoundly commit his work to the world, to the world's questions, yet suspend the commitment precisely where doctrines, political parties, groups, and cultures prompt him to an answer. The interrogation of literature is then infinitesimal (in relation to the world's needs) and also essential (since it is this interrogation which constitutes it). This interrogation is not: *what is the meaning of the world?* nor even perhaps: *does the world have a meaning?* but only: *here is the world: is there meaning in it?* Literature is then truth, but the truth of literature is at once its very impotence to answer the world's questions and its power to ask real questions, total questions, whose answer is not somehow presupposed in the very form of the question: an enterprise which no philosophy, perhaps, has brought off and which would then belong, truly, to literature.

IV. *Do you think Tel quel can be the locus of literary experiment? Does the notion of esthetic "completion" (however open) seem to you the only requirement which can justify this experiment? What advice would you offer us?*

I understand your endeavor: you face on the one hand certain literary reviews, whose literature was that of your elders, and on the other hand certain polygraph reviews, increasingly indifferent to literature; you are dissatisfied, you want to react both against a certain literature and against a certain contempt for literature. Yet the object which you produce is, to my mind, paradoxical, and this is why: to create a review, even a literary review, is not a literary act, it is an entirely social act: it is to decide that you will, in some sense, institutionalize reality. Now literature, being only form, supplies no reality (unless you substantialize its forms and make literature into a sufficient world); it is the world which is real, not literature: literature is only an indirect illumination. Can you make a review out of the indirect? I do not think so: if you treat an indirect structure directly, it flees, it empties out, or, on the contrary, it freezes, essentializes; in any case, a "literary" review can only fail literature: since Orpheus, we know we must never turn back to look at what we love, or risk destroying it; and being only "literary," such a review also fails the world, which is no small matter.

What, then, is to be done? Above all, create works, which is to say, unknown objects. You speak of *completion:* only the work can be completed, i.e., offer itself as a total question: for to complete a work cannot mean anything but to end it at the moment when it is about to signify something, when, having been a question, it is about to become an answer; we must construct the work as a complete system of signification, and yet so that this signification is inconclusive. This kind of completion is obviously impossible in the review, whose function is to keep giving answers to what the world proposes; in this sense, the so-called "committed" reviews are perfectly justified, and quite as justified in reducing still further the space allotted to literature: as reviews, they are right and you are wrong; for noncommitment can be the truth of literature, but it cannot be a general rule of conduct, quite the contrary: why should the review not commit itself, since nothing keeps it from doing so? Naturally, this does not mean that a review must be necessarily committed "to the left"; you can, for instance, profess a general *tel quelism* which would be, doctrinally, a "suspension of judgment"; but apart from the fact that this *tel quelism* could only avow its profound commitment to the history of our times (for no "suspension of judgment" is innocent), it would have a completed meaning only if it had a bearing day by day on everything that happens in the world, from Ponge's latest poem to Castro's latest speech, from Soraya's latest affair to the latest cosmonaut. The (straight and narrow) path for a review like yours would then be to see the world as it creates itself through a literary consciousness, to consider reality periodically as the raw material of a secret work, to locate yourselves at that very fragile and rather obscure moment when the relation of a real event is about to be apprehended by literary meaning.

V. *Do you think a criterion of quality exists for a literary work? Would it not be urgent to establish such a thing? Do you consider that we would be right in not defining this criterion a priori? to let it be revealed, if possible, of itself by an empirical choice?*

Recourse to empiricism is perhaps a creator's attitude, it cannot be a critical attitude; if you *consider* literature, the work is always the fulfillment of a project which has been deliberated at a certain level by the author (this level is not necessarily that of pure intellect), and you perhaps remember that Valéry proposed basing all criticism on an evaluation of the distance separating the work from its project; we might in fact define the work's "quality" as its shortest distance from its generating idea; but since this idea is ineffable, since in fact the author is condemned to communicate it only in the work, i.e., through the very mediation we are interrogating, we can define "literary quality" only in an indirect fashion: it is an impression of rigor, it is the feeling that the author is consistently subjecting himself to a single value; this imperative value, which gives the work its unity, can vary from age to age. We see, for instance, that in the traditional novel, description is subjected to no rigorous technique: the novelist innocently mixes what he sees, what he knows, what his character sees and knows; a page by Stendhal (take the description of Carville in *Lamiel*) implies several narative consciousnesses; the traditional novel's system of vision was very impure, doubtless because the "quality" was then absorbed by other values and because the familiarity of the novelist and of his reader did not constitute a problem. This disorder was first treated systematically (and no longer innocently), it seems to me, by Proust, whose narrator possesses, if one may say so, a single voice and several consciousnesses; this means that traditional rationality is replaced by a strictly novelistic rationality; but the entire classical novel is thereby called into question; we now have (to glance at this history very summarily) novels of a single angle of vision: the work's quality is then constituted by its rigor and continuity of vision: in Robbe-Grillet, in Butor, in all the other works of our "new novelists," I believe the vision, once inaugurated on a precise postulate, is "drawn" with a single line without any intervention of those parasitical consciousnesses which once permitted the novelist's subjectivity to intervene in his work declaratively (this is a wager: one cannot swear that it is always kept: we need, here, explications of the texts). In other words, the world is expressed from a single viewpoint, which considerably modi-

fies the respective "roles" of character and novelist. The work's
quality is then the rigor of the wager, the purity of a vision
which lasts and which is yet subject to all the contingencies of
the anecdote; for the anecdote, the "story," is the first enemy of
the angle of vision, and it is perhaps for this reason that these
novels "of quality" are so little anecdotal: this is a conflict which
must nonetheless be resolved, i.e., either declare the anecdote
null and void (but then, how to "interest"?) or incorporate it
into a system of vision whose purity considerably reduces the
reader's knowledge.

VI. *"We know how often our realistic literature is mythical,
just as we know that our 'unrealistic' literature has at least the
merit of being for the most part anything but 'unrealistic.'"*
*Can you distinguish these works concretely, giving your defini-
tion of a true literary realism?*

Hitherto, realism has been defined much more by its content
than by its technique; the *real* has first of all been the prosaic,
the trivial, the low; then, more broadly, the supposed infrastructure of society, disengaged from its sublimations and its
alibis; no one doubted that literature simply *copied* something;
according to the level of this something, the work was realistic
or unrealistic.

Yet, what is the *real?* We never know it except in the form
of effects (physical world), functions (social world), or fantasies (cultural world); in short, the *real* is never anything but
an inference; when we declare we are copying reality, this means
that we choose a certain inference and not certain others:
realism is, at its very inception, subject to the responsibility of a
choice; this is a first misunderstanding, proper to all the realistic
arts, as soon as we attribute to them a truth somehow rawer and
more indisputable than that of the other so-called interpretive
arts. There is a second misunderstanding, proper to literature,
and which makes literary realism still more mythical: literature
is never anything but language, its being is in language; now
language is already, anterior to any literary treatment, a system
of meaning: even before being literature, it implies particularity
of substances (the words), discontinuity, selection, categoriza-

tion, special logic. I am in my room, I *see* my room; but already, isn't *seeing* my room *speaking* it to myself? And even if this were not so, what am I to *say* about what I *see*? A bed? A window? A color? Already I wildly disrupt that continuity which is before my eyes. Further, these simple words are themselves values, they have a past, associations, their meaning is born perhaps less from their relation to the object they signify than from their relation to other words, at once adjacent and different: and it is precisely in this zone of oversignification, of secondary signification, that literature will be lodged and will develop. In other words, in relation to objects themselves, literature is fundamentally, constitutively unrealistic; literature is unreality itself; or more exactly, far from being an analogical copy of reality, *literature is on the contrary the very consciousness of the unreality of language*: the "truest" literature is the one which knows itself as the most unreal, to the degree that it knows itself as essentially language; is that search for an intermediary state between things and words; is that tension of a consciousness which is at once carried and limited by the words, which wields through them a power both absolute and improbable. Realism, here, cannot be the copy of things, therefore, but the knowledge of language; the most "realistic" work will not be the one which "paints" reality, but which, using the world as content (this content itself, moreover, is alien to its structure, i.e., to its being), will explore as profoundly as possible the *unreal reality* of language.

Concrete examples? The concrete is very expensive, and here it is a whole history of literature which would have to be reconstructed from this viewpoint. What we can say, I think, is that the exploration of language is at its inception, it constitutes an infinitely rich reservoir of creation; for we must not assume that this exploration is a poetic privilege, poetry being supposed to concern itself with words and the novel with "reality"; it is all literature which is a problematics of language; for instance, our classical literature is the exploration of a certain arbitrary rationality of language, our modern poetry of a certain irrationality, our "new novel" of a certain literalness, etc.; from this viewpoint, all the subversions of language are only very rudimentary experiments, they do not go far; the new, the unknown, the infinite wealth of literature, will instead be found on the side of the false rationalities of language.

VII. What do you think of our immediately contemporary literature? What do you expect of it? Does it have a meaning?

One might ask you to define, yourselves, what you mean by "immediately contemporary literature," and you would have, I think, great difficulty in answering; for if you draw up a list of authors, you will arrive at startling discrepancies, and you will have to explain yourselves in each case; and if you establish a body of doctrine, you will be defining a utopian literature (or, putting matters in the best light, your literature), but then, each real author will define himself chiefly by his divergence from this doctrine. The impossibility of a synthesis is not contingent; it expresses the difficulty we have in grasping the historical meaning of time and of the society we live in.

Despite the feeling one may have of a certain affinity among the various "new novelists," and which I referred to myself apropos of the novelistic vision, one may well hesitate to see the "new novel" as anything but a sociological phenomenon, a literary myth whose sources and function can be readily located; a community of friendships, of publishers, and of panel discussions does not suffice to sanction a genuine synthesis of works. Is such a synthesis possible? Perhaps it will be some day, but all things considered it seems today fairer and more fruitful to explore each writer in particular, to consider his work in isolation, i.e., as an object which has not reduced the tension between subject and history and which is even, as a completed and yet unclassifiable work, constituted by this tension. In short, it would be better to explore the meaning of Robbe-Grillet's *oeuvre* or Butor's, than the meaning of the "new novel"; by explicating the "new novel," as it presents itself, you may explain a tiny fraction of our society; but by explicating Robbe-Grillet or Butor, as they create themselves, you may, beyond your own historical opacity, arrive at some part of the profound history of your time: is not literature that particular language which makes the "subject" into the sign of history?

Taking Sides

Human mores are variable: this is the consensus of classical humanism, from Herodotus to Montaigne and Voltaire. But precisely: mores were then carefully detached from human nature, as the episodic attributes of an eternal substance: on the one side, timelessness, on the other, historical or geographical relativity; to describe the different ways of being cruel or generous was to acknowledge a certain essence of cruelty or generosity, and in consequence to diminish its variations; on classical terrain, relativity is never bewildering because it is not infinite; it stops very soon at the inalterable heart of things: it is a reassurance, not a disturbance.

Today, we are beginning to know, as a consequence of historians like Febvre and of ethnologists like Mauss, that not only mores but also the fundamental acts of human life are historical objects; and that we must redefine, in each case, according to each society observed, facts reputed to be natural by reason of their physical character. It was doubtless a great (still unexploited) conquest, the day historians and ethnologists began to describe the elementary behavior of past or distant societies, such as eating, sleeping, walking, or dying, as acts variable not only in their protocols of execution but also in the human meaning which constitutes them and, for some indeed, in their biological nature (I am thinking of Simmel's and Febvre's reflections on the historical variations in visual and auditory acuteness). This conquest might be defined as the intrusion of an ethnological viewpoint into civilized societies; and naturally, the more such a viewpoint is taken toward a society close to the observer, the more difficult it is to proceed: for it is then nothing but a distance from himself.

Michel Foucault's *Histoire de la Folie*[1] takes its place within this conquering movement of modern ethnology, or of ethnological history (though it also escapes it, as I shall show in a moment): how Lucien Febvre would have enjoyed this audacious book, since it restores to history a fragment of "nature" and transforms into a phenomenon of civilization what we hitherto took for a medical phenomenon: madness. For if we were obliged to envisage a history of madness, we should doubtless do so as if it were analogous to a history of cholera or the plague; we should describe the scientific endeavors of past centuries, the faltering steps of the first medical science, down to the enlightenment of present-day psychiatry; we should accompany this medical history with a notion of ethical progress, the stages articulated by the separation of the madman from the criminal, then his liberation from his chains by Pinel, then the modern physician's effort to listen to and to understand his patient. This mythic viewpoint (mythic since it reassures us) is not at all Michel Foucault's: he has not written the history of madness, as he says, in a style of positivity: from the start he has refused to consider madness as a nosographic reality which has always existed and to which the scientific approach has merely varied from century to century. Indeed Foucault never defines madness; madness is not the *object* of knowledge, whose history must be rediscovered; one might say instead that *madness is nothing but this knowledge itself*: madness is not a disease, it is a variable and perhaps heterogeneous *meaning,* according to the period; Foucault never treats madness except as a functional reality: for him it is the pure function of a couple formed by reason and unreason, observer and observed. And the observer (the man of reason) has no *objective* privilege

1. [Published in America as *Madness and Civilization.*]

over the observed (the madman). It would thus be futile to try
to find the modern names for dementia under its old names.

Here is a first shock to our intellectual habits; Foucault's
method partakes at once of an extreme scientific discretion and
of an extreme distance with regard to "science"; for on the one
hand, nothing happens in the book which is not nominally
given by documents of the period; there is never a projection
of a modern reality onto the old names; if we decide that madness is only what it is said to be (and what else could we decide,
since there is no discourse of madness about reason, corresponding to the discourse of reason about madness), this *saying* must
be treated literally, and not as the outmoded version of a phenomenon about which we now know the truth at last; and on
the other hand, the historian here studies an object whose
objective character he deliberately puts in parentheses; not only
does he describe collective representations (still rarely done in
history), but he even claims that without being mendacious
these representations somehow exhaust their object; we cannot
reach madness outside the notions of men of reason (which does
not mean, moreover, that these notions are illusory); it is therefore neither on the side of (scientific) reality nor on the side of
the (mythic) image that we shall find the historical reality
of madness: it is on the level of the interconstituent dialogue of
reason and unreason, though we must keep in mind that this
dialogue is faked: it involves a great silence, that of the mad:
for the mad possess no metalanguage in which to speak of
reason. In short, Michel Foucault refuses to constitute madness
either as a medical object or as a collective hallucination; his
method is neither positivist nor mythological; he does not even
shift, strictly speaking, the reality of madness from its nosographic content to the pure representation men have made of
it; he keeps identifying the reality of madness with a reality at
once extensive and homogeneous with madness: the couple
formed by reason and unreason. Now this shift has important
consequences, both historically and epistemologically.

The history of madness as a medical phenomenon had to be
nosographic: a simple chapter in the general—and triumphant
—history of medicine. The history of reason/unreason, on the

other hand, is a complete history which brings into play all the
data of a specific historical society; paradoxically, this "immaterial" history immediately satisfies our modern insistence
on a total history, which materialistic historians or ideologists
appeal to without always managing to honor it. For the constitutive observation of madness by men of reason is very
quickly seen to be a simple element of their *praxis:* the fate of
the mad is closely linked to the society's needs with regard to
labor, to the economy as a whole; this link is not necessarily
causal, in the crude sense of the word: *simultaneous* with these
needs appear representations which establish them in nature,
and among these representations, which for a long time were
moral ones, there is the image of madness; the history of madness always follows a history of the ideas of labor, of poverty,
of idleness, and of unproductivity. Michel Foucault has taken
great care to describe *simultaneously* the images of madness and
the economic conditions within the same society; this is doubtless in the best materialist tradition; but where this tradition is
—happily—transcended is in the fact that madness is never
offered as an effect: men produce in the one impulse both
solutions and signs; economic accidents (unemployment, for
example, and its various remedies) immediately take their place
in a structure of significations, a structure which may well pre-
exist them; we cannot say that the needs *create* values, that
unemployment *creates* the image of labor-as-punishment:
rather the two meet as the true units of a vast system of signifying relations: this is what Foucault's analyses of classical society
unceasingly suggest: the link which unites the foundation of
the Hôpital Général to the economic crisis of Europe (beginning of the seventeenth century), or on the contrary the link
which unites the disappearance of confinement to the more
modern sentiment that massive internment cannot solve the
new problems of unemployment (end of the eighteenth century)—these links are essentially signifying links.

This is why the history described by Michel Foucault is a
structural history (and I am not forgetting the abuse made of
this word today). It is structural on two levels, that of the
analysis and that of the project. Without ever breaking the
thread of a diachronic narrative, Foucault reveals, for each

period, what we should elsewhere call *sense units,* whose combination defines this period and whose translation traces the very movement of history; animality, knowledge, vice, idleness, sexuality, blasphemy, libertinage—these historical components of the demential image thus form signifying complexes, according to a kind of historical syntax which varies from epoch to epoch; they are, if you like, classes of what is signified, huge "semantemes" whose signifiers themselves are transitory, since reason's observation constructs the marks of madness only from its own norms, and since these norms are themselves historical. A more formalistic mind might have exploited more intensely the discovery of these sense units: in the notion of structure to which he appeals, Foucault emphasizes the notion of functional totality more than that of component units; but this is a matter of discourse; the meaning of the procedure is the same, whether we attempt a history of madness (as Foucault has done) or a syntax of madness (as we can imagine it): the question is still one of making forms and contents vary *simultaneously.*

Can we imagine that behind all these various *forms* of the demential consciousness there is something signified which is stable, unique, timeless, and, in a word, "natural"? From the medieval fools to the lunatics of the classical period, from these lunatics to Pinel's alienated sufferers, and from these to the new patients of modern psychopathology, the whole of Foucault's history answers: no, madness possesses no transcendent content. But what we can infer from Foucault's analyses (and this is the second way in which his history is structural) is that madness (always conceived, of course, as a pure function of reason) corresponds to a permanent, one might say to a transhistorical *form;* this form cannot be identified with the marks or signs of madness (in the scientific sense of the term), i.e., with the infinitely various signifiers of what is signified (itself diverse) which each society has invested in unreason, dementia, madness, or alienation; it is a question, rather, of a *form of forms,* i.e., of a specific structure; this form of forms, this structure, is suggested on each page of Foucault's book: it is a complementarity which opposes and unites, on the level of society as a whole, the excluded and the included (Lévi-Strauss has mentioned this structure apropos of witch doctors in his introduction to the work of Marcel Mauss). Naturally, we must repeat, each term of the function is fulfilled differently according to period, place, society; exclusion (or as we sometimes say today: deviation) has different contents (meanings), here madness, there shamanism, elsewhere criminality, homosexuality, etc. But a serious paradox begins here: in our societies, at least, the relation of exclusion is determined, and in a sense objectified, by only one of the two humanities participating in it; thus it is the excluded humanity which is named (mad, insane, alienated, criminal, libertine, etc.), it is the act of exclusion, by its very nomination, which in a positive sense accounts for both excluded and "included" ("exile" of the mad in the Middle Ages, confinement in the classical period, internment in the modern age). Thus it is on the level of this general form that madness can be structured (not defined); and if this form is present in any society (but never outside of a society), the only discipline which could account for madness (as for all forms of exclusion) would be anthropology (in the "cultural" and no longer "natural" sense the word increasingly acquires for us). In this perspective, Foucault might have found it advantageous to give some ethnographic references, to suggest the example of societies "without madmen" (but not without "excluded groups"); but also, no doubt, he would regard this additional distance, this serene purview of all humanity as a kind of reassuring alibi, a distraction from what is newest about his project: its bewilderment, its vertigo.

For this book, as we realize when we read it, is different from a book of history, even if such history were audaciously conceived, even if such a book were written, as is the case, by a philosopher. What is it, then? Something like a cathartic question asked of knowledge, of all knowledge, and not only of that knowledge which speaks about madness. Knowledge is no longer that calm, proud, reassuring, reconciling act which Balzac opposed to the will which burns and to the power which destroys; in the couple constituted by reason and madness, by included and excluded, knowledge is a taking of sides; the very act which apprehends madness no longer as an object but as the other face which reason rejects, thereby proceeding to the extreme verge of intelligence, this act too is an act of darkness: casting a brilliant light on the couple constituted by madness and reason, *knowledge* thereby illuminates its own solitude and its own particularity: manifesting the very history of the division, it cannot escape it.

This misgiving—unrelated to the Pirandellian doubt which the frequent confusion of "reasonable" and "demented" behavior can provoke in good minds, for it is not agnostic—this misgiving is inherent in Foucault's very project; once madness is no longer defined substantially ("a disease") or functionally ("antisocial conduct"), but structurally on the level of society as a whole as the discourse of reason about unreason, an implacable dialectic is set up; its origin is an obvious paradox: for a long time men have accepted the idea of reason's historical relativity; the history of philosophy is invented, written, taught, it belongs, one may say, to a hygiene of our societies; but there has never been a corresponding history of *unreason*; in this couple, outside of which neither term can be constituted, one of the partners is historical, participates in the values of civilization, escapes the fatality of being, conquers the freedom of doing; the other partner is excluded from history, fastened to an essence, either supernatural, or moral, or medical; doubtless a fraction—tiny, moreover—of culture acknowledges madness as a respectable or even inspired object, at least through certain of its mediators, Hölderlin, Nietzsche, Van Gogh; but this observation is very recent and, above all, it admits of no exchange: in short it is a liberal observation, an observation of good will, unfortunately powerless to dissipate bad faith. For our knowledge, which never divides itself from our culture, is essentially a rational knowledge, even when history persuades reason to broaden itself, to correct or even to contradict itself: it is a discourse of reason about the world: to discourse about madness starting from knowledge, whatever extreme one reaches, is therefore never to emerge from a functional antinomy whose truth is thus inevitably situated in a space as inaccessible to the mad as to men of reason; for to conceive this antinomy is always to conceive it starting from one of its terms: distance here is merely the ultimate ruse of reason.

In short, knowledge, whatever its conquests, its audacities, its generosities, cannot escape the relation of exclusion, and it cannot help conceiving this relation in terms of inclusion, even when it discovers this relation in its reciprocity; for the most part, it reinforces this relation of exclusion, often just when it thinks it is being most generous. Foucault shows very well that the Middle Ages were actually much more open to madness than our modernity, for madness then, far from being objectified in the form of a disease, was defined as a great passage toward the supernatural, in short as a communication (this is the theme of *The Ship of Fools*); and it is the very progressivism of the modern period which here seems to exert the densest form of bad faith; by removing their chains from the mad, by converting unreason into alienation, Pinel (here merely the representative of a period) masked the functional antinomy of two humanities, constituted madness as an object, i.e., deprived it of its truth; progressive on the physical level, Pinel's liberation was regressive on the anthropological one.

The history of madness could be "true" only if it were naïve, i.e., written by a madman; but then it could not be written in terms of history, so that we are left with the incoercible bad faith of knowledge. This is an inevitability which greatly exceeds the simple relations of madness and unreason; indeed, it affects all "thought," or to be more exact, all recourse to a metalanguage, whatever it might be: each time men speak about the world, they enter into a relation of exclusion, even when they speak in order to denounce it: a metalanguage is always terrorist. This is an endless dialectic, which can seem sophistical only to minds possessed of a reason substantial as a nature or a right; the others will experience it dramatically, or generously, or stoically; in any case, they know that bewilderment, that vertigo of discourse on which Michel Foucault has just cast so much light, a vertigo which appears not only upon contact with madness, but indeed each time that man, taking his distances, observes the world as different, which is to say, each time he writes.

Literature and Discontinuity

Behind every collective rejection of a book by our stock criticism we must look for *what has been offended*. *Mobile* offended the very idea of the Book.[1] A compilation—and even worse, for the compilation is a minor but received genre—a sequence of phrases, quotations, clippings, of paragraphs, words, block-letter capitals scattered over the (often nearly blank) surface of the page, all this concerning an object (America) whose very parts (the states of the Union) are presented in the most insipid of orders, which is the alphabetical order: here is a technique of exposition unworthy of the way our ancestors have taught us to make a book.

What aggravates *Mobile*'s case is that the liberty its author takes with regard to the Book is paradoxically associated with a genre, the *travel impression*, to which our society extends the greatest indulgence. A journey, we grant, may be freely described from day to day in frank subjectivity, in the manner of

---

1. Apropos of Michel Butor's *Mobile: Study for a Representation of the United States*. [The reference to a general disapproval by French critics was reflected by a characteristic American review—incredulous, derisive, outraged—which the translation of the book received from Truman Capote.—Trans.]

a private diary whose thread is continually broken by the pressure of days, sensations, ideas: a journey can be written elliptically (*Yesterday, ate an orange at Sibari*), the telegraphic style being sanctified by the genre's "naturalness." But society is reluctant to add to the liberty which it gives, a liberty which is taken. In a literature like ours where everything is in its place, and where only such an order generates security, morality, or, more exactly, for it consists of a complex mixture of both, hygiene, it is poetry and poetry alone whose function is to collect all the phenomena subversive of the Book's material nature: since Mallarmé and Apollinaire, no one can take exception to the typographical "eccentricity" or the rhetorical "disorder" of a poetic "composition." We recognize here a technique familiar to good society: to freeze such liberties as if they were an ulcer; consequently, aside from poetry, no outrage to the Book may be tolerated.

Butor's offense was all the graver in that his infraction was intentional. *Mobile* is not a "natural" or "familiar" book; no question here of "travel notes" or even of a "dossier" of various materials whose diversity might be accepted if one could call the thing, for instance, a *scrapbook* (for naming exorcises). For *Mobile* is a conscious composition: first of all, in its scope, which relates to those great poems, so foreign to us, which were the epic or the didactic poem; then, in its structure, which is neither a narrative nor an accumulation of notes, but a combination of selected units (to which we shall return); finally, in its very closure, since the object treated is defined by a number (the states of the Union) and since the book ends when this number has been honored. If, then, *Mobile* violates the consecrated (i.e., sacred) notion of the Book, this is not out of negligence but in the name of another idea of another Book. Which one? Before finding out, there are two lessons to be learned from *Mobile*'s reception, lessons concerning the traditional nature of the Book.

The first is that any upset an author imposes on the typographic norms of a work constitutes an essential disturbance: to deploy isolated words on a page, to mix italic, roman, and capital letters with a purpose which is visibly not that of intellectual demonstration (for when we are concerned to teach

English to our schoolchildren, we are quite indulgent of the splendid typographical eccentricity of our Carpentier-Fialip manuals), to break the material thread of the sentence by disparate paragraphs, to make a word equal in importance to a sentence—all these liberties contribute in short to the very destruction of the Book: *the Book-as-Object is materially identified with the Book-as-Idea,* the technique of printing with the literary institution, so that to attack the material regularity of the work is to attack the very idea of literature. In short, the typographical forms are a basic guarantee: normal printing attests to the normality of the discourse; to say of *Mobile* that "it's not a book" is obviously to enclose the being and the meaning of literature in a pure protocol, as if this same literature were a rite which would lose all effectiveness the day we formally violated any of its rules: the Book is a High Mass, and it matters little whether or not it is said with piety, provided its every element proceeds in order.

If everything which happens on the surface of the page wakens so intense a susceptibility, it is clear that this surface is the depository of an essential value, which is the continuity of literary discourse (and this will be the second lesson to be learned from *Mobile's* reception). The (traditional) Book is an object which *connects, develops, runs,* and *flows,* in short, has the profoundest horror vacui. Sympathetic metaphors of the Book are: fabric to be woven, water flowing, flour to be milled, paths to be followed, curtains parting, etc.; antipathetic metaphors are those of a fabricated object, i.e., an object assembled out of discontinuous raw materials: on one side, the "flow" of living, organic substances, the charming unpredictability of spontaneous liaisons; on the other, the ungrateful sterility of mechanical contraption, of cold and creaking machinery (this is the theme of the laborious). For what is hidden behind this condemnation of discontinuity is obviously the myth of life itself: the Book must flow because fundamentally, despite centuries of intellectualism, our criticism wants literature to be, always, a spontaneous, gracious activity conceded by a god, a muse, and if the god or muse happens to be a little reticent, one must at least "conceal one's labor": to write is to secrete words within that great category of the continuous which is narrative;

all literature, even if it is didactic or intellectual (after all, we must put up with some of the novel's poor relations), should be a narrative, a flow of words in the service of an event or an idea which "makes its way" toward its denouement or its conclusion: not to "narrate" its object is, for the Book, to commit suicide.

This is why, in the eyes of our stock criticism, guardian of the sacred Book, any analytical explanation of the work is ultimately mistrusted. The continuous work requires a corresponding cosmetic criticism which covers the work without dividing it up; the two preferred operations are: to summarize and to judge; but it is not good to break down the Book into parts which are too small: that is Byzantine, that destroys the work's ineffable life (by which is meant: its course, its murmuring stream, guarantee of its life); all the suspicion attached to thematic or structural criticism comes from this: to divide is to dissect, to destroy, to profane the Book's "mystery," i.e., its continuity. Granted, our criticism has gone to school, where it has been taught to discern "schemas" and to recognize those of others; but the divisions of the "schema" (three or four at most) are the main breaks of the journey, that is all; what underlies the "schema" is the *detail*: the detail is not a fundamental raw material, it is inessential small change: major ideas are coined into "details" without for a moment entertaining the notion that major ideas can be generated from the mere arrangement and disposition of "details." Paraphrase is therefore the rational operation of a criticism which demands of the Book, above all, that it be continuous: we "caress" the Book, just as we ask the Book's continuous language to "caress" life, the soul, evil, etc. Thus the discontinuous Book is tolerated only in very special circumstances: either as a compilation of fragments (Heraclitus, Pascal), the work's unfinished character (but are these works actually unfinished?) corroborating *a contrario* the excellence of continuity, outside of which there may be a sketch but never perfection; or as a compilation of aphorisms, for the aphorism is a tiny, dense piece of continuity, the theatrical affirmation that the void is horrible. In short, to be a Book, to satisfy its essence as Book, the work must either flow (like a narrative) or gleam (like a flash of light). Outside these two systems lies violation, outrage of the Book, a not very tempting sin against the hygiene of letters.

Confronted with this problem of continuity, the author of *Mobile* has proceeded to a rigorous inversion of rhetorical values. What does traditional rhetoric say? That we must construct a work in large masses and let the details take care of themselves: hats off to the "general schema," a scornful denial that the idea can be parceled out beyond the paragraph; this is why our entire art of writing is based on the notion of *development:* an idea "develops" and this development constitutes part of the "schema"; thus the Book is always reassuringly composed of a small number of well-developed ideas. (We might of course ask what a "development" is, contest the very notion, acknowledge its mythic character and affirm on the contrary that there is a profound solitude, a matte nature of the authentic idea, in which case the essential Book—if there must be such a thing as an essence of the Book—would be precisely Pascal's *Pensées* which "develop" nothing at all.) Now it is precisely this rhetorical order which the author of *Mobile* has reversed: in *Mobile* the "general schema" is of no account and the detail is raised to the rank of structure; the ideas are not "developed" but distributed.

To present America without any "rational" schema, as moreover to accomplish for any object whatever a schema of no account, is a very difficult thing, for every order has a meaning, even that of the absence of order, which has a name, which is disorder. To express an object without order and without disorder is a feat. Is it therefore necessary? It can be, insofar as any classification, whatever it may be, is responsible for a meaning. We are beginning to know, in small measure since Durkheim, in large measure since Lévi-Strauss, that taxonomy can be an important part of the study of societies: *tell me how you classify and I'll tell you who you are;* on a certain scale, there are neither natural nor rational schemas, but only "cultural" schemas, in which is invested either a collective representation of the world or an individual imagination, which we might call a taxonomic imagination, which remains to be studied but of which a man like Fourier furnishes a great example.

Since, then, *any* classification is a commitment, since men inevitably give a meaning to forms (and is there a purer form than a classification?), the neutrality of an order becomes not only an adult problem but even an esthetic problem—one difficult to solve. It will appear absurd (and provocative) to suggest that alphabetical order (which the author has used in part to present the states of the Union and for which he has been censured) is an intelligent order, i.e., an order concerned with an esthetic concept of the intelligible. Yet the alphabet— not to mention the profound circularity it can be given, as the mystic metaphor of "alpha and omega" testifies—the alphabet is a means of institutionalizing a zero degree of classification; it startles us because our society has always given an exorbitant privilege to charged signs and crudely identifies a zero degree of things with their negation: for us, there is little place and little consideration for the neutral, which is always felt morally as an impotence to be or to destroy. Yet it has been possible to consider the notion of mana as a zero degree of signification, which is enough to indicate the importance of the neutral in a realm of human thought.

It hardly need be said that in *Mobile* the alphabetical presentation of the states of the Union also *signifies,* insofar as it rejects all other classifications (of a geographical or picturesque type); it reminds the reader of the federal, hence arbitrary, nature of the country described, affords throughout the entire course of the book that civic expression which results from the fact that the United States is a constructed nation, a list of units, none of which takes pre-eminence over the rest. Michelet too, undertaking in his time a "study for a representation" of France, organized our country as if it were a chemical body, the negative at the center, the active parts at the edge, balancing each other across this central, this neutral void (for Michelet did not fear the neutral), out of which had come our royalty; for the United States, nothing of the kind is possible: the United States is an accumulation of stars: here the alphabet consecrates a history, a mythological way of thought, a civic sentiment; it is at bottom the classification of appropriation, that of encyclopedias, i.e., of any knowledge which seeks to dominate the plural of things without destroying their identity,

and it is true that the United States was won like an encyclopedic substance, thing after thing, state after state.

Formally, alphabetical order has another virtue: by breaking,
by rejecting the "natural" affinities of the states, it obliges the
discovery of other relations, quite as intelligent as the first, since
the meaning of this whole combination of territories has come
afterwards, once they have been laid out on the splendid alphabetical list of the Constitution. In short, the order of the letters
says that in the United States, there is no contiguity of spaces
except in the abstract; look at the map of the states: what order
are we to follow? No sooner does it set out than our forefinger
loses track, the accounting evades us; there is no such thing as
a "natural" contiguity; but precisely for this reason the poetic
contiguity is born, the powerful one which obliges an image to
leap from Alabama to Alaska, from Clinton (Kentucky) to
Clinton (Indiana), etc., under the pressure of this truth of
forms, of literal parallels, whose heuristic power we have
learned from all modern poetry: if Alabama and Alaska were
not such close alphabetical relatives, how would they be merged
in that night which is the same and different: simultaneous and
yet divided by a whole day?

Alphabetical classification is sometimes completed by other
associations of spaces, quite as formal. There is no lack in the
United States of cities of the same name; in relation to the
truth of the human heart, this circumstance is trivial enough;
the author of *Mobile* has nonetheless paid it the closest attention; in a continent marked by a permanent identity crisis, the
penury of proper names participates profoundly in the American
phenomenon: a continent that is too big, a lexicon that is too
small—a whole part of America is in this strange friction of
words and things. By connecting homonymic cities, by referring
spatial contiguity to a purely phonic identity, Butor reveals a
certain secret of things; and it is in this that he is a writer: the
writer is not defined by the use of specialized tools which parade
literature (*discourse, poem, concept, rhythm, wit, metaphor,*
according to the peremptory catalogue of one of our critics),
unless we regard literature as an object of hygiene, but by the
power of surprising, by some formal device, a particular collusion of man and nature, i.e., a meaning: and in this "surprise,"

it is form which guides, form which keeps watch, which in-
structs, which knows, which thinks, which "commits"; this is
why form has no other judge than what it reveals; and here,
what it reveals is a certain knowledge concerning America. That
this knowledge should not be enunciated in intellectual terms,
but according to a particular table of signs, is precisely . . .
literature: a code which we must agree to decipher. After all, is
Mobile more difficult to understand, is its knowledge more
difficult to reconstitute, than the rhetorical or *précieux* code of
our seventeenth century? It is true that in that century the
reader agreed to learn how to read: it did not seem exorbitant to
know mythology or rhetoric in order to receive the meaning of
a poem or of a discourse.

The fragmentary order of *Mobile* has another significance.
By destroying within discourse the notion of "part," it refers us
to an infinitely sensitive mobility of closed elements. What are
these elements? They have no form in themselves; they are
neither ideas nor images nor sensations nor even notations, for
they do not emerge from a projected restoration of experience;
they are, rather, an enumeration of signaletic objects, here a
press clipping, here a paragraph from a book, here a quote from
a prospectus, here finally, less than all that, the name of an ice-
cream flavor, the color of a car or a shirt, or just a simple proper
name. As if the writer resorts to "takes," various soundings, with
no regard for their material origin. Yet these "takes" without
stable form, anarchic as they seem on the level of the detail
(since, without rhetorical transcendence, they are indeed nothing but details), paradoxically become object units on the
broadest level there is, the most intellectual level, one might say,
which is the level of history. The units are categorized with
remarkable consistency, within three "bundles": the Indians,
1890, today. The "representation" which *Mobile* gives of
America is thus anything but modernist; it is a representation in
depth, in which the perspective dimension is constituted by the
past. This past is doubtless brief, its chief moments are contiguous, it is not far from peyote to Howard Johnson ice-cream
flavors. As a matter of fact, moreover, the extent of the American diachrony has no importance; what is important is that by
constantly mixing *ex abrupto* Indian narratives, an 1890 guide-

book, and today's automobiles, the author perceives, and allows us to perceive, America in an oneiric perspective, with this one stipulation—original when it concerns America—that the dream here is not exotic but historical: *Mobile* is a profound *anamnesis*, all the more singular in that it was written by a Frenchman, i.e., by a writer from a nation which has itself ample sustenance for memory, and in that it applies to a nation mythologically "new"; *Mobile* thus destroys the traditional function of the European in America, which consists of being astonished, in the name of his own past, to discover a nation without roots, the better to describe the surprises of a civilization at once endowed with technology and deprived of culture.

Now *Mobile* gives America a culture. Of course this enumerative, broken, a-rhetorical discourse offers no dissertation on values: it is precisely because American culture is neither moralistic nor literary, but, paradoxically, despite the eminently technological condition of the country, "natural," i.e., naturalistic: in no country of the world, perhaps, is nature, in the quasi-romantic sense of the term, so visible; Butor tells us that the first monument of American culture is precisely Audubon's work, i.e., a flora and a fauna represented by an artist outside of any school or tendency. This fact is in a sense symbolic: culture does not necessarily consist of experiencing nature in metaphors or styles, but in subjecting what is immediately given to an intelligible order; it is of little importance whether this order is that of a scrupulous recension (Audubon), of a mythic narrative (that of the young Indian peyote eater), of a newspaper chronicle (the *New York World* reporter), or of a canned-goods label: in all these cases, the American language constitutes a first transformation of nature into culture, i.e., essentially an act of institution. All *Mobile* does, in short, is to recuperate this institution of America for the Americans and to represent it: the book's subtitle is "Study for a Representation of the United States," and it has indeed a plastic finality: it aims to provide an equivalent for a great historical (or more precisely, transhistorical) tableau in which the objects, in their very discontinuity, are at once shards of time and first thoughts.

For there are objects in *Mobile*, and these objects assure the work its degree of credibility—not realistic, but oneiric credibility. The objects are starters: they are mediators of culture infinitely faster than ideas, producers of hallucinations just as active as the "situations"; they are most often at the very bottom of the situations and give them that exciting, i.e., strictly mobilizing character which makes a literature truly alive. In the murder of Agamemnon, there is the obsessional veil which serves to blind him; in Nero's love, there are those torches glittering on Junia's tears; in the humiliation of Boule de Suif, there is that basket of food, described to the last detail; in *Nadja* there is the Tour Saint-Jacques, the Hôtel des Grands-Hommes; in *Jealousy* there is an insect squashed on the wall; in *Mobile*, there is peyote, twenty-eight flavors of ice cream, ten colors of cars (there are also the different colors of the blacks). This is what makes a work into a memorable event; like a childhood memory in which, beyond all hierarchies learned and meanings imposed (genre: "truth of the human heart"), shimmers the light of the essential accessory.

A single wide horizon, in the form of a mythic history, a profound flavor of the objects cited in this great catalogue of the United States, such is the perspective of *Mobile*, i.e., what makes it, in short, a work of familiar culture. If this classicism of substance has been misunderstood, no doubt it is because Butor has given his discourse a discontinuous form (*crumbs of thought* was the scornful phrase). We have seen how subversive any attack on the myth of rhetorical "development" appears. But in *Mobile* there is worse still: discontinuity is here all the more scandalous in that the poem's "units" are not "varied" (in the sense this word can have in music) but merely repeated: unalterable cells are infinitely combined, without there ever having been any internal transformation of the elements. If indeed we grant that a work can be composed of several themes (though thematic criticism, if it parcels out the theme too much, is sharply contested): in spite of everything, the theme remains a literary object insofar as it submits itself to variation, i.e., to development. Now in *Mobile*, there is no theme, from this point of view, and therefore no obsession: the repetition of elements clearly has no psychological value here, but only a structural one: it does not "betray" the author, but, entirely interior to the object described, visibly derives from an art.

Whereas in the traditional esthetic, all literary effort consists in disguising the theme, in giving it unexpected variations, in *Mobile* there is no variation, but only variety, and this variety is purely combinatory. The units of discourse are, in short, essentially defined by their function (in the mathematical sense of the term), not by their rhetorical nature: a metaphor exists in itself; a structural unit exists only by distribution, i.e., by relation to other units. These units are—and must be—beings so perfectly *mobile* that by shifting them throughout his poem the author engenders a kind of huge animate body whose movement is one of perpetual transmission, not of internal "growth": thus, the title of the object: *Mobile*, i.e., a scrupulously articulated armature all of whose breaks, by shifting very slightly (which the delicacy of the combinatory method permits), produce paradoxically the most connected movements.

For there is, after all, a continuity of discourse in *Mobile* which is immediately perceptible, provided we forget the rhetorical model on which we are accustomed to pattern our reading. Rhetorical continuity develops, amplifies; it will agree to repeat only if it can transform. *Mobile*'s continuity repeats, but combines differently what it repeats. Thus rhetorical continuity never returns to what it has set forth, while *Mobile*'s continuity returns, recurs, recalls: the new is ceaselessly accompanied by the old: it is, one might say, a fugal continuity, in the course of which identifiable fragments ceaselessly reappear. The example of music is useful here, for the most connected of the arts actually possesses only the most discontinuous of raw materials: in music—at least, in our music—there are only thresholds, relations of differences, and constellations of these differences ("routines," one might say). *Mobile*'s composition derives from this same dialectic of difference, which we also find in other forms of continuity: though who would dare say that Webern or Mondrian have produced an art "in crumbs"? Moreover, all these artists have in no way invented discontinuity merely in order to defeat it: discontinuity is the fundamental status of all communication: signs never exist unless they are discreet. The esthetic problem is simply how to mobilize this inevitable discontinuity, how to give it a rhythm, a tempo, a history. Classical rhetoric has given its answer, a masterly one for centuries, by erecting an esthetic of variation (of which the notion of "development" is merely the crude myth); but there is another possible rhetoric, a rhetoric of transmission: modern, no doubt, since we find it only in certain *avant-garde* works, and yet, elsewhere, how old! Is not every mythic narrative, according to Lévi-Strauss, produced by a *mobilization* of recurrent units, of autonomous series (the musicians would say), whose infinitely possible shifts afford the work the responsibility of its choice, i.e., its singularity, i.e., its meaning?

For *Mobile* has a meaning, and this meaning is perfectly human (since the human is what our stock criticism calls for here), i.e., it refers on the one hand to the serious history of a man, who is the author, and on the other to the real nature of an object, which is America. *Mobile* occupies in Michel Butor's itinerary a place which is obviously not gratuitous. We know from the author himself that his *oeuvre* is constructed; this banal term covers a very precise project, one very different from the kind of "construction" recommended in the classroom; taken literally, it implies that the work reproduces an interior model assembled by the meticulous arrangement of parts: this model is, specifically, a *maquette*: the author works from a *maquette*, and we immediately see the structural signification of this art: the *maquette* is not, strictly speaking, a ready-made structure which the work must transform into an event; rather it is a structure to be realized starting from pieces of events, pieces which the author tries to bring together, to separate, to arrange, without altering their material figuration; this is why the *maquette* participates in that art of assemblage which Lévi-Strauss has just given its structural dignity (in *The Savage Mind*). It is possible that, starting from poetry—poetry, which is the exemplary art of literary assemblage (it is understood that the word has no pejorative nuance here), since in poetry word-events are transformed by mere arrangement into a system of meaning—Michel Butor has conceived his novels as a single structural investigation whose principle might be this: it is by *trying* fragments of events together that meaning is generated, it is by tirelessly transforming these events into functions that the structure is erected: the writer (poet, novelist, chronicler) *sees* the meaning of the inert units in front of him only by *relating* them: thus the work has that simultaneously ludic and serious character which marks every great question: it is a masterly puzzle, the puzzle of the best possibility. We then see how much *Mobile* represents, in this direction, an urgent investigation (corroborated by *Votre Faust,* which was written immediately afterwards, and in which the spectator himself is invited to organize the "routines" of the puzzle, to venture into the structural combination): art here serves a serious question, which we find throughout all of Michel Butor's *oeuvre,* a question which is that of the world's *possibility,* or to speak in a more Leibnitzian fashion, of its *compossibility.* And if the method is explicit in *Mobile,* it is because it has encountered in America (here we deliberately call the United States by its mythic name) a privileged object which art can account for only by an incessant trial of contiguities, of shifts, of returns, of entrances bearing on denominative enumerations, oneiric fragments, legends, flavors, colors, or simple toponymic noises, the sum of which represents this compossibility of the New World. And here again, *Mobile* is at once very new and very old: this great catalogue of America has for distant ancestors those epic catalogues, gigantic and purely denominative enumerations of ships, of regiments and captains, which Homer and Aeschylus inserted in their narratives in order to testify to the infinite "compossibility" of war and of power.

1962

Structure of the
Fait-Divers

A murder is committed: if political, it is news, otherwise we French call it a *fait-divers*.[1] Why? One might suppose that the difference here is between the particular and the general or, more precisely, between the named and the unnamed: the *fait-divers* (the term, at least, seems to indicate as much) would thus derive from a classification of the unclassifiable, it would be the unorganized discard of news; its essence would be privative, it would begin to exist only where the world stops being named, subject to a known catalogue (politics, economics, war, amusement, science, etc.); in a word, it would be a monstrous item, analogous to all the exceptional or insignificant, i.e., anomic phenomena classified under the modest rubric *Varia*, like the platypus which gave poor Linnaeus so much trouble. This taxonomic definition is obviously not satisfactory: it does not account for the extraordinary promotion of the *fait-divers* in today's press (we are beginning, moreover, to call it, more nobly, *general information*); it would be better

1. [Sometimes translated by the journalist's term *filler*. By retaining the French expression, emphasis is placed rather on the phenomenon itself than on its function for the compositor.]

to put the *fait-divers* and other kinds of information on a basis of equality and to try to discover, in all of them, a difference in structure and no longer a difference in classification.

This difference appears as soon as we compare our two murders; in the first (the assassination), the event (the murder) necessarily refers to an extensive situation outside itself, previous to and around it: "politics"; such news cannot be understood immediately, it can be defined only in relation to a knowledge external to the event, which is political knowledge, however confused; in short, a murder escapes the *fait-divers* whenever it is exogenous, proceeding from an already known world; we might then say that it has no sufficient structure of its own, for it is never anything but the manifest term of an implicit structure which pre-exists it: there is no political news without duration, for politics is a transtemporal category; this is true, moreover, of all news proceeding from a named horizon, from an anterior time: it can never constitute *faits-divers*;[2] in terms of literature, such items are fragments of novels,[3] insofar as every novel is itself an extensive knowledge of which any event occurring within it is nothing but a simple variable.

Thus an assassination is always, by definition, partial information; the *fait-divers*, on the contrary, is total news, or more precisely, immanent; it contains all its knowledge in itself; no need to know anything about the world in order to consume a *fait-divers*; it refers formally to nothing but itself; of course, its content is not alien to the world: disasters, murders, rapes, accidents, thefts, all this refers to man, to his history, his alienation, his hallucinations, his dreams, his fears: an ideology and a psychoanalysis of the *fait-divers* are possible, but they would concern a world of which knowledge is never anything but intellectual, analytical, elaborated at second-hand by the person who speaks of the *fait-divers*, not by the person who consumes it; on the level of reading, everything is given within the *fait-*

2. Phenomena which belong to what we might call the "gestae" of stars or personalities are never *faits-divers*, precisely because they imply a structure of episodes.

3. In a sense, it is correct to say that politics is a novel, i.e., a narrative which has duration, provided its actors are personalized.

divers; its circumstances, its causes, its past, its outcome; without duration and without context, it constitutes an immediate, total being which refers, formally at least, to nothing implicit; in this it is related to the short story and the tale, and no longer to the novel. It is its immanence which defines the *fait-divers*.[4]

Here, then, is a closed structure—what happens within it? An example, however slight, will perhaps afford the answer. *The Palais de Justice has just been cleaned . . .* That is insignificant. *. . . for the first time in over a century.* That becomes a *fait-divers*. Why? The anecdote matters little (there are even slighter examples); two terms are posited which invariably enforce a certain relation, and it is the problematics of this relation which will constitute the *fait-divers*; the cleaning of the Palais de Justice on the one hand, its infrequency on the other, are in a sense the two terms of a function: it is this function which is vital; it is this function which is regular, hence intelligible; presumably there is no simple *fait-divers*, constituted by a single notation: the simple is not notable; whatever its content's density, astonishment, horror, or poverty, the *fait-divers* begins only where the news divides and thereby involves the certainty of a relation; the brevity of the utterance or the importance of the information, elsewhere a guarantee of unity, can never efface the articulated character of the *fait-divers: five million dead in Peru?* The horror is total, the sentence is simple; yet the notable, here, is already the relation between the dead and a number. Granted, a structure is always articulated; but here the articulation is internal to the immediate narrative, whereas in political news, for example, it is transferred outside the discourse to an implicit context.

Thus every *fait-divers* involves at least two terms, or, one might say, two notations. And we can quite properly make a first analysis of the *fait-divers* without referring to the form and the content of these two terms: to their form, because the phraseology of narrative is alien to the structure of the phenomenon reported, or, more precisely, because this structure does not

---

4. Certain *faits-divers* are developed over several days; this does not violate their constitutive immanence, for they still imply an extremely short memory.

inevitably coincide with the structure of language, though one gains access to it only through journalistic language; to their content, because what matters is not the terms themselves, the contingent way in which they are saturated (by a murder, a fire, a theft, etc.), but the relation which unites them. It is this relation we must question first, if we would grasp the *fait-divers'* structure, i.e., its human meaning.

It appears that all relations immanent in the *fait-divers* can be reduced to two types. The first is the—very frequent—relation of causality: a crime and its motive, an accident and its circumstance. From this point of view, there are powerful stereotypes: crime of passion, greed, etc. But whenever causality is more or less normal, expected, the emphasis is not put on the relation itself, though the relation continues to form the structure of the narrative; the emphasis shifts to what might be called the *dramatis personae* (child, old man, mother, etc.), emotional essences responsible for vivifying the stereotype.[5] Each time, then, we would see the *fait-divers'* causality function in its pure state, it is a slightly aberrant causality we encounter. In other words, the pure (and exemplary) cases are constituted by the disturbances of causality, as if the spectacle ("notability," one should say) began where causality, without ceasing to be affirmed, already contained a germ of deterioration, as if causality could be consummated only when it began to rot, to disintegrate. There is no *fait-divers* without astonishment (to write is to be astonished); now, referred to a cause, astonishment always implies a disturbance, since in our civilization, every *elsewhere* of a cause seems to be situated more or less declaratively outside of nature, or at least outside of the natural. What, then, are these disturbances of causality, around which the *fait-divers* is articulated?

First of all, certainly, the fact that we cannot immediately determine the cause. Someday we must diagram our contem-

5. Moreover, in stereotyped *faits-divers* (the crime of passion, for example), the narrative increasingly emphasizes aberrant circumstances (*killed for bursting into laughter: her husband was behind the door; when he heard her laugh, he went down to the cellar and got his revolver . . .*).

porary inexplicability, as it is represented to us not by science but by common sense; it appears that in the *fait-divers*, the inexplicable is reduced to two categories of phenomena: prodigies and crimes. What used to be called the prodigy, and which would doubtless have pre-empted the *fait-divers* if the popular press had existed in those days, always has heaven for its locus, but in recent years it seems that there is only one such prodigy left: flying saucers; although a recent American army report has identified as natural objects (planes, balloons, birds) all the flying saucers reported, the object continues to have a mythic life: it is identified with a planetary vehicle, generally sent by the Martians: causality is thus projected into space, it is not abolished; moreover, the Martian theme has been considerably diminished by real flights into the cosmos: there is no need for a Martian to enter the earth's atmosphere now that Gagarin, Titov, and Glenn are leaving it: a whole supernature is disappearing. As for "mysterious" crime, we all know its fortunes in popular fiction; its fundamental relation is constituted by a postponed causality; the detective work consists in filling in, backwards, the fascinating and unendurable interval separating the event from its cause; the detective, emanation of the entire society in its bureaucratic form, then becomes the modern figure of the ancient solver of riddles (Oedipus), who puts an end to the terrible *why* of things; his patient and determined activity is the symbol of a profound desire: man feverishly plugs the causal breach, resolves frustration and anguish. In the press, of course, "mysterious" crimes are rare, the detective is rarely personalized, the logical enigma is drowned in the pathos of the actors; here, on the other hand, real ignorance of the cause obliges the *fait-divers* to extend over several days, to lose that ephemeral character so consonant with its immanent nature; this is why, in the *fait-divers*, contrary to the novel, a crime without a cause is not so much inexplicable as unexplained: the causal "delay" does not aggravate the crime, it destroys it: a crime without a cause is a crime which is forgotten: the *fait-divers* then vanishes, precisely because in reality its fundamental relation is exhausted.

Naturally, since it is the disturbed causality which is the most notable, the *fait-divers* is rich in causal deviations: by virtue of certain stereotypes, we look for one cause, and it is another which appears: *a woman stabs her lover* . . . A crime of passion? . . . *during a political argument*. Again, *a young nursemaid kidnaps her employer's baby* . . . For the ransom? No, . . . *because she adored the child*. Again, *a prowler attacks unaccompanied women* . . . A rapist? No: *a purse snatcher*. In all these examples, the cause revealed is in a sense *poorer* than the cause expected; crimes of passion, blackmail, sexual aggression have a long past; they are phenomena charged with emotion, in relation to which political differences, excessive affection, or simple theft are absurd motives; this kind of causal relation affords the spectacle of a frustration; paradoxically, the causality is all the more notable in that it is frustrated. To deficiency or deviation, those privileged disturbances of causality, we must add what might be called the surprises of number (or more broadly, of quantity). Here again, we return to that frustrated causality which engenders, for the *fait-divers*, a spectacle of surprise. *A train is derailed in Alaska: a stag had tripped the switch. An Englishman enlists in the Foreign Legion: to avoid spending Christmas with his mother-in-law. An American coed is forced to leave school: her bust measurements cause an uproar in all her classes.* All these examples illustrate the rule: minor causes, great effects. But the *fait-divers* sees in these disproportions no invitation to philosophize on the vanity of things or on the cowardice of men; it does not say, like Valéry, how many men die in an accident because they are unwilling to let go of their umbrella; it says instead, and in a fashion actually much more intellectualist: the causal relation is peculiar; the slight volume of a cause in no way diminishes the scope of its effect; a little equals a lot; and thereby this "deranged" causality can be everywhere: it is not constituted by a quantitatively accumulated force, but rather by a mobile energy, active in very small doses.

We must include in these absurd circuits all the important events tributary to a prosaic, humble, familiar object: *gangster routed by a poker. Murderer identified by his bicycle clips. Old man strangled by the cord of his hearing aid.* This figure is familiar to the detective novel, by its nature avid for the "miracle of the index": it is the most discreet index which finally solves the mystery. Two ideological themes are implicated here: on the one hand, the infinite power of signs, the panic sentiment that signs are everywhere, that anything can be a sign; and on the other hand, the responsibility of objects, as active ultimately as persons: there is a false innocence of objects; the object hides behind its inertia-as-thing, but only to emit an even stronger causal force, which may derive from itself or from elsewhere.

All these paradoxes of causality have a double meaning; on the one hand, the notion of causality is reinforced by them, since we feel that the cause is everywhere: here the *fait-divers* tells us that man is always linked to something else, that nature is full of echoes, relations, and movements; but on the other hand, this same causality is constantly undermined by forces which escape it; disturbed but not disappearing, causality remains "suspended" between the rational and the unknown, subject to a fundamental astonishment distant from its effect (and this distance, for the *fait-divers*, is the very essence of the *notable*), the cause seems inevitably imbued with an alien force: chance; in the world of the *fait-divers*, all causality is under suspicion of chance.

Here we encounter the second type of relation which can articulate the structure of the *fait-divers*: the relation of coincidence. It is chiefly the repetition of an event, however anodyne, which marks it out for the notation of coincidence: *the same diamond brooch is stolen three times; a hotelkeeper wins the lottery whenever he buys a ticket*, etc.: why? Repetition always commits us to imagining an unknown cause, so true is it that in the popular consciousness, the aleatory is always distributive, never repetitive: chance is supposed to vary events; if it repeats them, it does so in order to signify something through them; to repeat is to signify, this belief [6] is at the source of all ancient *manteia*; today, of course, repetition does not openly suggest a supernatural interpretation; however, even

6. A belief obscurely consonant with the formal nature of signifying systems, since the use of a code always implies the repetition of a limited number of signs.

when reduced to the rank of a "curiosity," repetition cannot be noted without its occurring to us that it possesses a certain meaning, even if this meaning remains suspended: the "peculiar," the "uncanny," the "curious" cannot be a matte, "innocent" notion, so to speak (except for the absurd consciousness, which is not the case of the popular consciousness): it inevitably institutionalizes an interrogation.

Another relation of coincidence is the one which relates two terms which are qualitatively distant: *a woman routs four burglars; a judge vanishes in Pigalle; Iceland fishermen net a cow*, etc.; there is a kind of logical distance between the woman's weakness and the number of the burglars, between the magistracy and Pigalle, between fishing and a cow, and the *fait-divers* immediately begins to suppress this distance. In logical terms, we might say that since each term belongs in principle to an autonomous circuit of signification, the relation of coincidence has as its paradoxical function the reduction of two different circuits to one, as if suddenly the magistracy and "Pigallity" were to be found in the same realm.

And since the original distance of the circuits is spontaneously felt as a relation of opposition, we approach here a fundamental rhetorical figure in the discourse of our civilization: antithesis.[7] Coincidence is indeed all the more spectacular in that it *reverses* certain stereotyped situations: *in Little Rock, the chief of police kills his wife. Burglars are frightened away by another burglar. Thieves sic their police dog on the night watchman*, etc. The relation becomes vectorized, it is steeped in intelligence: *not only* is there a murderer, but *furthermore* this murderer is the chief of police: causality is reversed by virtue of an exactly symmetrical design. This movement was familiar to our classical tragedy, where it even had a name: *le comble*, the acme:

---

7. The figures of rhetoric have always been treated disdainfully by historians of literature or of language, as if they were merely gratuitous language games; the "living" expression is always contrasted to the rhetorical expression. Yet rhetoric can constitute a crucial evidence of civilization, for it represents a certain mental selection of the world, i.e., finally, an ideology.

Je n'ai donc traversé tant de mers, tant d'Etats,
Que pour venir si loin préparer son trépas.

Then have I crossed all these seas and states,
Only to come so far to work her doom.

says Orestes, speaking of Hermione. The examples on both sides are numberless: it is precisely when Agamemnon condemns his daughter to death that she praises his kindness; it is precisely when Aman believes himself to have triumphed that he is ruined; it is precisely when she has invested her savings in an annuity that the seventy-year-old woman is strangled; it is precisely the blowtorch-manufacturer's safe that the burglars manage to open with a blowtorch; it is precisely when they are summoned to a reconciliation session that the husband kills his wife: the list of acmes is inexhaustible.[8]

What does this predilection signify? The acme is the expression of a situation of mischance. Yet just as repetition "limits" the anarchic (or innocent) nature of the aleatory, so luck and mischance are not neutral, they invincibly call up a certain signification—and the moment chance signifies, it is no longer chance; the acme's precise function is this conversion of chance into sign, for the exactitude of a reversal cannot be conceived outside of an intelligence which performs it; in mythic terms, Nature (Life) is not an exact force; wherever a symmetry is manifested (and the acme is the very figure of symmetry), there has to be a hand to guide it.

Thus, each time it appears by itself, unrelated to the emotional values which generally attach to the archetypical role of the characters, the relation of coincidence implies a certain idea of Fate. Every coincidence is a sign at once indecipherable and intelligent: it is actually by a kind of transference, whose motive is only too obvious, that men accuse Fate of being blind: on the contrary, Fate is cunning, it constructs signs, and it is men who

8. The French language expresses the acme clumsily, for it requires a periphrasis: *c'est précisément quand . . . que;* Latin possesses a very strong and indeed an archaic correlative: *cum . . . tum.*

are blind, impotent to decipher them. When safecrackers open the blowtorch manufacturer's safe with a blowtorch, this notation can ultimately belong only to the category of signs, for the meaning (if not its content, at least its idea) inevitably derives from the conjunction of two oppositions: antithesis or paradox, all contrariety belongs to a deliberately constructed world: a god prowls behind the *fait-divers*.

Nor does this intelligent—but unintelligible—fatality animate only the relation of coincidence. We have seen that the explicit causality of the *fait-divers* was in fact a faked causality, or at least one under suspicion, dubious, absurd, since in some sense the effect frustrates the cause; we might say that the causality of the *fait-divers* is constantly subject to the temptation of coincidence and, inversely, that coincidence here is constantly fascinated by the order of causality. Aleatory causality, organized coincidence—it is at the junction of these two movements that the *fait-divers* is constituted: both ultimately refer to an ambiguous zone where the event is experienced as a sign whose content is nonetheless uncertain. We are thus in a world not of meaning but of signification,[9] which is probably the status of literature, a formal order in which meaning is both posited and frustrated: and it is true that the *fait-divers* is literature, even if this literature is reputed to be bad.

Doubtless we have here a general phenomenon which greatly exceeds the category of the *fait-divers*. But in the *fait-divers*, the dialectic of meaning and signification has a historical function much clearer than in literature, because the *fait-divers* is a mass art: its role is probably to preserve at the very heart of contemporary society an ambiguity of the rational and the irrational, of the intelligible and the unfathomable; and this ambiguity is historically necessary insofar as man still must have signs (which reassure him), but also insofar as these signs must be of uncertain content (which releases him from responsibility): he can then be supported through the *fait-divers* by a certain cul-

---

9. By *meaning* I have in mind the content (the signified) of a signifying system, and by *signification* the systematic procedure which unites a meaning and a form, signifier and signified.

ture, for any sketch of a system of signification is a sketch of a culture; but at the same time, he can *in extremis* fill this culture with nature, since the meaning he gives to the concomitance of phenomena escapes cultural artifice by remaining mute.

1962

The Last Word on Robbe-Grillet?

> Don't give them any name. . . . They could
> have had so many other adventures.
> *Last Year at Marienbad*

Literary realism has always presented itself as a certain way of *copying* reality. As if reality were on one side and language on the other, as if reality were antecedent to language and the latter's task were somehow to pursue the former until it had caught up. No doubt the reality available to the writer can be of many kinds: psychological, theological, social, political, historical, even imaginary, each in its turn supplanting the other; nonetheless, such realities have one common feature which explains the constancy of their projection: they all seem immediately imbued with meaning: passion, sin, conflict, dream inevitably refer to a certain transcendence, soul, divinity, society, or supernature, so that our whole realistic literature is not only analogical but *signifying*.

Among all these realities, psychological and social, the object itself had virtually no original place; for a long time, literature dealt only with a world of interhuman relations (if a harp is mentioned in *Les Liaisons dangereuses*, it is because the instrument serves to conceal a love letter); and when things, tools, spectacles, or substances began to appear with some frequency in our novels, it was as esthetic elements or human indices, to refer to some mood (romantic landscape) or some social evil (realistic detail). As we know, Alain Robbe-Grillet's work deals with this problem of the literary object; do things induce meanings, or on the contrary are they "matte"? Can and should the writer describe an object without referring it to some human transcendence? Signifying or nonsignifying, what is the function of objects in a fictional narrative? How does the way they are described modify the story's meaning? the character's consistency? the work's relation to the idea of literature? Now that Robbe-Grillet's *oeuvre* has developed, now that the cinema has given it another dimension and another public, we can ask these questions in a new way. Depending on the answer, we soon realize that we possess, with the help of the novelist himself, *two* Robbe-Grillets: on the one hand, the Robbe-Grillet of immediate things, destroyer of meaning, sketched chiefly by the early criticism; and on the other, the Robbe-Grillet of mediate things, creator of meaning, whom Bruce Morrissette has analyzed in his study of the novels, to which these remarks serve as a preface.

The first Robbe-Grillet (no question here of a temporal antecedence, but only of an order of classification) decides that things signify nothing, not even the absurd (he rightly adds), for it is obvious that the absence of meaning can also be a meaning. But since these very things are buried under the assorted meanings with which men, through sensibilities, through poetry, through different uses, have impregnated the name of each object, the novelist's labor is in a sense cathartic: he purges things of the undue meaning men ceaselessly deposit upon them. How? Obviously by description. Robbe-Grillet thus produces descriptions of objects sufficiently geometrical to discourage any induction of poetic meaning and sufficiently detailed to break the fascination of the narrative; but thereby he encounters realism; like the realists, he copies, or at least seems to copy, a model; in formal terms, we might say that he proceeds as if his novel were only the event which satisfies an antecedent structure: it matters little whether or not this structure is *true*, and whether Robbe-Grillet's realism is objective or subjective; for what defines realism is not the origin of its model but its exteriority in relation to the language which expresses it.

The Last Word on Robbe-Grillet?

On the one hand, the realism of this first Robbe-Grillet remains classical because it is based on a relation of analogy (the slice of tomato described by Robbe-Grillet resembles a real slice of tomato); and on the other hand, it is new because this analogy refers to no transcendence but claims to survive as a closed system, satisfied when it has necessarily and sufficiently designated the notorious *Dasein* (being-there) of the object (this slice of tomato is described so as to provoke neither desire nor disgust, and to signify neither season nor site nor even sustenance).

It is obvious that description can neither exhaust the fabric of the novel nor satisfy the interest traditionally expected of it: there are many genres besides description in Robbe-Grillet's novels. But it is also obvious that a small number of descriptions at once analogical and nonsignifying, according to the place the author gives them and the variations he introduces into them, suffice to modify the novel's meaning as a whole. Every novel is an intelligible organism of an infinite sensibility: the least point of opacity, the least (mute) resistance to the desire which animates and sustains any reading, constitutes an *astonishment* which affects the entire work. Thus Robbe-Grillet's famous objects have no anthological value whatever; they engage the anecdote itself, and the characters which the anecdote collects, in a kind of silence of signification. This is why our conception of a "thing-oriented" Robbe-Grillet must be unitary, and even totalitarian: there is an inevitable inference from the nonsignifying nature of things to the nonsignifying nature of situations and men. It is indeed quite possible to read Robbe-Grillet's entire *oeuvre* (at least up to *In the Labyrinth*) in a matte fashion; it suffices to remain on the surface of the text, once we clearly understand that a superficial reading can no longer be condemned in the name of the old values of interiority. It is even, in fact, the merit of this first Robbe-Grillet (even if he is a figment) to demystify the "natural" qualities of the literature of introspection (the profound being by rights preferable to the superficial) for the sake of a *Dasein* of the text (which we must be careful not to mistake for the *Dasein* of the thing itself), and to keep the reader from enjoying a "rich," "profound," "secret," in short, a signifying world. It is obvious that accord-

ing to Robbe-Grillet number 1, the neurotic or pathological
state of his characters (one oedipal, the next sadistic, the third
obsessed) has none of the traditional values of a content, of
which the novel's elements would be the more or less mediate
symbols and which would offer themselves to the reader's (or
the critic's) decoding: this state is only the formal term of a
function: Robbe-Grillet *seems* to deal with a certain content
because there is no literature without a sign, and no sign without
a signified; but his entire art consists precisely in disappointing
meaning precisely when he makes it possible. To name this
content, to speak of madness, sadism, or even jealousy, is therefore to exceed what we might call the novel's best level of
perception, the level on which it is perfectly and immediately
intelligible, just as to look at a photographic reproduction at
very close range is doubtless to penetrate its typographic secret,
but it is also to understand no longer anything about the object
it represents. It follows that this disappointment of meaning, if
authentic, is anything but gratuitous: to provoke meaning in
order to arrest it is precisely to continue an experiment which
has its modern origin in the surrealist movement and which
involves literature's very being, i.e., its anthropological function
within a given historical society. Such is the image of Robbe-
Grillet number 1 that we can form from certain theoretical
texts and novels, to which we must add in general the early
commentaries on them.

From these same texts and novels (but not, of course, from
these same commentaries) we may also form the image of a
Robbe-Grillet number 2, no longer "thing-oriented" but "humanist," since the objects, without quite turning back into
symbols in the full sense of the word, do regain a mediating
function with regard to "something else." Of this second image,
Professor Morrissette has made himself, in the course of his
study, the thoroughgoing constructor. His method is both
descriptive and comparative: on the one hand, he patiently
recounts Robbe-Grillet's novels, and this retelling serves to
reconstruct the often intricate arrangement of episodes, i.e., the
structure of the work, which no one has dealt with hitherto; and
on the other hand, extensive learning enables him to relate

these episodes (scenes or descriptions of objects) to models, archetypes, sources, echoes, and thus to re-establish the cultural continuity which unites a reputedly "matte" work to a whole literary, and consequently human, context. Morrissette's method certainly produces an "integrated" image of Robbe-Grillet or, better still, an image reconciled with the novel's traditional goals; doubtless it reduces the revolutionary share of the work; but in return it establishes the excellent reasons the public may have for recognizing itself in Robbe-Grillet (and the critical success of *In the Labyrinth* in France, the public career of *Last Year at Marienbad* the world over seem to prove him entirely right). This Robbe-Grillet number 2 does not say, like Chénier: *out of new thoughts, let us make classical verses.* He says on the contrary: *out of classical thoughts, let us make new novels.*

What does this reconciliation affect? First of all, obviously, it affects those famous "objects" whose neutral, nonsignifying character had once seemed so evident. Morrissette recognizes the originality of Robbe-Grillet's vision of objects, but he does not regard the object, in this vision, as cut off from all reference —as radically ceasing to be a sign; he has no difficulty discovering in Robbe-Grillet's repertoire several objects which if not obsessional are at least repeated often enough to induce a meaning (for what is repeated is supposed to signify). The eraser (in *The Erasers*), the piece of string (in *The Voyeur*), the centipede (in *Jealousy*), these objects, recurring in various ways throughout the novels, all refer to a criminal or sexual act and, beyond this act, to an interiority. Morrissette nevertheless does not permit himself to take them as symbols; in a more restrained (but perhaps rather specious?) manner, he prefers to define them as no more than the props of sensations, sentiments, memories; in this way the object becomes a contrapuntal element of the work; it participates in the story to the same degree as a peripeteia, and it is certainly one of Morrissette's great contributions to Robbe-Grillet criticism to have managed to discover a narrative in each of these novels; as a consequence of these detailed, scrupulous summaries, Morrissette shows very clearly that the Robbe-Grillet novel is a "story" and that this story has a meaning: oedipal, sadistic, obsessional, or even simply literary, if *In the Labyrinth,* as he regards it, is the story of a creation; of

course this "story" is not composed in a traditional way, and
Morrissette, attentive to the modernism of the technique,
emphasizes the variations and complexities of the narrative
"point of view," the distortions Robbe-Grillet imposes on
chronology and his rejection of psychological analysis (but not
of psychology). The fact remains, nonetheless, that once more
furnished with a story, with a (pathological) psychology, and
with a referential if not a symbolic substance, the Robbe-Grillet
novel is no longer the "flat" diagram of the early criticism; it is
an object in the round, and one full of secrets; criticism must
then begin scrutinizing what is behind this object and around it:
must become a deciphering process: it seeks "keys" (and usually
finds them). This is what Morrissette has done for Robbe-
Grillet's novels: his courage is evident, for he has dared, immediately and apropos of a writer not only contemporary but
still quite young, to use a deciphering method we have taken
more than half a century to apply to authors like Nerval and
Rimbaud.

Must we choose between the two Robbe-Grillets—the
"thing-oriented" Robbe-Grillet number 1 and the "humanist"
Robbe-Grillet number 2, between the Robbe-Grillet of the
early criticism and the Robbe-Grillet of Bruce Morrissette?
Robbe-Grillet himself will not help us here; like every author,
and despite his theoretical declarations, he is constitutively
ambiguous about his own work; moreover his work is obviously
changing, which is its right. And it is actually this ambiguity
which counts, which concerns us, which bears the historical
meaning of an *oeuvre* which seems peremptorily to reject history. What is this meaning? The very opposite of a meaning,
i.e., *a question*. What do things signify, what does the world
signify? All literature is this question, but we must immediately
add, for this is what constitutes its speciality, *literature is this
question minus its answer*. No literature in the world has ever
answered the question it asked, and it is this very suspension
which has always constituted it as literature: it is that very
fragile language which men set between the violence of the
question and the silence of the answer: religious and also

critical when it questions, it is irreligious and conservative when it does not answer: a question itself, what the ages interrogate in literature is the question, not the answer. What god, Valéry once said, would dare take as his motto "I disappoint"? Literature would be that god; perhaps it will some day be possible to describe all literature as the art of disappointment, of frustration. The history of literature will then no longer be the history of the contradictory answers writers have given to the question of meaning but, quite the contrary, the history of the question itself.

For it is obvious that literature cannot ask directly the only question which constitutes it: it never was and never will be able to extend its questioning to the duration of discourse, without passing through the stage of certain techniques; and if the history of literature is ultimately the history of these techniques, it is not because literature is only technique (as was claimed in the days of *art for art's sake*), but because technique is the only power capable of suspending the world's meaning and of keeping open the imperative question addressed to it; for it is not *answering* which is difficult, it is questioning. From this point of view, Robbe-Grillet's "technique" was, at a certain moment, radical: the moment when the author believed it was possible to "kill" meaning directly, so that the work let pass only the fundamental astonishment which constitutes it (for to write is not to affirm, it is to be astonished). The originality of the attempt proceeded, then, from the fact that the question was not supplied with false answers, though it was never formulated, of course, in terms of a question; Robbe-Grillet's (theoretical) error was merely to suppose that there is a *Dasein* of things, antecedent and exterior to language, which he believed literature was obliged to rediscover in a final impulse of realism. As a matter of fact, anthropologically, things signify immediately, always, and with good reason; and it is precisely because signification is their "natural" condition that, by simply stripping them of their meaning, literature can affirm itself as an admirable artifice: if "nature" signifies, it can be a certain acme of "culture" to make it "designify." Whence, quite properly, these matte descriptions of objects, these anecdotes narrated "on the surface," these characters without secrets—all of which constitute, at least according to a certain reading, the style or, if we prefer, the choice of Robbe-Grillet.

Yet these empty forms irresistibly invite a content, and we gradually see—in criticism, in the author's own work—certain temptations of feelings, returns of archetypes, fragments of symbols, in short, everything that belongs to the realm of the adjective, creeping into the splendid *Dasein* of things. In this sense, there is an evolution of Robbe-Grillet's *oeuvre*, an evolution produced simultaneously by the author, by criticism, and by the public: we are all part of Robbe-Grillet, insofar as we are all busy relaunching the meaning of things, as soon as we open one of his books. Considered in its development and in its future (which we cannot assign), Robbe-Grillet's *oeuvre* then becomes the ordeal of meaning experienced by a certain society, and the history of this *oeuvre* will be, in its way, the history of this society. Already meaning returns: driven out of the famous slice of tomato in *The Erasers* (but doubtless already present in the eraser itself, as Morrissette shows), it fills *Marienbad*, its gardens, its paneled walls, its feather capes. Nonetheless, if it is no longer null and void, meaning is still variously conjectural here: everyone has explained *Marienbad*, but each explanation was a meaning immediately contested by the next one: meaning is no longer disappointed, but it remains suspended. And if it is true that each of Robbe-Grillet's novels contains its own symbol *en abyme*, doubtless the last allegory of this work is that statue of Charles III and his wife, discussed by the lovers in *Marienbad*: an admirable symbol, moreover, not only because the statue itself induces various meanings, uncertain yet named (*you, me, Helen, Agamemnon,* etc.), but also because the prince and his wife are pointing quite specifically at some unspecified object (situated in the story? in the garden? in the theater?): *this,* they say. But what is *this—this* what? Perhaps all literature is in this anaphoric suspension which at one and the same time designates and keeps silent.

1962

The Imagination
of the Sign

Every sign includes or implies three relations. To start with, an interior relation which unites its signifier to its signified; then two exterior relations: a virtual one that unites the sign to a specific reservoir of other signs it may be drawn from in order to be inserted in discourse; and an actual one that unites the sign to other signs in the discourse preceding or succeeding it. The first type of relation appears clearly in what is commonly called a *symbol*; for instance, the Cross "symbolizes" Christianity, red "symbolizes" a prohibition to advance; we shall call this first relation, then, a *symbolic* relation, though we encounter it not only in symbols but also in signs (which are, roughly speaking, purely conventional symbols). The second type of relation implies the existence, for each sign, of a reservoir or organized "memory" of forms from which it is distinguished by the smallest difference necessary and sufficient to effect a change of meaning; in *lupum*, the element *-um* (which is a sign, and more precisely a morpheme) affords its meaning of "accusative case" only insofar as it is opposed to the (virtual) remainder of the declension (*-us, -i, -o*, etc.); red signifies prohibition only insofar as it is *systematically* opposed to green and yellow (of course, if there were no other color but red, red would still be opposed to the absence of color); this second type of relation is therefore that of the system, sometimes called paradigm; we shall therefore call it a *paradigmatic* relation. According to the third type of relation, the sign is no longer situated with regard to its (virtual) "brothers," but with regard to its (actual) "neighbors"; in *homo homini lupus, lupus* maintains certain connections with *homo* and with *homini*; in garment systems, the elements of an outfit are associated according to certain rules: to wear a sweater and a leather jacket is to create, between these two garments, a temporary but signifying association, analogous to the one uniting the words of a sentence; this level of association is the level of the syntagm, and we shall call the third relation the *syntagmatic relation.*

Now it seems that when we consider the signifying phenomenon (and this interest may proceed from very different horizons), we are obliged to focus on one of these three relations more than on the other two; sometimes we "see" the sign in its symbolic aspect, sometimes in its systematic aspect, sometimes in its syntagmatic aspect; this is occasionally the result of mere ignorance of the other relations: symbolism has long been blind to the formal relations of the sign; but even when the three relations have been defined (for example, in linguistics), each school tends to base its analysis on one of the sign's dimensions: one vision overflows the whole of the signifying phenomenon, so that we may speak, apparently, of different semiological consciousnesses (I refer, of course, to the consciousness of the analyst, not of the user, of the sign). Now, on the one hand, the choice of a dominant relation implies a certain ideology; and, on the other hand, one might say that each consciousness of the sign (symbolic, paradigmatic, and syntagmatic) corresponds to a certain moment of reflection, either individual or collective: structuralism, in particular, can be defined historically as the passage from symbolic consciousness to paradigmatic consciousness: there is a history of the sign, which is the history of its "consciousnesses."

The symbolic consciousness sees the sign in its profound, one might almost say its geological, dimension, since for the symbolic consciousness it is the tiered arrangement of signifier and signified which constitutes the symbol; there is a consciousness of a kind of vertical relation between the Cross and Christianity: Christianity is *under* the Cross, as a profound mass of beliefs, values, practices, more or less disciplined on the level of its form. The verticality of the relation involves two consequences: on the one hand, the vertical relation tends to seem solitary: the symbol seems to stand by itself in the world, and even when we assert that it is abundant, it is abundant in the fashion of a "forest"—i.e., by an anarchic juxtaposition of profound relations which communicate, so to speak, only by their roots (by what is signified); and on the other hand, this vertical relation necessarily appears to be an analogical relation: to some degree the form resembles the content, as if it were actually produced by it, so that the symbolic consciousness may sometimes mask an unacknowledged determinism: thus there is a massive privilege of resemblance (even when we emphasize the inadequate character of the sign). The symbolic consciousness has dominated the sociology of symbols and of course a share of psychoanalysis in its early stages, though Freud himself acknowledged the inexplicable (nonanalogical) character of certain symbols; this moreover was the period when the very word *symbol* prevailed; during all this time, the symbol possessed a mythic prestige, the glamor of "richness": the symbol was rich, hence it could not be reduced to a "simple sign" (today we may doubt the sign's "simplicity"): its form was constantly exceeded by the power and the movement of its content; indeed, for the symbolic consciousness, the symbol is much less a (codified) form of communication than an (affective) instrument of participation. The word *symbol* has now gone a little stale; we readily replace it by *sign* or *signification*. This terminological shift expresses a certain crumbling of the symbolic consciousness, notably with regard to the analogical character of signifier and signified; nonetheless the symbolic consciousness remains typical, insofar as its analytical consideration is not interested in the formal relations of signs, for the symbolic consciousness is essentially the rejection of form; what interests it in the sign is the signified: the signifier is always a determined element.

Once the forms of two signs are compared, or at least perceived in a somewhat comparative manner, a certain paradigmatic consciousness appears; even on the level of the classical symbol, the least subtle of signs, if there is some occasion to perceive the variation of two symbolic forms, the other dimensions of the sign are immediately discovered; as in the case, for instance, of the opposition between *Red Cross* and *Red Crescent:* on the one hand, *Cross* and *Crescent* cease to entertain a "solitary" relation with what they respectively signify (Christianity and Islam), they are included in a stereotyped syntagm; and, on the other hand, they form between themselves an interplay of distinctive terms, each of which corresponds to a different signified: the paradigm is born. The paradigmatic consciousness therefore defines meaning not as the simple encounter of signifier and signified, but, according to Merleau-Ponty's splendid expression, as a veritable "modulation of coexistence"; it substitutes for the bilateral relation of the symbolic consciousness a quadrilateral or more precisely a homological relation. It is the paradigmatic consciousness which permitted Lévi-Strauss to reconceive the problem of totemism: whereas the symbolic consciousness vainly seeks the "dimensional," more or less analogical characters which unite a signifier (the totem) to a signified (the clan), the paradigmatic consciousness establishes a homology (as Lévi-Strauss calls it) between the relation of two totems and that of two clans. Naturally, by retaining in the signified only its demonstrative role (it designates the signifier and makes it possible to locate the terms of the opposition), the paradigmatic consciousness tends to empty it: but it does not thereby empty the signification. It is obviously the paradigmatic consciousness which has permitted (or expressed) the extraordinary development of phonology, a science of exemplary paradigms (*marked/non-marked*): it is the paradigmatic consciousness which, through the work of Lévi-Strauss, defines the structuralist threshold.

The syntagmatic consciousness is a consciousness of the relations which unite signs on the level of discourse itself, i.e., essentially a consciousness of the constraints, tolerances, and liberties of the sign's associations. This consciousness has marked the linguistic endeavors of the Yale school and, outside linguistics, the investigations of the Russian formalist school, notably those of Propp in the domain of the Slavic folk tale (hence we may expect that it will eventually illuminate analysis of the major contemporary "narratives," from the *fait-divers* to the popular novel). But this is not the only orientation of the syntagmatic consciousness; of the three, it is certainly the syntagmatic consciousness which most readily renounces the signified: it is more a structural consciousness than a semantic one, which is why it comes closest to practice: it is the syntagmatic consciousness which best permits us to imagine operational groups, "dispatchings," complex classifications: the paradigmatic consciousness permits the fruitful return from decimalism to binarism; but it is the syntagmatic consciousness which actually permits us to conceive cybernetic "programs," just as it has permitted Propp and Lévi-Strauss to reconstruct the myth-"series."

Perhaps we shall some day be able to return to the description of these semantic consciousnesses, attempt to link them to a history; perhaps we shall some day be able to create a semiology of the semiologists, a structural analysis of the structuralists. All we are endeavoring to say here is that there is probably a genuine imagination of the sign; the sign is not only the object of a particular knowledge, but also the object of a vision, analogous to the vision of the celestial spheres in Cicero's *Somnium Scipionis* or related to the molecular representations used by chemists; the semiologist *sees* the sign moving in the field of signification, he enumerates its valences, traces their configuration: the sign is, for him, a sensuous idea. Of the three (still fairly technical) consciousnesses discussed here, we must presume an extension toward much wider types of imagination, which we may find mobilized in many other objects than the sign.

The symbolic consciousness implies an imagination of depth; it experiences the world as the relation of a superficial form and a many-sided, massive, powerful *Abgrund*, and the image is reinforced by a very intense dynamics: the relation of form and content is ceaselessly renewed by time (history), the super-structure overwhelmed by the infrastructure, without our ever being able to grasp the structure itself. The paradigmatic consciousness, on the contrary, is a formal imagination; it *sees* the signifier linked, as if in profile, to several virtual signifiers which it is at once close to and distinct from: it no longer sees the sign in its depth, it sees it in its perspective; thus the dynamics attached to this vision is that of a summons: the sign is chosen from a finite organized reservoir, and this summons is the sovereign act of signification: imagination of the surveyor, the geometrician, the owner of the world who finds himself at his ease on his property, since man, in order to signify, has merely to choose from what is presented to him already prestructured either by his brain (in the binarist hypothesis), or by the material finitude of forms. The syntagmatic imagination no longer sees the sign in its perspective, it *foresees* it in its extension: its antecedent or consequent links, the bridges it extends to other signs; this is a "stemmatous" imagination of the chain or the network; hence the dynamics of the image here is that of an arrangement of mobile, substitutive parts, whose combination produces meaning, or more generally a new object; it is, then, a strictly fabricative or even *functional* imagination (the word is conveniently ambiguous, since it refers both to the notion of a variable relation and to that of a usage).

Such are (perhaps) the three imaginations of the sign. We may doubtless attach to each of them a certain number of different creations, in the most diverse realms, for nothing constructed in the world today escapes meaning. To remain in the realm of recent intellectual creation, among the works of the profound (symbolic) imagination, we may cite biographical or historical criticism, the sociology of "visions," the realist or introspective novel, and in a general way, the "expressive" arts or languages, postulating the signified as sovereign, extracted either from an interiority or from a history. The formal (or paradigmatic) imagination implies an acute attention to the *variation* of several recurrent elements; thus this type of imagination accommodates the dream and oneiric narratives, powerfully thematic works and those whose esthetic implies the interplay of certain commutations (Robbe-Grillet's novels, for example). The functional (or syntagmatic) imagination nourishes, lastly, all those works whose fabrication, by arrangement of discontinuous and mobile elements, constitutes the spectacle itself: poetry, epic theater, serial music, and structural compositions, from Mondrian to Butor.

1962

The Structuralist
Activity

What is structuralism? Not a school, nor even a movement (at least, not yet), for most of the authors
ordinarily labeled with this word are unaware of being
united by any solidarity of doctrine or commitment. Nor is it a
vocabulary. *Structure* is already an old word (of anatomical and
grammatical provenance), today quite overworked: all the social
sciences resort to it abundantly, and its use can distinguish no
one, except to polemicize about the content assigned to it;
functions, forms, signs, and *significations* are scarcely more
pertinent: they are, today, words in common use from which
one asks (and obtains) whatever one wants, notably the
camouflage of the old determinist schema of cause and product;
we must doubtless resort to pairings like those of *signifier/
signified* and *synchronic/diachronic* in order to approach what
distinguishes structuralism from other modes of thought: the
first because it refers to the linguistic model as originated by
Saussure and because, along with economics, linguistics is, in
the present state of affairs, the true science of structure; the
second, more decisively, because it seems to imply a certain
revision of the notion of history, insofar as the idea of synchrony
(although in Saussure this is a pre-eminently operational con-

cept) accredits a certain immobilization of time, and insofar as diachrony tends to represent the historical process as a pure succession of forms. This second pairing is all the more distinctive in that the chief resistance to structuralism today seems to be of Marxist origin and in that it focuses on the notion of history (and not of structure); whatever the case, it is probably the serious recourse to the nomenclature of signification (and not to the word itself, which is, paradoxically, not at all distinctive) which we must ultimately take as structuralism's spoken sign: watch who uses *signifier* and *signified*, *synchrony* and *diachrony*, and you will know whether the structuralist vision is constituted.

This is valid for the intellectual metalanguage, which explicitly employs methodological concepts. But since structuralism is neither a school nor a movement, there is no reason to reduce it a priori, even in a problematical way, to the activity of philosophers; it would be better to try and find its broadest description (if not its definition) on another level than that of reflexive language. We can in fact presume that there exist certain writers, painters, musicians in whose eyes a certain exercise of structure (and no longer merely its thought) represents a distinctive experience, and that both analysts and creators must be placed under the common sign of what we might call *structural man*, defined not by his ideas or his languages, but by his imagination—in other words, by the way in which he mentally experiences structure.

So the first thing to be said is that in relation to all its users, structuralism is essentially an *activity*, i.e., the controlled succession of a certain number of mental operations: we might speak of structuralist activity as we once spoke of surrealist activity (surrealism, moreover, may well have produced the first experience of structural literature, a possibility which must some day be explored). But before seeing what these operations are, we must say a word about their goal.

The goal of all structuralist activity, whether reflexive or poetic, is to reconstruct an "object" in such a way as to manifest thereby the rules of functioning (the "functions") of this object. Structure is therefore actually a *simulacrum* of the object, but a directed, *interested* simulacrum, since the imitated object makes something appear which remained invisible or, if one prefers, unintelligible in the natural object. Structural man takes the real, decomposes it, then recomposes it; this appears to be little enough (which makes some say that the structuralist enterprise is "meaningless," "uninteresting," "useless," etc.). Yet from another point of view, this "little enough" is decisive: for between the two objects, or the two tenses, of structuralist activity, there occurs something new, and what is new is nothing less than the generally intelligible: the simulacrum is intellect added to object, and this addition has an anthropological value, in that it is man himself, his history, his situation, his freedom, and the very resistance which nature offers to his mind.

We see, then, why we must speak of a structuralist *activity*: creation or reflection are not, here, an original "impression" of the world, but a veritable fabrication of a world which resembles the primary one, not in order to copy it but to render it intelligible. Hence one might say that structuralism is essentially *an activity of imitation*, which is also why there is, strictly speaking, no *technical* difference between structuralism as an intellectual activity, on the one hand, and literature in particular, art in general, on the other: both derive from a *mimesis*, based not on the analogy of substances (as in so-called realist art), but on the analogy of functions (what Lévi-Strauss calls *homology*). When Troubetskoy reconstructs the phonetic object as a system of variations; when Dumézil elaborates a functional mythology; when Propp constructs a folk tale resulting by structuration from all the Slavic tales he has previously decomposed; when Lévi-Strauss discovers the homologic functioning of the totemic imagination, or Granger the formal rules of economic thought, or Gardin the pertinent features of prehistoric bronzes; when Richard decomposes a poem by Mallarmé into its distinctive vibrations—they are all doing nothing different from what Mondrian, Boulez, or Butor are doing when they articulate a certain object—what will be called, precisely, a *composition*—by the controlled manifestation of certain units and certain associations of these units. It is of little consequence whether the initial object submitted to the simulacrum activity is given by the world in an already assembled fashion (in the case of the structural analysis made of a constituted language or society or work) or is still dispersed (in the case of the structural "composition"); whether this initial object is drawn from a social reality or an imaginary reality. It is not the nature of the copied object which defines an art (though this is a tenacious prejudice in all realism), it is the fact that man adds to it in reconstructing it: technique is the very being of all creation. It is therefore to the degree that the goals of structuralist activity are indissolubly linked to a certain technique that structuralism exists in a distinctive fashion in relation to other modes of analysis or creation: we recompose the object in order to make certain functions appear, and it is, so to speak, the way that makes the work; this is why we must speak of the structuralist activity rather than the structuralist work.

The structuralist activity involves two typical operations: dissection and articulation. To dissect the first object, the one which is given to the simulacrum-activity, is to find in it certain mobile fragments whose differential situation engenders a certain meaning; the fragment has no meaning in itself, but it is nonetheless such that the slightest variation wrought in its configuration produces a change in the whole; a *square* by Mondrian, a *series* by Pousseur, a *versicle* of Butor's *Mobile*, the "mytheme" in Lévi-Strauss, the phoneme in the work of the phonologists, the "theme" in certain literary criticism—all these units (whatever their inner structure and their extent, quite different according to cases) have no significant existence except by their frontiers: those which separate them from other actual units of the discourse (but this is a problem of articulation) and also those which distinguish them from other virtual units, with which they form a certain class (which linguistics calls a *paradigm*); this notion of a paradigm is essential, apparently, if we are to understand the structuralist vision: the paradigm is a group, a reservoir—as limited as possible—of objects (of units) from which we summon, by an act of citation, the object or unit we wish to endow with an actual meaning; what characterizes the paradigmatic object is that it is, vis-à-vis other objects of its class, in a certain relation of affinity and of dissimilarity: two units of the same paradigm must resemble each other somewhat *in order* that the difference which separates them be indeed evident: *s* and *z* must have both a common feature (dentality) and a distinctive feature (presence or absence of sonority) so that we cannot, in French, attribute the same meaning to *poisson* and *poison;* Mondrian's squares must have both certain affinities by their shape as squares, and certain dissimilarities by their proportion and color; the American automobiles (in Butor's *Mobile*) must be constantly regarded in the same way, yet they must differ each time by both their make and color; the episodes of the Oedipus myth (in Lévi-Strauss's analysis) must be both identical and varied—in order that all these languages, these works may be intelligible. The dissection-operation thus produces an initial dispersed state of the simulacrum, but the units of the structure are not at all anarchic: before being distributed and fixed in the continuity of the composition, each one forms with its own virtual group or reservoir an intelligent organism, subject to a sovereign motor principle: that of the least difference.

Once the units are posited, structural man must discover in them or establish for them certain rules of association: this is the activity of articulation, which succeeds the summoning activity. The syntax of the arts and of discourse is, as we know, extremely varied; but what we discover in every work of structural enterprise is the submission to regular constraints whose formalism, improperly indicted, is much less important than their stability; for what is happening, at this second stage of the simulacrum-activity, is a kind of battle against chance; this is why the constraint of recurrence of the units has an almost demiurgic value: it is by the regular return of the units and of the associations of units that the work appears constructed, i.e., endowed with meaning; linguistics calls these rules of combination *forms,* and it would be advantageous to retain this rigorous sense of an overtaxed word: form, it has been said, is what keeps the contiguity of units from appearing as a pure effect of chance: the work of art is what man wrests from chance. This perhaps allows us to understand on the one hand why so-called non-figurative works are nonetheless to the highest degree works of art, human thought being established not by the analogy of copies and models but by the regularity of assemblages; and on the other hand why these same works appear, precisely, fortuitous and thereby useless to those who discern in them no form: in front of an abstract painting, Khrushchev is certainly wrong to see only the traces of a donkey's tail whisked across the canvas; at least he knows in his way, though, that art is a certain conquest of chance (he simply forgets that every rule must be learned, whether one wants to apply or interpret it).

The simulacrum, thus constructed, does not render the world as it has found it, and it is here that structuralism is important. First of all, it manifests a new category of the object, which is neither the real nor the rational, but the *functional*, thereby joining a whole scientific complex which is being developed around information theory and research. Subsequently and especially, it highlights the strictly human process by which men give meaning to things. Is this new? To a certain degree, yes; of course the world has never stopped looking for the meaning of what is given it and of what it produces; what is new is a mode of thought (or a "poetics") which seeks less to assign completed meanings to the objects it discovers than to know how meaning is possible, at what cost and by what means. Ultimately, one might say that the object of structuralism is not man endowed with meanings but man fabricating meanings, as if it could not be the *content* of meanings which exhausted the semantic goals of humanity, but only the act by which these meanings, historical and contingent variables, are produced. *Homo significans*: such would be the new man of structural inquiry.

According to Hegel, the ancient Greek was amazed by the natural in nature; he constantly listened to it, questioned the meaning of mountains, springs, forests, storms; without knowing what all these objects were telling him by name, he perceived in the vegetal or cosmic order a tremendous shudder of meaning, to which he gave the name of a god: *Pan*. Subsequently, nature has changed, has become social: everything given to man is already human, down to the forest and the river which we cross when we travel. But confronted with this social nature, which is quite simply culture, structural man is no different from the ancient Greek: he too listens for the natural in culture, and constantly perceives in it not so much stable, finite, "true" meanings as the shudder of an enormous machine which is humanity tirelessly undertaking to create meaning, without which it would no longer be human. And it is because this fabrication of meaning is more important, to its view, than the meanings themselves, it is because the function is extensive with the works, that structuralism constitutes itself as an activity, and refers the exercise of the work and the work itself to a single identity: a serial composition or an analysis by Lévi-Strauss are not objects except insofar as they have been made: their present being *is* their past act: they are *having-been-mades*; the artist, the analyst recreates the course taken by meaning, he need not designate it: his function, to return to Hegel's example, is a *manteia*; like the ancient soothsayer, he speaks the locus of meaning but does not name it. And it is because literature, in particular, is a mantic activity that it is both intelligible and interrogating, speaking and silent, engaged in the world by the course of the meaning which it remakes with the world, but disengaged from the contingent meanings which the world elaborates: an answer to the man who consumes it yet always a question to nature, an answer which questions and a question which answers.

How then does structural man deal with the accusation of "unreality" which is sometimes flung at him? Are not forms in the world? are not forms responsible? Was it really his Marxism that was revolutionary in Brecht? Was it not rather the decision to link to Marxism, in the theater, the placing of a spotlight or the deliberate fraying of a costume? Structuralism does not withdraw history from the world: it seeks to link to history not only certain contents (this has been done a thousand times) but also certain forms, not only the material but also the intelligible, not only the ideological but also the esthetic. And precisely because all thought about the historically intelligible is also a participation in that intelligibility, structural man is scarcely concerned to last; he knows that structuralism, too, is a certain form of the world, which will change with the world; and just

as he experiences his validity (but not his truth) in his power
to speak the old languages of the world in a new way, so he
knows that it will suffice that a new language rise out of history,
a new language which speaks *him* in his turn, for his task to be
done.

1963

La Bruyère

La Bruyère occupies an ambiguous place in French culture: he is taught as a "major author"; his maxims, his art, his historical role are assigned as dissertation subjects; his knowledge of Man and his premonition of a more equitable society are extolled: *The notion of humanity*, Brunetière used to say, *dawns with La Bruyère*; he is made (O precious paradox!) at once a classic and a democrat. Yet outside our schools, the La Bruyère myth is a meager one: he has not yet been caught up in any of those great dialogues which French writers have always engaged in from one century to another (Pascal and Montaigne, Voltaire and Racine, Valéry and La Fontaine); criticism itself has scarcely bothered to renew our entirely academic image of him; his work has not lent itself to any of the new languages of our age, has stimulated neither historians nor philosophers nor sociologists nor psychoanalysts; in short, if we except the sympathy of a Proust quoting some penetrating maxim ("Being with the people one loves is enough; dreaming, talking to them or not talking to them, thinking about them or about indifferent things in their presence, it is all one." *Du coeur*, No. 23), our modernity, though quite ready to appropriate classical authors, seems to have great difficulty recuperating him: though he stands with the great names of our literature, La Bruyère is nonetheless disinherited, one might almost say *deconsecrated:* he lacks even that final fortune of the writer: to be neglected.

In short, this glory is a little drowsy, and it must be admitted that La Bruyère himself is not a likely agent for great awakenings; he remains, in everything, temperate (Thibaudet used to speak of La Bruyère's *chiaroscuro*), avoids exhausting the subjects he initiates, renounces that radicality of viewpoint which assures the writer a violent posthumous life; close as it is to La Rochefoucauld's, for example, his pessimism never exceeds the prudence of a good Christian, never turns to obsession; though capable of producing a short, lightninglike form, he prefers the somewhat longer fragment, the portrait which repeats itself: he is a moderate moralist, he does not scald (except perhaps in the chapters on women and money, of an unyielding aggressiveness); and furthermore, although an avowed painter of a society and, within that society, of the most social passion there is, worldliness, La Bruyère does not become a chronicler, a Retz or a Saint-Simon; it is as if he wanted to avoid the choice of a specific genre; as a moralist, he persistently refers to a real society, apprehended in its persons and events (as the number of "keys" to his book testifies); and as a sociologist, he nonetheless experiences this society in its moral substance alone; we cannot really deduce from him the image of man's "eternal flaw"; nor can we find in him, beyond good and evil, the lively spectacle of a pure sociality; perhaps this is why modernity, which always seeks certain pure nutriments in the literature of the past, has difficulty acknowledging La Bruyère: he escapes it by the most delicate of resistances: it cannot name him.

This uneasiness is doubtless that of our modern reading of La Bruyère. We might express it differently: the world of La Bruyère is at once *ours* and *different; ours* because the society he paints conforms so closely to our academic myth of the seventeenth century that we circulate quite comfortably among these old figures from our childhood: Ménalque, the plum lover, the savage beast-peasants, the "everything has been said and we have come too late," the city, the court, the parvenus, etc.; *different* because the immediate sentiment of our modernity tells us that these customs, these characters, these passions even, are not ourselves; the paradox is a cruel one: La Bruyère is ours by his anachronism and alien to us by his very project of eternity; the moderation of this author (what used to be called *mediocrity*), the weight of academic culture, the pressure of contiguous readings, everything makes La Bruyère transmit an image of classical man which is neither distant enough for us to relish its exoticism, nor close enough for us to identify ourselves with it: it is a familiar image which does not concern us.

To read La Bruyère would of course have no reality today (once we have left school), if we could not violate that suspect equilibrium of distance and identity, if we did not let ourselves be swayed toward one or the other; we can certainly read La Bruyère in a spirit of confirmation, searching, as in any moralist, for the maxim which will account in a perfect form for that very wound we have just received from the world; we can also read him and underline all that separates his world from ours and all that this distance teaches us about ourselves; such is our enterprise here: let us discuss everything in La Bruyère which concerns us little or not at all: perhaps we shall then, at last, collect the modern meaning of his work.

And first of all, what is the world, for someone who speaks? An initially formless field of objects, beings, phenomena which must be organized, i.e., divided up and distributed. La Bruyère does not fail this obligation; he divides up the society he lives in into great regions, among which he will distribute his "characters" (which are, roughly, the chapters of his book). These regions or classes are not a homogeneous object, they correspond, one may say, to different sciences (and this is natural enough, since every science is itself a dividing up of the world); first of all, there are two sociological classes, which form the "basis" of the classical world: the court (the nobility) and the city (the bourgeoisie); then an anthropological class: women (a particular race, whereas man is general: he says *de l'homme* but *des femmes*); a political class (the monarchy), psychological classes (heart, judgment, merit), and ethnological classes, in which social behavior is observed at a certain distance (fashion, customs); the whole is framed (an accident, or a secret signifi-

cance?) by two singular "operators": literature, which opens
the work (we shall discuss, later on, the relevance of this inauguration), and religion, which closes it.

This variety of objects manipulated by La Bruyère, the disparity of the classes he has constituted as chapters, suggest two
remarks; first of all: *Les Caractères* is in a sense a book of total
knowledge; on the one hand, La Bruyère approaches social man
from every angle, he constitutes a kind of indirect *summa* (for
it is always literature's function to circumvent science) of the
various kinds of knowledge of the *socius* available at the end of
the seventeenth century (it will be noted that this man is indeed
much more social than psychological); and on the other hand,
more disturbingly, the book corresponds to a kind of initiatory
experience, it seeks to reach that supreme point of existence
where knowledge and conduct, science and consciousness meet
under the ambiguous name of *wisdom*; in short, La Bruyère has
sketched a kind of cosmogony of classical society, describing
this world by its aspects, its limits and interferences. And this
leads to our second remark: the regions out of which La Bruyère
composes his world are quite analogous to logical classes: every
"individual" (in logic, we would say every x), i.e., every "character," is defined first of all by a relation of membership in some
class or other, the tulip fancier in the class *Fashion*, the coquette
in the class *Women*, the absent-minded Ménalque in the class
Men, etc.; but this is not enough, for the characters must be
distinguished among themselves within one and the same class;
La Bruyère therefore performs certain operations of intersection
from one class to the next; cross the class of *Merit* with that of
Celibacy and you get a reflection on the stifling function of
marriage (*Du mérite*, No. 25); join Tryphon's former virtue and
his present fortune: the simple coincidence of these two classes
affords the image of a certain hypocrisy (*Des biens de fortune*,
No. 50). Thus the diversity of the regions, which are sometimes
social, sometimes psychological, in no way testifies to a rich
disorder; confronting the world, La Bruyère does not enumerate
absolutely varied elements like the surveyor writers of the next
century; he combines certain rare elements; the man he constructs is always made up of several principles: age, origin,
fortune, vanity, passion; only the formula of composition varies,

the interplay of intersecting classes: a "character" is always the product of the encounter of at least two constants.

Now this is a treatment of man which to us has become if not alien at least impossible. It has been said of Leibnitz, more or less La Bruyère's contemporary, that he was the last man able to know everything; La Bruyère, too, was perhaps the last moralist able to speak of *all* of man, to enclose all the regions of the human world in a book; less than a century later, this would require the thirty-three volumes of the *Encyclopédie;* today, there is no longer a writer in the world who can treat man-in-society by regions: not all the human sciences combined can manage to do it. To borrow an image from information theory, we might say that from the classical century to our own, the *level of perception* has changed: we see man on another scale, and the very meaning of what we see is thereby transformed, like that of an ordinary substance under the microscope; the chapters of *Les Caractères* are so many brakes applied to the vision of man; today we cannot stop man anywhere; any partition we impose upon him refers him to a particular science, his totality escapes us; if I speak, *mutatis mutandis,* of the city and the court, I am a social writer; if I speak of the monarchy, I am a political theorist; of literature, a critic; of customs, an essayist; of the heart, a psychoanalyst, etc.; further, at least half the classes of objects to which La Bruyère refers have no more than a decrepit existence; no one today would write a chapter on women, on merit, or on conversation; though we continue to marry, to "arrive," or to speak, such behavior has shifted to another level of perception; a new dispatching refers them to human regions unknown to La Bruyère: social dynamics, interpersonal psychology, sexuality, though these realms can never be united under a single kind of writing: narrow, clear, "centered," finite, obsessive, La Bruyère's man is always *here;* ours is always elsewhere; if it occurs to think of someone's character, we do so either in terms of its insignificant universality (the desire for social advancement, for instance), or of its ineffable complexity (of whom would we dare say quite simply that he is a *dolt?*). In short, what has changed, from La Bruyère's world to ours, is what is notable: we no longer *note* the world the way La Bruyère did; our speech is different not because the vocabulary has developed, but because to speak is to fragment reality in an always committed fashion and because our dividing-up refers to a reality so broad that reflection cannot accommodate it and because the new sciences, those we call the human sciences (whose status, moreover, is not clearly defined), must intervene: La Bruyère notes that a father-in-law loves his daughter-in-law and that a mother-in-law loves her son-in-law (*De la société*, No. 45); this is a notation which would concern us more today if it came from a psychoanalyst, just as it is Freud's Oedipus who sets us thinking now, not Sophocles'. A matter of language? But the only *power* history has over the "human heart" is to vary the language which utters it. "Everything has been said now that men have been living and thinking for seven thousand years": yes, no doubt; but it is never too late to invent new languages.

Such, then, is La Bruyère's "world," accounted for by several great classes of "individuals": court, city, Church, women, etc.; these same classes can easily be subdivided into smaller "societies." Merely reread fragment 4 of the chapter *De la ville*: "The city is divided into various societies, which are like so many little republics, each with its own laws, customs, jargon, and jokes . . ." One might say in modern terms that the world is made up of a juxtaposition of *isolates*, impermeable to one another. In other words, the human group, as La Bruyère sees it, is not in the least constituted in a substantial fashion; beyond the purely contingent way in which these little societies are filled with bourgeois or with nobles, La Bruyère seeks out some feature which might define them all; this feature exists; it is a form; and this form is enclosure; La Bruyère is concerned with worlds, with *the* world, insofar as they—and it—are closed. We are dealing here, poetically, with what we might call an imagination of partition which consists in mentally exhausting every situation which the simple enclosure of a space gradually engenders in the general field where it occurs: choice of the partition, different substances of *inside* and *outside*, rules of admission, of exit, of exchange—it suffices that a line be closed in the world for a host of new meanings to be generated, and this is what La Bruyère realized. Applied to the social substance, the imagination of enclosure, whether experienced or analyzed, produces in fact an object which is both real (for it can be derived from sociology) and poetic (for writers have treated it with predilection): this object is worldliness. Before literature raised the problem of political realism, worldliness was a precious means for the writer to observe social reality yet remain a writer; worldliness is indeed an ambiguous form of reality: committed and uncommitted; referring to the disparity of the human condition but remaining in spite of everything a pure form, enclosure guarantees access to the psychological and the social without passing through the political; this is why, perhaps, we have had a great literature of worldliness in France, from Molière to Proust: and it is in this tradition of an entire imaginary world focused on the phenomena of social enclosure that La Bruyère obviously takes his place.

There can exist a great number of little worldly societies, since they need merely be closed in order to exist; but it follows that enclosure, which is the original form of all worldliness, and which we can consequently describe on the level of infinitesimal groups (the coterie of fragment 4 of *De la ville,* or the Verdurin salon), assumes a precise historical meaning when it is applied to the world as a whole; for what is then inside and outside it inevitably correspond to the economic partition of society; this is the case for the general worldliness described by La Bruyère; it has necessarily social roots: what is inside the enclosure are the privileged classes, nobility and bourgeoisie; what is outside are men without birth and money, the people (workers and peasants). La Bruyère, however, does not define social classes; he variously populates an inland and an outland; everything which occurs inside the enclosure is thereby called into Being; everything which remains outside it is rejected into nothingness; one might say, paradoxically, that social substructures are only the reflection of the forms of rejection and admission. The primacy of the form thus renders indirect the notations we would today call political. La Bruyère's democratic sentiments are often hailed, generally supported by fragment 128, *De l'homme,* which is a grim description of the peasants ("Certain wild animals . . . are to be seen about the countryside . . ."). Nonetheless, *the people,* in this literature, has no more than a purely functional value: it remains the object of a charity, of which the subject alone, the charitable man, is called upon to exist; in order to exercise pity, there must be a pitiable object: *the people* obliges. In formal terms (and it has been said how much the closed form predetermined this world), the poor classes, enlightened by no political consideration, are that pure exterior without which bourgeoisie and aristocracy could not realize their own being (see fragment 31, *Des biens de fortune*, in which the people watches the nobility live their emphatic existence, as though on a stage); the poor are the thing starting from which one exists: they are the constitutive limit of the enclosure. And of course, as pure functions, the men of the exterior have no essence. We can attribute to them none of those "characters" which mark the inhabitants of the interior with a full existence: a man of the people is neither a dolt nor absent-minded nor vain nor greedy nor gluttonous (greedy, gluttonous—how could he be?); he is merely a pure tautology: *a gardener is a gardener, a mason is a mason*, no more can be said of him; the only double quality, the only relation to Being which, from the interior and beyond his utensil nature (to tend the garden, to build a wall), he can occasionally be granted is to be a man: not a human being, but a male whom the women of the world discover when they are too sequestered (*Des femmes*, No. 34): the questioner (the torturer who applies the question) is not a bit cruel (that would be a "character"); he is simply "a young man with broad shoulders and a stocky figure, a Negro moreover, a black man" (*Des femmes*, No. 33).

The "character" is a metaphor: it is the development of an adjective. Forbidden definition (being merely a limit), the people can receive neither adjective nor character: therefore the people vanishes from discourse. By the very weight of the formal postulate which consigns what is enclosed to Being, all the writing of *Les Caractères* is focused on the interior plenitude of the enclosure: it is here that characters, adjectives, situations, anecdotes abound. But this abundance is, one might say, rare, purely qualitative; it is not a quantitative abundance; the inland of worldliness, though filled to bursting with Being, is a narrow and sparsely populated territory; there occurs here a phenomenon of which our mass societies are losing all notion:

everybody knows everybody else, everyone has a name. This interior familiarity, based on an openly sociological circumstance (nobles and bourgeois were a small minority) suggests what happens in societies of minor demography: tribes, villages, even American society before the great immigration. Paradoxically, La Bruyère's readers could conceive the universal better than the anonymous: thus any description of a character coincides with the sentiment of an identity, even if this identity is uncertain; the many "keys" which followed the publication of *Les Caractères* do not constitute a paltry phenomenon which would indicate, for instance, contemporary incomprehension in the face of the book's general scope; it is perhaps indifferent that the glutton *Cliton* was actually Count de Broussin or Louis de la Trémouille; it is not indifferent that the "characters" were almost all drawn from a personalized society: nomination here is a strict function of enclosure: the worldly type (and it is here that it probably differs from the typical roles of comedy) is not born of abstraction, quintessence of countless individuals: the worldly type is an immediate unit, defined by his place among adjacent units whose "differential" contiguity forms the inland of worldliness: La Bruyère does not purify his characters, he recites them like the successive cases of one and the same worldly declension.

Enclosure and individuation, these are dimensions of a sociality we no longer know anything about. Our world is open, we circulate in it; and above all, if enclosure still exists, it is anything but a rare minority which is confined within it and emphatically finds its being there; on the contrary, it is the countless majority; worldliness, today, is normality; it follows that the psychology of partition has entirely changed; we are no longer sensitive to characters resulting from the principle of vanity (decisive when it is the minority which is associated with both Being and Having), but rather to all the variations of the abnormal; for us, characters exist only marginally: it is no longer La Bruyère who gives a name to men now, it is the psychopathologist or the psychosociologist, those specialists who are called upon to define not essences but (quite the contrary) divergences. In other words, our enclosure is extensive, it confines the majority. There ensues a complete reversal of the interest we can take in characters; in the past, the character referred to a "key," the (general) *person* to a (particular) *personality*; today, it is the opposite; our world certainly creates, for its spectacle, a closed and personalized society: that of the stars and celebrities which we might group under the name of modern Olympians; but this society does not yield characters, only functions or roles (the love goddess, the mother, the queen enslaved by her duty, the vixen princess, the model husband, etc.); and contrary to the classical circuit, these "personalities" are treated as persons in order that the greatest number of human beings can recognize themselves in them; the Olympian society we create for our own consumption is, in short, only a world set within the world so as to represent it—not an enclosure but a mirror: we no longer seek out the typical but the identical; La Bruyère condensed a character in the fashion of a metaphor; we develop a star like a narrative; Iphis, Onuphre, or Hermippe lent themselves to an art of the portrait; Margaret, Soraya, or Marilyn renew that of the epic gesture.

This "structural" distance of La Bruyère's world in relation to ours does not cause our lack of interest in his, but merely exempts us from trying to identify ourselves with it; we must get used to the idea that La Bruyère's truth is, in the full sense of the term, elsewhere. Nothing will prepare us to do this better than a glance at what we would call today his political position. As we know, his century was not subversive. Born of the monarchy, fed by it, entirely immersed within it, writers of the period were as united in approving the establishment as those of today are in contesting it. Sincere or not (the question itself was virtually meaningless), La Bruyère declares himself as submissive to Louis XIV as to a god; not that his submission is not experienced as such; simply, it is inevitable: a man born a Christian and a Frenchman (i.e., subject to the king) cannot, by nature, approach the great subjects, which are the forbidden subjects: nothing remains for him except to write well (*Des ouvrages de l'esprit*, No. 65); the writer will therefore fling himself into the sanctification of what exists, *because it exists* (*Du souverain*, No. 1); it is the immobility of things which shows their truth; the Siamese welcome Christian missionaries but refrain from sending theirs to Europe: this is because their gods are false and "ours" true (*Des esprits forts*, No. 29). La Bruyère's submission to the most emphatic (and therefore to the most banal) forms of the royal cult is of course not at all strange in itself: every writer of his day employed this style; but all the same, there is one singularity about it: it suddenly reins in what today we would call a demystifying attitude: moralism, which is by definition a substitution of rationales for appearances and of motives for virtues, ordinarily operates like vertigo: applied to the "human heart," the investigation of truth seems unable to stop anywhere; yet in La Bruyère, this implacable movement, pursued by means of tiny notations throughout a whole book (which was the book of his life) concludes with the dullest of declarations: that the things of this world remain finally as they were, motionless under the gaze of the god-king; and that the author himself joins this immobility and "takes refuge in mediocrity" (*mediocrity* in the sense of the *juste milieu*; see *Des biens de fortune*, No. 47): it is as if we were hearing a new profession of dharma, the Hindu law which prescribes the immobility of things and of castes. Thus there appears a kind of distortion between book and author, a discrepancy at once surprising and exemplary; surprising because, whatever effort the author makes to submit, the book continues to ignite everything in its path; exemplary because by founding an order of signs on the distance between the witness and his testimony, the work seems to refer to a particular fulfillment of man in the world, a fulfillment which we call, precisely, *literature*. It is, finally, just when La Bruyère seems farthest from us that a figure suddenly appears who concerns us very closely and who is, quite simply, the *writer*.

It is not a question, of course, of "writing well." We believe today that literature is a technique at once more profound than that of style and less direct than that of thought; we believe that it is both language and thought, thought which seeks itself on the level of words, language which considers itself philosophically. Is that what La Bruyère is?

One might say that the first condition of literature is, paradoxically, to produce an *indirect* language: to name things in detail in order not to name their ultimate meaning, and yet to retain this threatening meaning, to designate the world as a repertoire of signs without saying what it is they signify. Now, by a second paradox, the best way for a language to be indirect is to refer as constantly as possible to objects and not to their concepts: for the object's meaning always vacillates, the concept's does not; whence the concrete vocation of literary writing. Now *Les Caractères* is an admirable collection of substances, sites, customs, attitudes; man here is almost constantly dominated by an object or an incident: clothing, language, movement, tears, colors, cosmetics, faces, foods, landscapes, furniture, visits, baths, letters, etc. Everyone knows that La Bruyère's book has none of the algebraic dryness of La Rochefoucauld's maxims, for instance, which are based on the articulation of pure human essences; La Bruyère's technique is different: it consists of *putting on record*, and always tends to mask the concept under the percept; if he wants to say that the motive of modest actions is not necessarily modesty, La Bruyère will produce a little story of apartments or meals ("The man who, lodged in a palace, with two sets of apartments for the two seasons, comes to the Louvre to sleep in a vestibule," etc. *Du mérite*, No. 41); every truth begins this way, in the fashion of a riddle which separates the thing from its signification; La Bruyère's art (and we know that art, i.e., technique, coincides with the very Being of literature) consists in establishing the greatest possible distance between the evidence of the objects and events by which the author inaugurates most of his notations and the idea which actually seems to choose, to arrange, to move them retroactively. Most of the characters are thus constructed like a semantic equation: the concrete has the function of the signifier; the abstract, that of the signified; and between them comes a suspense, for we never know in advance the final meaning the author will draw from the things he treats.

The semantic structure of the fragment is so powerful in La Bruyère that we can readily attach it to one of the two fundamental aspects which Roman Jakobson so usefully distinguishes in any system of signs: a selective aspect (to choose a sign from a reservoir of similar signs) and a combinatory aspect (to connect the signs thus chosen within a discourse); each of these aspects corresponds to a typical figure of the old rhetoric, by which we can designate it: the selective aspect corresponds to *metaphor*, which is the substitution of one signifier for another, both having the same meaning, if not the same value; the combinatory aspect corresponds to *metonymy*, which is the shift, starting from a same meaning, from one sign to another; esthetically, a resort to metaphorical procedure is at the origin of all the arts of variation; a resort to metonymic procedure is at the origin of all the arts of narrative. A portrait by La Bruyère, then, has an eminently metaphorical structure; La Bruyère chooses features which have the same signified, and he accumulates them in a continuous metaphor, whose unique signified is given at the end; consider, for instance, the portrait of the rich man and of the poor man at the end of the chapter *Des biens de fortune*, No. 83: in *Giton* are enumerated, one right after another, all the signs which make him a rich man; in *Phédon*, all the signs of the poor man; we thus see that everything which happens to Giton and to Phédon, although apparently recounted, does not derive, strictly speaking, from the order of narrative; it is entirely a matter of an extended metaphor, of which La Bruyère himself has very pertinently given the theory when he says of his Ménalque that he is "less a particular character than a collection of examples of distraction" (*De l'homme*, No. 7); by this we are to understand that all the distractions enumerated are not really those of a single man, even one fictively named, as would occur in a real narrative (metonymic order); but that they belong instead to a lexicon of distraction from which can be chosen, "according to taste," the most significant feature (metaphoric order). Here perhaps we approach La Bruyère's art: the "character" is a false narrative, it is a metaphor which assumes the quality of narrative without truly achieving it (we recall moreover La Bruyère's scorn for storytelling: *Des jugements*, No. 52): the indirect nature of literature is thus fulfilled: ambiguous, intermediate between definition and illustration, the discourse constantly grazes one and the other and deliberately misses both: the moment we think we perceive the clear meaning of an entirely metaphorical portrait (lexicon of the features of distraction), this meaning shifts under the appearances of an experienced narrative (one of Ménalque's days).

A false narrative, a masked metaphor: this situation of La Bruyère's discourse perhaps explains the formal structure (what used to be called the composition) of the *Caractères*: it is a book of fragments precisely because the fragment occupies an intermediary place between the maxim which is a pure metaphor, since it defines (see La Rochefoucauld: "Self-love is the worst flatterer"), and the anecdote, which is pure narrative: the discourse extends a little because La Bruyère cannot be content with a simple equation (he explains this at the end of his preface); but it stops as soon as it threatens to turn into a story. *Les Caractères* exploits, in fact, a very special language, one which has few equivalents in a literature so imbued with the excellence of determined genres, fragmented language (the maxim), or continuous language (the novel); yet we might cite precedents—a prosaic reference and a sublime one. The prosaic reference of the fragment would be what we call today the *scrapbook*, a varied collection of reflections and items (press cuttings, for instance) whose mere *notation* leads to a certain meaning: *Les Caractères* is indeed the scrapbook of worldliness: a timeless fragmented gazette whose pieces are in a sense the discontinuous significations of a continuous reality. The sublime reference would be what we call today *poetic language*; by a historical paradox, poetry in La Bruyère's day was essentially a continuous discourse, of metonymic and not metaphoric structure (to return to Jakobson's distinction); it has taken the profound subversion worked upon language by surrealism to obtain a fragmentary utterance which derives its poetic meaning from its very fragmentation (see for instance Char's *La Parole en archipel*); if it were poetic, La Bruyère's book would certainly not be a poem but, in the manner of certain modern compositions, a pulverized language: that the example refers us on the one hand to a classical rationality (characters) and on the other to a poetic "irrationality" in no way alters a certain shared experience of the fragment: the radical discontinuity of language could be experienced by La Bruyère as it is experienced today by René Char.

And indeed it is on the level of language (and not of style) that *Les Caractères* can perhaps touch us most closely. Here we see a man conducting a certain experiment upon literature: its object may seem to us anachronistic, as we have seen, though the word ("literature") is not. This experiment is conducted, one may say, on three levels.

First of all, on the level of the institution itself. It seems that La Bruyère very consciously worked out a certain reflection on the Being of that singular language which we now call *literature* and which he himself named, by an expression more substantial than conceptual, *the works of the mind*: in addition to his preface, which is a definition of his enterprise on the level of discourse, La Bruyère dedicates to literature a whole chapter of his work, and this chapter is the first one, as if all reflection on man must initially establish in principle the language which sustains it. No one at that time, of course, could imagine that *to write* was an intransitive verb, without moral justification: La Bruyère therefore writes in order to instruct. This finality is nonetheless absorbed in a group of much more modern definitions: writing is a métier, which is a way of demoralizing it and at the same time of giving it the seriousness of a technique (*Des ouvrages de l'esprit*, No. 3); the man of letters (a new notion at the time) is open to the world yet occupies a place in it shielded from worldliness (*Des biens de fortune*, No. 12); one engages in writing *or* in not-writing, which signifies that writing is a choice. Without trying to force the modernity of such notations, all this suggests the project of a singular language, distant both from the playfulness of the *précieux* (naturalness is a theme of the period) and from moral instruction, a language which finds its secret goal in a certain way of dividing up the world into words and of making it signify on the level of an exclusively verbal labor (which is *art*).

This brings us to the second level of the literary experiment, which is the writer's commitment to words. Speaking of his predecessors (Malherbe and Guez de Balzac), La Bruyère remarks: "Discourse has been given all the order and all the clarity of which it is capable (which it can receive): it can now be given only wit." Wit designates here a kind of *ingenuity* between intelligence and technique; such, indeed, is literature: a thought formed by words, a meaning resulting from form. For La Bruyère, to be a writer is to believe that in a certain sense content depends on form, and that by modifying the structure of form, a particular intelligence of things is produced, an original contour of reality, in short, a new meaning: language, to La Bruyère, is an ideology in and of itself; he knows that his vision of the world is somehow determined by the linguistic revolution of the beginning of his century and, beyond this revolution, by his personal utterance, that ethic of discourse which has made him choose the fragment and not the maxim, metaphor and not narrative, the *naturel* and not the *précieux*.

Thus he affirms a certain responsibility of writing which is, after all, quite modern. And which leads to the third determination of the literary experiment. This responsibility of writing is not at all identified with what we now call commitment and what was then called *instruction*. Of course the classical writers could quite well believe that they were instructing, just as our writers believe they are bearing witness. But even though it is substantially linked to the world, literature is elsewhere; its function, at least at the heart of that modernity which begins with La Bruyère, is not to answer the world's questions directly but—at once more modestly and more mysteriously—to lead the question to the verge of its answer, to construct the signification technically without fulfilling it. La Bruyère was certainly not a revolutionary nor even a democrat, as the positivists of the last century used to claim; he had no idea that servitude, oppression, poverty could be expressed in political terms; yet his description of the peasants has the profound value of an awakening; the light his writing casts on human misery remains indirect, issuing for the most part from a blinded consciousness, powerless to grasp causes, to foresee corrections; but this very indirectness has a cathartic value, for it preserves the writer from bad faith: in literature, through literature, the writer has no rights; the solution of human misery is not a triumphant possession; his language is there only to designate a disturbance. This is what La Bruyère has done: because he chose to be a writer, his description of man touches on the real questions.

1963

The Metaphor
of the Eye

Although Georges Bataille's *Historie de l'oeil* includes several named characters and the narrative of their erotic adventures, he certainly does not give us the story of Simone, Marcelle, or the narrator (as Sade could write the story of Justine or Juliette). *Histoire de l'oeil* is actually the story of an object. How can an object have a story? No doubt it can pass from hand to hand (thereby occasioning insipid fictions like *The Story of My Pipe* or *Memoirs of an Armchair*); it can also pass from image to image, so that its story is that of a migration, the cycle of the avatars it traverses far from its original being, according to the tendency of a certain imagination which distorts yet does not discard it: this is the case with Bataille's book.

What happens to the Eye (and no longer to Marcelle, Simone, or the narrator) cannot be identified with ordinary fiction; the "adventures" of an object which simply changes owner derive from a novelistic imagination content to arrange reality; on the other hand, its "avatars," since they must be absolutely imaginary (and no longer simply "invented"), can be only the imagination itself: they are not its product but its substance; describing the Eye's migration toward other objects (and consequently other functions than that of "seeing"), Bataille makes no commitment to the novel, which accommodates itself by definition to a partial imaginary world, derivative and impure (i.e., polluted by reality); he proceeds, quite the contrary, only within what is essentially an image system. Must we call such compositions "poems"? No other name seems available to set in opposition to the novel, and this opposition is necessary: the novelistic imagination is "probable": the novel is what, all things considered, might happen: a timid imagination (even in the most luxuriant of creations) which will declare itself only when guaranteed by reality; the poetic imagination, on the contrary, is improbable: the poem is what could never happen, except precisely in the shadowy or fiery region of fantasies which, thereby, the poem alone can designate; the novel proceeds by aleatory combinations of real elements; the poem by an exact and complete exploration of virtual elements.

This opposition—if it is justified—will suggest the two great categories (operations, objects or figures) which linguistics has recently taught us to distinguish and to name: arrangement and selection, syntagm and paradigm, metonymy and metaphor. *Histoire de l'oeil* is, then, a metaphoric composition (we shall see that metonymy nonetheless intervenes subsequently): one term, the Eye, is here varied through a certain number of substitutive objects which sustain with it the strict relation of affinitative objects (since they are globular) and yet dissimilar objects too (since they are variously named); this double property is the necessary and sufficient condition of every paradigm: the Eye's substitutes are actually declined, in all the senses of the term: recited like the inflectional forms of the same word; revealed as the states of the same identity; eluded like propositions no one of which can detain us more than the rest; extended like the successive moments of the same story. Thus, in its metaphoric trajectory, the Eye both abides and alters: its fundamental form subsists through the movement of a nomenclature, like that of a topological space; for here each inflection is a new name and utters a new usage.

The Eye seems, then, the matrix of a new trajectory of objects which are in a sense the different "stations" of the ocular metaphor. The first variation is that of eye and egg; this is a double variation, both of form (in French, the two words, *oeil* and *oeuf* have a common sound and a differentiated sound) and of content (although absolutely discrepant, both objects are globular and white). Once posited as invariant elements, whiteness and rotundity permit new metaphorical extensions: that of the cat's milk dish, for instance, which functions in the first erotic exchange between Simone and the narrator; and when this whiteness becomes nacreous (like that of a dead, rolled-up eye), it introduces a new development of the metaphor—sanctioned by current French usage which calls the testicles of certain animals *eggs*. Here we find fully constituted the metaphoric sphere in which the whole of *Histoire de l'oeil* functions, from the cat's milk dish to Granero's enucleation and the bull's castration ("the bull's testicles, the size and shape of an egg, were of a pearly whiteness tinged with blood, analogous to that of the ocular globe").

This is the first metaphor of the poem. It is not, however, the only one; a secondary series derives from it, constituted by all the avatars of the liquid whose image is equally linked to eye, egg, and testicles; and this series is not only the liquor itself (tears, milk, egg yolk, sperm, urine), it is, so to speak, the very mode of the moist; the metaphor here is much richer than in the case of the globular; from damp to runny, it is all the varieties of the inundant which complete the original metaphor of the globe; objects apparently quite remote from the eye are suddenly caught up in the metaphoric chain—like the guts of the gored horse, released "like a cataract" by the bull's horn thrust. Indeed (for the metaphor's power is infinite), the mere presence of one of the two series invokes the other; what is "dryer" than the sun? Yet it suffices that in the metaphoric field which Bataille traces like an haruspex, the sun should be a disc, then a globe, for light to *flow* from it and thereby join, through the notion of a soft luminosity or a urinary liquefaction of the sky, the theme of eye, egg, and testicle.

Here, then, are two metaphorical series, or better, according to the definition of metaphor, two series of signifiers; for in both, each term is merely the signifier of the next. Do all these signifiers "in series" refer to a stable signified, the more secret for being buried under a whole architecture of masks? In short, is there a core of metaphor, and thereby a hierarchy of its terms? This is a question for depth psychology, which is irrelevant here. We may merely note this: if there exists a beginning of the chain, if the metaphor involves a generating (and consequently privileged) term from which the paradigm is gradually constructed, it must at least be acknowledged that *Histoire de l'oeil* does not designate the sexual as a first term of the chain: nothing authorizes us to say that the metaphor begins with the genital in order to conclude with apparently unsexualized objects like the eye, the egg, or the sun; the image system developed here has no sexual obsession for its "secret"; if this were the case, we should first have to explain why the erotic theme is never directly phallic (what we have is a "round phallism"); but above all, Bataille himself has made any decipherment of his poem futile by giving (at the book's end) the (biographical) sources of his metaphor; he thus leaves no other recourse than to consider, in *Histoire de l'oeil*, a perfectly spherical metaphor: each of the terms is always the signifier of another (no term is a simple signified), without our ever being able to stop the chain; doubtless the Eye, since this is its story, seems to predominate—the Eye which we know to be that of the blind father himself whose whitish globe rolled up when he urinated in front of the child; but in this case, it is the very equivalence of ocular and genital which is original, not one of its terms: the paradigm *begins* nowhere. This indeterminacy of the metaphoric order, generally forgotten by the psychology of archetypes, merely reproduces, moreover, the unorganized character of the associative fields, as has been forcefully affirmed by Saussure: no single term of a declension can be assigned pre-eminence. The critical consequences are important: *Histoire de l'oeil* is not a "profound" work: everything is given on the surface and without hierarchy, the metaphor is displayed in its entirety; circular and explicit, it refers to no secret: we have here a signification without a signified (or one in which everything is signified); and it is neither the least beauty nor the least novelty of this text to compose, by the technique we are attempting to describe, an open literature which is situated beyond any decipherment and which only a formal criticism can—at a great distance—accompany.

Now we must return to the two metaphoric chains, that of the Eye (as we shall call it for simplicity's sake) and that of the tears. As a reservoir of virtual signs, a metaphor in the pure state cannot constitute discourses in and of itself: if we *re-cite* its terms—i.e., if we insert them in a narrative which cements them together, their paradigmatic nature already yields to the dimension of all speech, which is inevitably a syntagmatic extension;[1] *Histoire de l'oeil* is actually a narrative whose episodes remain predetermined, nonetheless, by the different stations of the double metaphor: the narrative is only a kind of flowing matter, a vehicle for the precious metaphoric substance: if we are in a park at night, it is so that a thread of moonlight can turn translucent the moist patch of Marcelle's sheet, which floats out the window of her room; if we are in Madrid, it is so that there can be a *corrida*, an offering of the bull's testicles, the enucleation of Granero's eye, and if in Seville, it is so that the sky there can express that yellowish liquid luminosity whose metaphoric nature we know by the rest of the chain. Even in the interior of each series, the narrative is a *form* whose constraint, fruitful on the same basis as the old metrical rules or the unities of tragedy, permits us to *extend* the terms of the metaphor beyond their constitutive virtuality.

Yet *Histoire de l'oeil* is something quite different from a narrative, even a thematic narrative. This is because, once the double metaphor is posited, Bataille proceeds to a new technique: he *exchanges* the two chains. This exchange is possible by nature, since he is not dealing with the same paradigm (the same metaphor), and because, consequently, the two chains can es-

---

1. Need we explain these terms which derive from linguistics and which a certain literature is beginning to acclimate? The *syntagm* is the connection and combination of signs on the level of actual discourse (for instance, the *linear sequence* of the words); the *paradigm* is, for each sign of the syntagm, the reservoir of related yet dissimilar signs from which it is chosen.

tablish relations of contiguity between themselves: we can
fasten a term of the first to a term of the second: the syntagm
is immediately possible: on the level of common sense, nothing
opposes—and one might even say that everything suggests—a
discourse in which *the eye weeps*, in which the *broken egg runs*,
or in which *the (sun) light spreads*; in a first moment, which is
that of the quotidian, the terms of the first metaphor and those
of the second proceed together, dutifully paired according to
the ancestral archetypes. Quite classically generated by the intersection of the two chains, these traditional syntagms obviously involve little enough information: to break an egg or to
poke out an eye are total assertions which have virtually no
effect except in relation to their context, and not in relation to
their components: what can you do with an egg, if not break
it; and what with an eye, except to poke it out?

Yet everything changes once we disturb the correspondence
of the two chains; if, instead of pairing objects and actions according to the laws of traditional kinship (to break an egg, to
poke out an eye), we dislocate the association by assigning each
of its terms to different lines; in short, if we permit ourselves
to break an eye and to poke out an egg; in relation to the two
parallel metaphors (of eye and tear), the syntagm then becomes *crossed*, for the link it proposes will seek from the two
series not complementary but distant terms: here we encounter
the law of the surrealist image, formulated by Reverdy and
adopted by Breton (*the more distant and accurate the relations
of two realities, the stronger the image*). Bataille's image is,
however, much more concerted; it is neither a wild image nor
even a free image, for the coincidence of its terms is not aleatory, and the syntagm is limited by a constraint: that of selection, which obliges us to choose the terms of the image from
only two finite series. This constraint, obviously, generates a
very powerful kind of information, located at an equal distance
from the banal and the absurd, since the narrative is encom-
passed by the metaphorical sphere, whose regions it can exchange (whence its energy) but whose limits it cannot
transgress (whence its meaning); according to the law which
decrees that the Being of literature is never anything but its

technique, the insistence and the freedom of this "song" are therefore products of an exact art which is able at once to measure the associative field and to liberate within it the contiguities of terms.

There is nothing gratuitous about this art, since it is apparently identified with eroticism itself, at least with Bataille's eroticism. We can of course imagine other definitions for eroticism than linguistic ones (as Bataille himself has shown). But if we call *metonymy* [2] *this transfer of meaning from one chain to the other, at different levels of the metaphor* (*eye sucked like a breast, my eye sipped by her lips*), we will doubtless realize that Bataille's eroticism is essentially metonymic. Since poetic technique consists, in this case, of undoing the usual contiguities of objects in order to substitute for them new encounters limited, nonetheless, by the persistence of a single theme within each metaphor, there occurs a kind of general contagion of qualities and actions: by their metaphoric dependence, eye, sun, and egg participate closely in the genital; and by their metonymic freedom, they endlessly exchange their meanings and their usages, so that to break eggs into a bathtub, to swallow or to shell (soft-boiled) eggs, to enucleate an eye or to play with it erotically, to associate milk dish and sexual organ, a thread of moonlight and a jet of urine, to bite into the bull's testicle as if it were an egg or to insert it into one's own body—all these associations are both the same and different; for metaphor, which *varies* them, manifests a regulated difference among them, a difference which metonymy, which *exchanges* them, immediately undertakes to abolish: the world becomes disturbed, its properties are no longer divided; to flow, to sob, to urinate, to ejaculate—these form a vacillating meaning, and the whole of *Histoire de l'oeil* signifies in the manner of a vibration which always produces the same sound (but what sound?). Thus the transgression of values—that declared principle of eroticism—corresponds to (if it does not indeed estab-

2. I refer here to the opposition established by Roman Jakobson between *metaphor*, a figure of similarity, and *metonymy*, a figure of contiguity.

lish) a technical transgression of the forms of language, for metonymy is precisely a forced syntagm, the violation of a signifying limit of space; it permits, on the very level of discourse, a counterdivision of objects, usages, meanings, spaces, and properties, which is eroticism itself: thus what the interplay of metaphor and metonymy, in *Histoire de l'oeil*, ultimately makes it possible to transgress is sex: not, of course, to sublimate it; quite the contrary.

It remains to be discovered if the rhetoric just described permits us to account for *all* eroticism or if it belongs strictly to Bataille. A glance at Sade's work, for instance, permits us to sketch the answer. It is true that Bataille's narrative owes a great deal to Sade's; but this is because Sade has established all erotic narrative, insofar as his eroticism is by nature essentially syntagmatic; given a certain number of erotic sites, Sade deduces from them every figure (or conjunction of characters) which can mobilize them; the primary units are finite in number, for nothing is more limited than erotic material; they are nonetheless sufficiently numerous to sustain an apparently infinite combination (the erotic sites combining into postures and the postures into scenes), whose profusion forms the entire narrative. Sade never resorts to a metaphoric or metonymic imagination, his erotics is simply combinatory; but thereby it doubtless has an entirely different meaning from Bataille's. By metonymic exchange, Bataille exhausts a metaphor, doubtless a double metaphor, each chain of which is weakly saturated; Sade, on the contrary, thoroughly explores a field of combinations free of any structural constraint; his eroticism is encyclopedic, he participates in the same inventorial spirit which animates Newton or Fourier. For Sade, what matters is to work out, to exhaust an erotic combination, a project which involves (technically) no transgression of the sexual. For Bataille, what matters is to traverse the vacillation of several objects (an entirely modern notion, unknown to Sade), so that they exchange the functions of the obscene and those of substance (the consistency of the soft-boiled egg, the bloody and nacreous tinge of the bull's testicles, the vitreous quality of the eye). Sade's erotic language has no other connotation than that of his century, it is writing [*une écriture*]; Bataille's erotic language is connoted by Georges Bataille's very being, it is a style; between the two, something is born, something which transforms every experience into a warped language and which is literature.

1963

The Two Criticisms

We have in France at the present time two parallel criticisms: one which we shall call, for simplicity's sake, *academic* and which practices, in essentials, a positivist method inherited from Lanson; and another which we shall call *interpretive*, whose representatives—as various as Sartre, Bachelard, Goldmann, Poulet, Starobinski, Weber, Girard, and Richard—have this in common, that their approach to the literary work can be attached, more or less explicitly but in any case consciously, to one of the major ideologies of the moment, existentialism, Marxism, psychoanalysis, phenomenology; hence we might also call this criticism *ideological*, in opposition to the first kind, which rejects every ideology and claims to derive only from an objective method. Between these two criticisms there exist, of course, certain links: on the one hand, ideological criticism is largely practiced by professors, for in France, traditionally and professionally, intellectual status is easily confused with academic status; and on the other hand, the university sometimes acknowledges interpretive criticism, since examples of it are offered as doctoral theses (more freely sanctioned, apparently, by philosophy faculties than by faculties of letters). Nonetheless, without labeling it a conflict, the separation of the two criticisms is real. Why?

If academic criticism were nothing but its avowed program —the rigorous establishment of biographical or literary facts— it would be hard to see why it should sustain any tension with ideological criticism. The achievements and indeed the demands of positivism are irreversible: no one today, whatever his philosophy, would dream of contesting the usefulness of erudition, the value of historical accuracy, the advantages of a subtle analysis of literary "circumstance," and if the importance academic criticism grants to the problem of sources already implies a certain notion of what a literary work is (we shall return to this), there can be no objection, at least, to treating this problem with exactitude, once it is raised; so at first glance there is no reason why the two criticisms should not acknowledge each other and collaborate: positivist criticism would establish and discover the "facts" (since that is its requirement) and would leave the other criticism free to interpret them, or more precisely to make them "signify" with reference to an ideological system. If this pacifying view is also a utopian one, it is because in reality there is no division of labor between academic criticism and interpretive criticism, a simple difference of method and philosophy, but instead a real competition of two ideologies. As Mannheim has shown, positivism is an ideology like the rest (which in no way keeps it from being useful). And when it inspires literary criticism, positivism clearly reveals its ideological nature at two (essential) points.

First of all, by deliberately limiting its investigations to the "circumstances" of the work (even if these are internal circumstances), positivist criticism espouses an entirely partial notion of literature; for to refuse to question the Being of literature is thereby to accredit the notion that this Being is eternal or "natural"—in short, that literature is *a matter of course*. And yet, what is literature? Why does one write? Did Racine write for the same reasons as Proust? Not to ask these questions is also to answer them, for it is to adopt the traditional notion of common sense (which is anything but historical) that a writer writes quite simply *to express himself,* and that the Being of literature is in the "translation" of sensibility and the passions. Unfortunately, once we touch upon human intentionality (and how speak of literature without doing so?), positivist psychology no longer suffices: not only because it is rudimentary, but also because it involves an altogether dated determinist philosophy. The paradox is that historical criticism here rejects history; history tells us that there is no such thing as a timeless essence of literature, but under the rubric "literature" (itself quite recent, moreover) a process of very different forms, functions, institutions, reasons, and projects whose relativity it is precisely the historian's responsibility to discern; otherwise he will be, precisely, unable to explain the "facts": by abstaining from telling us *why Racine wrote* (what literature could be for a man of his period), criticism keeps itself from discovering why at a certain moment (after *Phèdre*) Racine *stopped writing*. Everything connects: the most trivial literary problem, however anecdotal, can have its "key" in the mental context of an age; and this context is not ours. The critic must admit that it is his very object, in its most general form, literature, which resists or evades him, not the biographical "secret" of his author.

The second point where academic criticism clearly reveals its ideological commitment is what we might call the postulate of analogy. We know that this criticism is chiefly constituted by the investigation of "sources": it always puts the work to be studied in relation with *something else,* an *elsewhere* of literature; this elsewhere may be another (antecedent) work, a biographical circumstance, or even a "passion" actually experienced by the author and "expressed" (always the *expression*) in his work (Oreste is Racine at twenty-six, in love, jealous, etc.); the second term of the relation matters, moreover, much less than its nature, which is constant in all "objective" criticism: this relation is always analogical: it implies the certitude that to write is invariably to *reproduce, to copy, to be inspired by,* etc.; the (incontestible) differences between the model and the work are always ascribed to "genius," a notion whose presence causes the most determined, the most indiscreet critic to renounce his right to speak and the most unflinching rationalist to turn into a credulous psychologist, deferential to the mys-

terious alchemy of creation, once the analogy is no longer
visible: the *resemblances* of the work thus derive from the
most rigorous positivism, but by a singular abdication, its *differences* derive from magic. Now this is a typical postulate; it
is just as likely that the literary work begins precisely where it
distorts its model (or, more discreetly: its point of departure);
Bachelard has shown that the poetic imagination consists not
in *forming* images but rather in *deforming* them; and according to psychology, which is the privileged realm of analogical
explanations (for the written passion must always, apparently,
emerge from an experienced passion), we now know that phenomena of denial are at least as important as phenomena of
conformity: a desire, a passion, a frustration can very well produce *precisely* contrary representations; a real motive can be
inverted in an alibi which contradicts it; a work can be the very
fantasy which compensates the negative life: Oreste in love
with Hermione is perhaps Racine secretly disgusted with Mlle
Duparc: similarity is not a privileged relation which creation
entertains with reality. *Imitation* in the broadest sense takes a
labyrinthine path; defined in Hegelian or psychoanalytic or
existential terms, a powerful dialectic ceaselessly warps the
model away from the work, subjects it to forces of fascination,
compensation, derision, aggression, whose value must be established not with regard to the model itself but with regard to
their place in the work's general organization. Which brings
us to one of the gravest responsibilities of academic criticism:
focused on a genetics of literary detail, it risks missing the detail's functional meaning, which is its truth: to expend prodigies of ingenuity, rigor, and tenacity to discover whether Oreste
was Racine, or whether the Baron de Charlus was the Count de
Montesquiou is thereby to deny that Oreste and Charlus are
essentially the terms of a functional system of figures, a system
whose operation can be grasped only within the work; the
homologue of Oreste is not Racine but Pyrrhus; the homologue
of Charlus is not Montesquiou but the narrator precisely insofar as the narrator *is not* Proust. In short, it is the work which
is its own model; its truth is not to be sought in depth, but in
extent; and if there is a relation between the author and his
work (who would deny it? The work does not descend from

Heaven: only positivist criticism still believes in the Muse), it
is not a pointillist relation which accumulates parcellary, discontinuous, and "profound" resemblances, but on the contrary a relation between the *entire* author and the *entire* work,
a relation of relations, a homological not an analogical correspondence.

We approach the heart of the matter here; for if we now
consider the implicit rejection our academic criticism makes of
interpretive criticism, we see at once that this rejection has
nothing to do with the banal fear of the new; academic criticism is neither retrograde nor obsolete (a little slow, perhaps):
it is quite capable of adapting itself. Thus, though it has for
years espoused a conformist psychology of normality (inherited
from Théodule Ribot, a contemporary of Lanson's), it has
lately "acknowledged" psychoanalysis, consecrating (in a particularly well-received doctorate) the strictly Freudian criticism
of Charles Mauron. But this very consecration reveals the line
of resistance of academic criticism: for psychoanalytic criticism
is still a psychology, it postulates an *elsewhere* of the work (the
writer's childhood), a secret of the author, a substance to be
deciphered, which remains the human soul, even at the price of
a new vocabulary: better a psychopathology of the writer than
no psychology at all; by coordinating the details of a work with
the details of a life, psychoanalytic criticism continues to practice an esthetic of motivations entirely based on a relation of
exteriority: it is because Racine himself was an orphan that there
are so many fathers in his plays: biographical transcendence is
saved: there are, there will always be writers' lives to "excavate."
In short, academic criticism is prepared to concede (gradually
and after successive resistances) the very principle of interpretive criticism; but it denies that this interpretation can function in a realm purely internal to the work; in short, what is rejected here is immanent analysis: anything is acceptable, once
the work can be put in relation to something besides itself,
i.e., something besides literature: history (even if it turns out
to be Marxist), psychology (even if it becomes psychoanalytical)—these *elsewheres* of the work will gradually be allowed;
what will not be allowed is a criticism which establishes itself
within the work and posits its relation to the world only after

having entirely described it from within, in its functions or, as we say today, in its structure; what is rejected, then, is phenomenological criticism (which explicates the work instead of explaining it), thematic criticism (which reconstructs the internal metaphors of the work), and structural criticism (which regards the work as a system of functions).

Why this rejection of immanence (whose principle moreover is often misunderstood)? For the moment we can give only contingent answers; perhaps it is because of a stubborn adherence to determinist ideology which holds that the work is the "product" of a "cause" and that exterior causes are more "causal" than others; perhaps, too, because to shift from a criticism of determinations to a criticism of functions and significations would imply a profound conversion of the norms of knowledge, hence of technique, hence of the academic critic's very profession; we must not forget that since literary research is not yet separated from teaching, the university researches but it also issues diplomas; it therefore requires an ideology articulated around a technique difficult enough to constitute an instrument of selection; positivism affords it the obligation of a vast, difficult, patient knowledge; immanent criticism—at least, so it seems—requires, in the work's presence, only a power of astonishment, a power not easily measurable: we can understand that the university hesitates to convert its requirements.

1963

What Is Criticism?

It is always possible to prescribe major critical principles in
accord with one's ideological situation, especially in France,
where theoretical models have a great prestige, doubtless
because they give the practitioner an assurance that he is participating at once in a combat, a history, and a totality; French
criticism has developed in this way for some fifteen years, with
various fortunes, within four major "philosophies." First of all,
what is commonly—and questionably—called existentialism,
which has produced Sartre's critical works, his *Baudelaire*, his
Flaubert, the shorter articles on Proust, Mauriac, Giraudoux,
and Ponge, and above all his splendid *Genet*. Then Marxism:
we know (the argument is already an old one) how sterile
orthodox Marxism has proved to be in criticism, proposing a
purely mechanical explanation of works or promulgating slogans rather than criteria of values; hence it is on the "frontiers"
of Marxism (and not at its avowed center) that we find the
most fruitful criticism: Lucien Goldmann's work explicitly
owes a great deal to Lukacs; it is among the most flexible and
the most ingenious criticism which takes social and political
history as its point of departure. And then psychoanalysis; in
France today, the best representative of Freudian criticism is

Charles Mauron, but here too it is the "marginal" psycho-analysis which has been most fruitful; taking its departure from an analysis of substances (and not of works), following the dynamic distortions of the image in a great number of poets, Bachelard has established something of a critical school, so influential that one might call French criticism today, in its most developed form, a criticism of Bachelardian inspiration (Poulet, Starobinski, Richard). Finally structuralism (or to simplify to an extreme and doubtless abusive degree: formalism): we know the importance, even the vogue of this movement in France since Lévi-Strauss has opened to it the methods of the social sciences and a certain philosophical reflection; few critical works have as yet resulted from it, but they are in preparation, and among them we shall doubtless find, in particular, the influence of linguistic models constructed by Saussure and extended by Jakobson (who himself, early in his career, participated in a movement of literary criticism, the Russian formalist school): it appears possible, for example, to develop an entire literary criticism starting from the two rhetorical categories established by Jakobson: metaphor and metonymy.

As we see, this French criticism is at once "national" (it owes little or nothing to Anglo-American criticism, to Spitzer and his followers, to the Croceans) and contemporary (one might even say "faithless"): entirely absorbed in a certain ideological present, it is reluctant to acknowledge any participation in the critical tradition of Sainte-Beuve, Taine, or Lanson. This last model nonetheless raises a special problem for our contemporary criticism. The work, method, and spirit of Lanson, himself a prototype of the French professor, has controlled, through countless epigones, the whole of academic criticism for fifty years. Since the (avowed) principles of this criticism are rigor and objectivity in the establishment of facts, one might suppose that there is no incompatibility between Lansonism and the ideological criticisms, which are all criticisms of interpretation. However, though the majority of French critics today are themselves professors, there is a certain tension between interpretive criticism and positivist (academic) criticism. This is because Lansonism is itself an ideology; not content to demand the application of the objective rules of all scientific investigation, it implies certain general convictions about man, history, literature, and the relations between author and work; for example, the psychology of Lansonism is utterly dated, consisting essentially of a kind of analogical determinism, according to which the details of a work must *resemble* the details of a life, the soul of a character must *resemble* the soul of the author, etc.—a very special ideology, since it is precisely in the years following its formulation that psychoanalysis, for example, has posited contrary relations, relations of denial, between a work and its author. Indeed, philosophical postulates are inevitable; Lansonism is not to be blamed for its prejudices but for the fact that it conceals them, masks them under the moral alibi of rigor and objectivity: ideology is smuggled into the baggage of scientism like contraband merchandise.

If these various ideological principles are possible at the same time (and for my part, in a certain sense I subscribe to each of them at the same time), it is doubtless because an ideological choice does not constitute the Being of criticism and because "truth" is not its sanction. Criticism is more than discourse in the name of "true" principles. It follows that the capital sin in criticism is not ideology but the silence by which it is masked: this guilty silence has a name: *good conscience,* or again, *bad faith.* How could we believe, in fact, that the work is an object exterior to the psyche and history of the man who interrogates it, an object over which the critic would exercise a kind of extraterritorial right? By what miracle would the profound communication which most critics postulate between the work and its author cease in relation to their own enterprise and their own epoch? Are there laws of creation valid for the writer but not for the critic? All criticism must include in its discourse (even if it is in the most indirect and modest manner imaginable) an implicit reflection on itself; every criticism is a criticism of the work *and* a criticism of itself. In other words, criticism is not at all a table of results or a body of judgments, it is essentially an activity, i.e., a series of intellectual acts profoundly committed to the historical and subjective existence (they are the same thing) of the man who performs them. Can an activity be "true"? It answers quite different requirements.

Every novelist, every poet, whatever the detours literary theory may take, is presumed to speak of objects and phenomena, even if they are imaginary, exterior and anterior to language: the world exists and the writer speaks: that is literature. The object of criticism is very different; the object of criticism is not "the world" but a discourse, the discourse of someone else: criticism is discourse upon a discourse; it is a second language, or a *metalanguage* (as the logicians would say), which operates on a first language (or *language object*). It follows that the critical language must deal with two kinds of relations: the relation of the critical language to the language of the author studied, and the relation of this language object to the world. It is the "friction" of these two languages which defines criticism and perhaps gives it a great resemblance to another mental activity, logic, which is also based on the distinction between language object and metalanguage.

For if criticism is only a metalanguage, this means that its task is not at all to discover "truths," but only "validities." In itself, a language is not true or false, it is or is not valid: valid, i.e., constitutes a coherent system of signs. The rules of literary language do not concern the conformity of this language to reality (whatever the claims of the realistic schools), but only its submission to the system of signs the author has established (and we must, of course, give the word *system* a very strong sense here). Criticism has no responsibility to say whether Proust has spoken "the truth," whether the Baron de Charlus was indeed the Count de Montesquiou, whether Françoise was Céleste, or even, more generally, whether the society Proust described reproduces accurately the historical conditions of the nobility's disappearance at the end of the nineteenth century; its role is solely to elaborate a language whose coherence, logic, in short whose *systematics* can collect or better still can "integrate" (in the mathematical sense of the word) the greatest possible quantity of Proustian language, exactly as a logical equation tests the validity of reasoning without taking sides as to the "truth" of the arguments it mobilizes. One can say that the critical task (and this is the sole guarantee of its universality) is purely formal: not to "discover" in the work or the author something "hidden," "profound," "secret" which hitherto passed unnoticed (by what miracle? Are we more perspicacious than our predecessors?), but only to adjust the language his period affords him (existentialism, Marxism, psychoanalysis) to the language, i.e., the formal system of logical constraints elaborated by the author according to his own period. The "proof" of a criticism is not of an "alethic" order (it does not proceed from truth), for critical discourse—like logical discourse, moreover—is never anything but tautological: it consists in saying ultimately, though placing its whole being within that delay, what thereby is not insignificant: Racine is Racine, Proust is Proust; critical "proof," if it exists, depends on an aptitude not to *discover* the work in question but on the contrary to *cover* it as completely as possible by its own language.

Thus we are concerned, once again, with an essentially formal activity, not in the esthetic but in the logical sense of the term. We might say that for criticism, the only way of avoiding "good conscience" or "bad faith" is to take as a moral goal not the decipherment of the work's meaning but the reconstruction of the rules and constraints of that meaning's elaboration; provided we admit at once that a literary work is a very special semantic system, whose goal is to put "meaning" in the world, but not "a meaning"; the work, at least the work which ordinarily accedes to critical scrutiny—and this is perhaps a definition of "good" literature—the work is never entirely nonsignifying (mysterious or "inspired"), and never entirely clear; it is, one may say, a *suspended* meaning: it offers itself to the reader as an avowed signifying system yet withholds itself from him as a signified object. This disappointment of meaning explains on the one hand why the literary work has so much power to ask the world questions (undermining the assured meanings which ideologies, beliefs, and common sense seem to possess), yet without ever answering them (there is no great work which is "dogmatic"), and on the other hand why it offers itself to endless decipherment, since there is no reason for us ever to stop speaking of Racine or Shakespeare (unless by a disaffection which will itself be a language): simultaneously an insistent proposition of meaning and a stubbornly fugitive meaning, literature is indeed only a *language*, i.e., a system of signs; its being is not in its message but in this "system." And thereby the critic is not responsible for reconstructing the work's message but only its system, just as the linguist is not responsible for deciphering the sentence's meaning but for establishing the formal structure which permits this meaning to be transmitted.

It is by acknowledging itself as no more than a language (or more precisely, a metalanguage) that criticism can be—paradoxically but authentically—both objective and subjective, historical and existential, totalitarian and liberal. For on the one hand, the language each critic chooses to speak does not come down to him from Heaven; it is one of the various languages his age affords him, it is objectively the end product of a certain historical ripening of knowledge, ideas, intellectual passions— it is a *necessity*; and on the other hand, this necessary language is chosen by each critic as a consequence of a certain existential organization, as the exercise of an intellectual function which belongs to him in his own right, an exercise in which he puts all his "profundity," i.e., his choices, his pleasures, his resistances, his obsessions. Thus begins, at the heart of the critical work, the dialogue of two histories and two subjectivities, the author's and the critic's. But this dialogue is egoistically shifted toward the present: criticism is not an "homage" to the truth of the past or to the truth of "others" —it is a construction of the intelligibility of our own time.

1963

Literature and Signification
Answers to a Questionnaire in *Tel Quel*

I. You have always been interested in problems of signification, but only recently, it would seem, have you given this interest the form of a systematic investigation inspired by structural linguistics, an investigation which you and others have called, after Saussure, semiology. From the viewpoint of a "semiological" conception of literature, does the particular attention you once paid to the theater still seem justified today by an exemplary status of theatricality? And specifically by Brecht's work, which you have championed since 1955, i.e., before the systematization just mentioned?

What is theater? A kind of cybernetic machine. When it is not working, this machine is hidden behind a curtain. But as soon as it is revealed, it begins emitting a certain number of messages. These messages have this peculiarity, that they are simultaneous and yet of different rhythm; at a certain point in the performance, you receive at the same time six or seven items of information (proceeding from the set, the costumes, the lighting, the placing of the actors, their gestures, their speech), but some of these remain (the set, for example) while others change (speech, gestures); what we have, then, is a real informational polyphony, which is what theatricality is: *a density of signs* (in relation to literary monody and leaving aside the question of cinema). What relations do these counterpointed signs (i.e., at once dense and extensive, simultaneous and successive) have among themselves? They do not have the same signifiers (by definition); but do they always signify the same thing? Do they combine in a single meaning? What is the relation which unites them during an often very long interval to that final meaning which is, one may say, retrospective, since it is not contained in the last speech and yet is not clear until the play is over? Further, how is the theatrical signifier formed? What are its models? We know that the linguistic sign is not "analogical" (the word "cow" does not resemble a cow), it is formed by reference to a digital code; but what about the other signifiers—let us call them, for simplicity's sake, the *visual* signifiers—which prevail on the stage? Every performance is an extremely dense semantic act: the nature of the theatrical sign, whether analogical, symbolic, or conventional, the significant variations of this sign, the constraints of linkage, the denotation and connotation of the message—all these fundamental problems of semiology are present in the theater; one can even say that the theater constitutes a privileged semiological object since its system is apparently original (polyphonic) in relation to that of language (which is linear).

Brecht has brilliantly illustrated—and justified—this semantic status of the theater. First of all he understood that the theatrical phenomenon might be treated in cognitive and not purely emotive terms; he was able to conceive the theater intellectually, abolishing the (stale but still tenacious) mythic distinction between creation and reflection, nature and system, the spontaneous and the rational, the "heart" and the "head"; his theater is neither pathetic nor cerebral: it is a *justified* theater. Next he decided that the dramatic forms had a political responsibility; that the placing of a spotlight, the interruption of a scene by a song, the use of placards, the degree to which a costume was made to look threadbare, the way an actor spoke, *signified* a certain choice, not with regard to art but with regard to man and the world; in short, that the materiality of the spectacle derived not only from an esthetic or a psychology of emotion, but also and chiefly from a technique of signification; in other words, that the meaning of a theatrical work (generally an insipid notion identified with the author's "philosophy") depended not on a sum of intentions and "discoveries," but on what we must call an intellectual system of signifiers. Finally, Brecht divined the variety and relativity of semantic systems: the theatrical sign does not appear as a matter of course; what we call the *naturalness* of an actor or the *truth* of a performance is merely one language among others (a language fulfills its function, which is to communicate, by its validity not by its truth), and this language depends on a certain mental context, i.e., a certain history, so that to change the signs (and not just what they say) is to give nature a new apportionment (an enterprise which precisely defines art), and to base this apportionment not on "natural" laws but, quite the contrary, on man's freedom to make things signify.

But above all, precisely when he was linking this theater of signification to political thought, Brecht *affirmed* meaning but did not *fulfill* it. Of course his theater is ideological, more openly so than many others: it takes sides with regard to nature, labor, racism, fascism, history, war, alienation; yet it is a theater of consciousness not of action, of problems not of answers; like every literary language, it serves to "formulate" not to "execute"; all Brecht's plays end on an implicit "find the solution" addressed to the spectator in the name of that decipherment to which the spectacle's materiality must lead him: *consciousness of unconsciousness*, consciousness the audience must have of the unconsciousness prevailing on the stage—that is Brecht's theater. It doubtless explains why this theater signifies so powerfully and preaches so little; the role of the system here is not to transmit a positive message (this is not a theater of the signified) but to show that the world is an object to be deciphered (this is a theater of the signifier). Brecht thus elaborates the tautological status of all literature, which is a message of the signification of things and not of their meaning (by *signification* I refer to the process which produces the meaning and not this meaning itself). What makes Brecht's enterprise exemplary is that it takes more risks than others:

Brecht proceeds to the extreme of a certain meaning (which we may call, roughly, a Marxist meaning), but precisely when it "takes" (solidifies into a positive signified) he suspends this meaning as a question (a suspension we encounter in the particular quality of historical time represented in Brecht's theater, a time of the not-yet). This very subtle friction between a (fulfilled) meaning and a (suspended) signification is an enterprise which far surpasses, in audacity, in difficulty, in necessity, too, the suspension of meaning which the *avant-garde* believed it had produced by a pure subversion of ordinary language and of theatrical conformism. A vague question (the kind which a philosophy of the "absurd" could ask the world) has much less power (disturbs less) than a question whose answer is imminent yet arrested (like Brecht's): in literature, which is an order of connotation, there is no pure question: a question is never anything but its own scattered answer, dispersed in fragments among which meaning erupts and escapes at the same time.

II. How do you interpret the shift you yourself have remarked from the "committed" literature of the Camus-Sartre period to today's "abstract" literature? What do you think of this massive and spectacular depoliticization of literature on the part of writters who for the most part are not apolitical and who are even, on the whole, "leftist"? Do you believe that this zero degree of history is a silence pregnant with meaning?

One can always link a cultural fact with some historical "circumstance"; one can see a relation (either causal or analogical or affinitive) between a work's depoliticization and Khrushchevism or Gaullism on the other, as if the writer had let himself be won over by a general climate of nonparticipation (though we should then have to say why it was that Stalinism or the Fourth Republic had incited writers to "commitment"!). But if we want to deal with cultural phenomena in terms of an authentic historical perspective, we must wait until history itself can be read in depth (no one has yet told us what Gaullism was); what is *under* an avowedly "committed" literature and *under* an apparently "uncommitted" literature, which is perhaps the same thing, can be read only later; it is possible that the historical meaning will appear only when we can group, for instance, surrealism, Sartre, Brecht, "abstract" literature, and even structuralism as so many modes or even fashions of the same idea. These "pieces" of literature have a meaning only if we can relate them to much larger groups; today, for example—or in any case very soon—it is no longer possible to understand "heuristic" literature (a literature of search) without relating it functionally to mass culture, with which it maintains complementary relations of resistance, subversion, exchange, or complicity (it is acculturation which dominates our period, and we can imagine a parallel—and relational—history of the "new novel" and the advice-to-the-lovelorn columns). In reality, I cannot see "committed" literature or "abstract" literature as anything but a diachrony, not a history; these two literatures (exiguous, moreover; nothing comparable to the expansion of classicism, of romanticism, of realism) are actually *fashions* (I do not use the word, of course, in any trivial sense), and I am tempted to see in their alternation that entirely formal phenomenon, the rotation of possibilities, which precisely defines Fashion: an exhaustion of a language and a shift to the antinomic language: here it is *difference* which is the motor, not of history but of diachrony; history intervenes only when these micro-rhythms are perturbed and when this kind of differential orthogenesis of forms is blocked by a whole group of historical functions: it is what lasts that must be explained, not what "changes." We might say, allegorically, that the (motionless) history of the alexandrine is more significant than the (fugitive) mode of the trimeter: the longer forms persist, the closer they approach that historical intelligibility which seems to me the object of all criticism today.

*III. You have said that literature is "constitutively reactionary,"
and elsewhere that it constitutes a fruitful interrogation of the
world. How do you resolve this apparent contradiction? Would
you say the same thing of the other arts, or do you consider
literature to have a special status which makes it more reactionary, or more fruitful, than the others?*

Literature has a particular status in that it is made of language, i.e., of a substance which already signifies when literature takes possession of it: literature must secrete itself in a system which does not belong to it but which nonetheless functions to the same ends as literature, which are: to communicate. It follows that the strife between language and literature forms in some sense literature's very being: structurally, literature is only a parasitical object of language; when you read a novel, you do not first of all consume the signified, a "novel"; the idea of literature (or of other themes subsidiary to it) is not the message you receive, it is a signified which you receive *in addition,* marginally; you sense it vaguely, floating in a paroptic zone; what you consume are the units, the relations, in short the words and the syntax of the first system (which is the language you are reading); and yet the "reality" of this discourse you are reading is indeed literature, and not the anecdote it transmits to you; in short it is the parasitical system here which is principal, for it controls the final intelligibility of the whole: in other words, it is this system which is "real." This complex inversion of functions explains the familiar ambiguities of literary discourse: it is a discourse we believe without believing it, for the act of reading is based on an endless exchange between the two systems: look at my words, I am language; look at my meaning, I am literature.

The other "arts" do not know this constitutive ambiguity. Of course a figurative painting transmits (by its "style," its cultural references) many other messages than the "scene" it represents, starting with the very notion of painting; but its "substance" is constituted by lines, colors, relations which do not signify in themselves (contrary to the linguistic substance which serves only to signify); if you isolate a sentence from the dialogue of a novel, nothing can distinguish it a priori from a portion of ordinary language, i.e., from the reality which serves it in principle as a model; but you can choose the most veristic detail from the most realistic painting, and you will never obtain anything but a flat, painted surface and not the substance of the object represented: a distance of substance remains between the model and its copy. There ensues a curious exchange of positions; in (figurative) painting, there is an analogy between the elements of the sign (signifier and signified) and a disparity between the substance of the object and that of its copy; in literature, on the contrary, there is a coincidence of the two substances (language, in both cases), but a dissimilarity between reality and its literary version, since the link is effected here not through analogical forms but through a digital code, that of language. We are thus brought back to the inevitably unrealistic status of literature, which can "evoke" reality only through a relay, language, this relay itself having an *institutional* relation to reality, not a *natural* one. Pictorial art, whatever the detours and dicta of culture, can still aspire to nature (and does so, even in its so-called abstract forms); literature has for its aspiration and its immediate nature only language.

This "linguistic" status of literature explains sufficiently, I think, the ethical contradictions which plague it. Each time we assign value, even a sacred value, to "reality" (which has hitherto been the concern of progressive ideologies), we realize that literature is only language, and a second language at that, a parasitical meaning which can only connote reality, not denote it: *logos* thus appears irremediably severed from *praxis*; impotent to fulfill language, i.e., to transcend it in the direction of a transformation of reality, deprived of all transitivity, forever doomed to signify itself just when it wants to signify only the world, literature is a motionless object, separated from a world in the making. But also, each time we do not *close* the description, each time we write ambiguously enough to suspend meaning, each time we proceed as if the world signified though without saying *what*, then writing releases a question, it troubles what exists, though without ever preforming what does not yet exist, it gives the world an energy: in short, literature does not permit us to walk, but it permits us to breathe. This is a limited status, and moreover one occupied—or exceeded—very diversely by our authors; take, for instance, one of Zola's last novels (one of the "Four Gospels"): what poisons the work is that Zola answers the question he asks (he speaks, declares, names the Social Good), but what leaves intact its energy, its power, is the fictional technique itself, in which the notation becomes a sign.

One could say that literature is Orpheus returning from the underworld; as long as literature walks ahead, aware that it is leading someone, the reality behind it which it is gradually leading out of the unnamed—that reality breathes, walks, lives, heads toward the light of a meaning; but once literature turns around to look at what it loves, all that is left is a named meaning, which is a dead meaning.

IV. *You have several times defined literature as an "unfulfilled" system of signification, in which meaning is both "posited and disappointed." Does this definition apply to all literature, or only to modern literature? Or again, only to the modern reader, who thereby gives a new function even to earlier texts? Or again, does modern literature manifest more distinctly a status which was hitherto latent? and in this case, what is the source of this revelation?*

Does literature possess if not an eternal, at least a transhistorical form? To answer this question seriously, we lack an essential instrument: a history of the *idea* of literature. We keep writing (at least since the nineteenth century, which is already significant) the history of works, of schools, of movements, of authors, but we have not yet written the history of literature's being. *What is literature?*: this famous question remains paradoxically a philosopher's question or a critic's question, it is not yet a historian's question. I can therefore venture only a hypothetical—and above all, a very general—answer.

An unfulfilled technique of meaning—what does this mean? It means that the writer is concerned to multiply significations without filling or closing them, and that he uses language to constitute a world which is emphatically signifying but never finally signified. Is this the case for *all* literature? Yes, for to define literature by its technique of meaning is to assign it, as its sole limit, a contrary language which can only be the transitive language; this transitive language is the one which seeks to transform reality immediately, not to double it: "practical" utterances linked to acts, to techniques, to behavior, invocatory utterances linked to rites, since rites too are presumed to open nature; but once a language ceases to be incorporated into a

praxis, once it begins to recount, to recite reality, thereby becoming a language for itself, second meanings appear, reversed
and evasive, and consequently the institution of something
which we call, precisely, *literature*, even when we speak of
works produced at a time when the word did not exist; such
a definition must therefore shift "nonliterature" into a pre-
history we know nothing about, where language was only
religious or practical. There must be, then, a great literary form
which covers all we know about man. This (anthropological)
form has received, of course, subsidiary forms, contents, and
uses ("genres") which differ greatly according to histories and
societies. Further, within a limited history like that of our own
Occident (though in truth, from the viewpoint of the technique of literary meaning, there is no difference between an ode
by Horace and a poem by Prévert, a chapter of Herodotus and
an article in *Paris-Match*), the institution and the "disappointment" of meaning have been achieved through extremely
varied secondary techniques; the elements of signification can
be accentuated differently, so as to produce very dissimilar
writing and more or less "fulfilled" meanings; we can, for example, strongly codify the literary signifiers, as in classical writing, or on the contrary give them over to chance, creating unheard-of meanings, as in certain modern poetics; we can
extenuate them, make them invisible, bring them, at one extreme, very close to denotation, or on the contrary we can exalt
them, exasperate them (as in the writing of a Léon Bloy, for
example): in short the *play* of signifiers can be endless, but the
literary sign remains immutable; since Homer and including
even Polynesian narratives, no one has ever transgressed the
simultaneously signifying and unfulfilled nature of this intransitive language which "doubles" reality (without joining it)
and which we call *literature*: perhaps precisely because it is a
luxury, the exercise of man's useless power to make several
meanings out of a single utterance.

However, if literature has always been, by its very technique
(which is its being), a system of meaning at once posited and
unfulfilled, and if that is its anthropological nature, there is a
viewpoint (which is no longer that of history) where the opposition of these two literatures—the literature of a fulfilled

meaning and the literature of a suspended meaning—recovers
a certain reality: this is the normative viewpoint. It seems that
today we accord a half-esthetic, half-ethical privilege to openly
unfulfilled systems, to the degree that literary investigation is
ceaselessly brought to the limits of meaning: it is, in short, the
explicitness of literary status which becomes a criterion of
value: "bad" literature is the one which proclaims a good
conscience of fulfilled meanings, and "good" literature is on
the contrary the one which struggles openly with the temptation
of meaning.

V. It appears that there are two divergent attitudes in contemporary criticism: on the one hand "critics of signification"
like Richard, Poulet, Starobinski, Mauron, Goldmann, all of
whom tend, despite obvious discrepancies, to "give meaning,"
and even ceaselessly new meanings, to works; on the other
hand, Blanchot, who tends to withdraw works from the world
of meaning, or at least to interrogate them in their silence outside of any technique of producing meaning. You yourself give
the impression of participating in both these attitudes. If this
is the case, how do you envision the reconciliation or the possible transcendence of the two attitudes? Is the task of criticism
to make the work speak, or to amplify its silence, or both, and
according to what distribution?

The "criticism of signification" you speak of can itself be
divided into two distinct groups; on one hand, a criticism which
gives a great plenitude and a very firm contour to the signified
of the literary work, since it names that signified. This signified
which is named is, in Goldmann's case, the real political situation of a certain social group; in the case of Mauron, it is the
writer's biographical situation during his childhood. This accentuation—or this nomination—of the signified develops the
signifying character of the work much less than one might
think, but the paradox is only apparent, if we recall that the
force of a sign (or rather of a system of signs) does not depend
on its complete character (fulfilled presence of a signifier and
of a signified) but much more on the relations the sign sustains with its (real or virtual) neighbors; in other words, it is

the attention paid to the organization of the signifiers which establishes a true "criticism of signification," much more than the discovery of the signified and of the relation which unites it to its signifier. This explains why Goldmann and Mauron, with their named signifiers, are ceaselessly threatened by two ghosts, usually quite hostile to signification; in Goldmann's case the signifier always risks appearing as the *product* of the social situation, the signification really serving to mask the old determinist schema; and in Mauron's case, this same signifier is difficult to separate from that *expression* so dear to the old psychology (which is doubtless why the Sorbonne so easily ingested literary psychoanalysis in the form of Mauron's thesis).

Still part of the "criticism of signification" is another group of critics we might call for convenience' sake *thematic* (Poulet, Starobinski, Richard); their criticism can be defined by the accent it puts on the "cutting up" of the work and its organization into vast networks of signifying forms. Of course this criticism acknowledges an implicit signified in the work, which is, roughly, the author's existential project, and on this point, just as the sign was threatened in the first group by the *product* or by *expression*, so it is difficult here to dissociate it from the *index*; but here, this signified is not named, the critic regards it as extensive with the forms he analyzes; it appears only upon the cutting up of these forms, it is not external to the work, and so this criticism remains an immanent criticism (which is no doubt why the Sorbonne still resists it somewhat); further, by bringing all its effort (its activity) to bear on a kind of reticular organization of the work, this criticism constitutes itself chiefly as a criticism of the signifier and not as a criticism of the signified.

We see that even in the "criticism of signification," there is a gradual evanescence of the signified, which seems indeed to be the crux of this entire critical debate; however, the signifiers are still present, attested in the first group by the "reality" of the signified, in the second by the "cutting up" of the work according to a pertinence which is no longer esthetic but structural, and it is for this reason that we can set, as you do, all "criticism of signification" in opposition to Blanchot's discourse, a language moreover rather than a metalanguage, which is why Blanchot occupies an indeterminate place between criticism and literature. However, while refusing any semantic "solidification" with the work, Blanchot merely shows the empty shell, the void of meaning, and this is an enterprise whose very difficulty concerns the "criticism of signification" (and will perhaps concern it increasingly); we must not forget that nonmeaning is only a tendential object, a kind of philosophers' stone, perhaps a (lost or inaccessible) paradise of the intellect; to create meaning is very easy, our whole mass culture elaborates meaning all day long; to suspend meaning is already an infinitely more complicated enterprise—it is an "art"; but to "annihilate" meaning is a desperate project in proportion to its impossibility. Why? because what is "outside meaning" is infallibly absorbed (at a certain moment which the work has the power only to delay) into nonmeaning which itself is of course a meaning (under the name of the *absurd*): what could "signify" more than questions about meaning or the subversions of meaning, from Camus to Ionesco? Indeed, meaning can know only its contrary, which is not absence but opposition, so that any "nonmeaning" is always a "countermeaning": there is no such thing as a zero degree of meaning. Blanchot's work, in criticism or fiction, therefore represents a kind of epic of meaning, an Adamite epic one might say, since it is the epic of the first man *before meaning*.

VI. *You have observed that Racine is open to every modern critical language, and you seem to hope that he will be open to still others. At the same time you seem to have adopted unhesitatingly the language of psychoanalytical criticism for Racine, as you adopted the language of the psychoanalysis of substances for Michelet. Apparently, in your eyes, a certain author spontaneously calls for a certain critical language; does this fact indicate a certain relation between that author and yourself (other approaches seeming to you quite as legitimate in principle), or do you believe there is an objective adequation between a certain author and a certain critical language?*

Undeniably there is a personal relation between a critic (or even a certain moment of his life) and his language. But this

is precisely a determination which the "criticism of signification" seeks to transcend: we do not choose a language because
it seems necessary to us, but we make necessary the language
we choose. Confronting his object, the critic therefore enjoys
an absolute freedom; it remains only to be seen what the world
permits him to do with it.

If, in effect, criticism is a language—or more exactly, a
metalanguage—it has for its sanction not truth but its own
validity, and any criticism can grasp any object; this freedom
of principle is, however, subject to two conditions, and these
conditions, though they are internal, are precisely the ones
which permit the critic to join the intelligibility of his own
history: on one hand, the critical language he has chosen must
be homogeneous, structurally coherent, and on the other it
must saturate the entire object of which it speaks. In other
words, at the outset, there is no prohibition in criticism, only
requirements and subsequently resistances. These resistances
have a meaning, the critic cannot treat them in an indifferent
and irresponsible fashion; he must on the one hand confront
them (if he wants to "discover" the work), but on the other
hand he must also understand that just where they are too
powerful, they reveal a new problem and thus oblige him to
change critical languages.

On the first point, we must not forget that criticism is an
activity, a "manipulation," and that it is therefore legitimate to
attempt at once the most difficult problem and the most
elegant "arrangement"; it is therefore fruitful that criticism
should seek in its object the pertinence which best permits it
to fulfill its nature as both coherent and total language, i.e.,
to signify its own history. What would be the use of subjecting Michelet to ideological criticism, since Michelet's
ideology is perfectly clear? What calls for a reading are the
distortions Michelet's language imposes upon the *petit-bourgeois* credo of his century, the refraction of this ideology in a
poetics of substances, moralized according to a certain idea of
political Good and Evil, and it is here that the psychoanalysis
of substances, in Michelet's case, has some chance of being
total: it can recuperate the ideology, whereas ideological criticism recuperates nothing of Michelet's experience of things:

we must always choose the most comprehensive criticism, the one which ingests the greatest possible quantity of its object. Goldmann's criticism, for instance, is justified, insofar as nothing, at first glance, predisposes Racine, an apparently uncommitted author, to an ideological reading; Richard's criticism of Stendhal is exemplary in the same way, because the "cerebral" submits more reluctantly to psychoanalysis than the "humoral"; it is not a question, of course, of prizing originality for its own sake (although criticism, like every art of communication, must submit to informational values), but of determining the distance critical language must traverse in order to join its object.

This distance, however, cannot be infinite; for if criticism is something of a game, it is in its mechanical sense that we must take the word here (criticism seeks to reveal the functioning of a certain apparatus, testing the articulation of its parts, but also letting them function, allowing them to play), not in its ludic sense: criticism is free, but its freedom is ultimately under the surveillance of certain limits of the object it chooses; thus, studying Racine, I first proposed a psychoanalysis of substances (already indicated by Starobinski), but this criticism, at least as I saw it then, encountered too many resistances, and I veered toward a psychoanalysis both more classical (since it gives a major importance to the father) and more structural (since it makes the Racinean theater into a purely relational game of figures). However, this unconquered resistance is not insignificant: for if it is difficult to psychoanalyze Racine in terms of substances, it is because most Racinean images belong to a kind of period folklore or general code, which was the rhetorical language of a whole society, the Racinean image system being merely a dialect of this language; the collective character of this image system in no way disqualifies it from a psychoanalysis of substance, it merely obliges us to broaden our investigation and to attempt a psychoanalysis of the period and not of the author: Professor Pommier is already asking, for instance, for a study of the theme of metamorphosis in classical literature. Such a psychoanalysis of the period (or of the "society") would be an entirely new enterprise (at least in literature): again, there must be the means to effect it.

These determinations may appear empirical, and they are

so in large measure, but the empirical is itself significant insofar as it consists of difficulties one chooses to confront, to avoid, or to postpone. I have often dreamed of a peaceful coexistence of critical languages or, perhaps, of a "parametric" criticism which would modify its language to suit the work proposed to it, not of course in the conviction that the sum of these languages would finally exhaust the truth of the work forever, but in the hope that out of these varied languages would appear a general form, which would be the very intelligibility our age gives to things and which critical activity helps, dialectically, both to decipher and to constitute; in short, it is because there might exist, here and now, in ourselves, a general form of analyses, a classification of classifications, a criticism of criticisms, that the simultaneous plurality of critical languages could be justified.

VII. *On the one hand, the human sciences, and perhaps other sciences as well, increasingly tend to see language as the model of every scientific object and linguistics as an exemplary science; on the other, many writers (Queneau, Ionesco, etc.) or essayists (Brice Parain) indict language and base their work upon its derision. What does this coincidence of a scientific "mode" and a literary "crisis" of language signify?*

Apparently, our interest in language is always ambiguous, and this ambiguity is acknowledged and consecrated by the very myth which makes language "the best and worst of things" (perhaps by reason of the close links between language and neurosis). In literature, particularly, any subversion of language is identified contradictorily with an exaltation of language, for to oppose language by means of language itself is always a claim to liberate a "second" language which is then the profound, "abnormal" (protected from norms) energy of utterance; hence the destructions of language often have something sumptuous about them. As for the "derision" of language, it is always extremely partial; I know only one example which actually hits the target, by which I mean makes us feel the vertigo of a wrecked system: Lucky's monologue in *Waiting for Godot*. Ionesco's derision deals with common-

places, domestic, political, and intellectual clichés, in short, it
deals with writing [*écritures*] not with language (as is proved
by the fact that this mockery is comic, but not at all terrible:
it is Molière putting on the *précieuses* or the doctors). Queneau is certainly a different matter: in all Queneau's complex
oeuvre there is no "negativity" with regard to language, but
rather an extremely confident exploration, based moreover upon
an intellectual knowledge of these problems. And if we consider
a younger generation, that of the "new novel" or of *Tel Quel*,
for instance, we see that the old subversions of language seem
entirely digested or transcended; neither Cayrol nor Robbe-
Grillet nor Simon nor Butor nor Sollers is concerned to destroy
the primary constraints of the verbal system (indeed we see a
revivescence of a certain rhetoric, of a certain poetics, or of a
certain "invisibility" of writing), and the investigation bears
rather on the meanings of the literary system, not on those of
the linguistic system; in technical terms, one might say that the
preceding generation, with surrealism and its epigones, provoked
a certain crisis of denotation (by attacking the elementary norms
of the system), but that this crisis (experienced moreover as an
expansion of the language) has been surmounted or abandoned, and that the present generation is particularly interested in the second communication invested in the literary
language: what is problematic today is not denotation but
connotation. Which comes down to saying that with regard to
this problem of language, there is doubtless no real opposition
between the "positive" and the "negative."

What remains true (and obvious) is that language has
become at once a problem and a model, and the moment
may be approaching when these two "roles" can communicate;
on the one hand, insofar as literature seems to have transcended the elementary subversions of the denoted language, it
should be able to carry its exploration more freely to the
real frontiers of language, which are not those of "words" or
of "grammar," but those of the connoted meaning, or of
"rhetoric"; and on the other hand, linguistics itself (as we
see already in some of Jakobson's work) may be preparing to
systematize the phenomena of connotation, to offer at last
a theory of "style" and to illuminate literary creation (perhaps

even to enliven it) by revealing its true watersheds of meaning; this consolidation designates a common activity of a classifying nature, and which we might call: structuralism.

VIII. *You have said that there is no technical difference between the activity of a structuralist scientist like Propp or Dumézil and that of an artist like Boulez or Mondrian. Is this similarity purely technical or deeper, and if the latter is true, do you see it as the beginning of a synthesis between science and art?*

The unity of structuralism is established, one may say, at the work's first moments and at its last; when the scientist and the artist endeavor to construct or to reconstruct their object, their activity is the same; and once these operations are terminated and consumed, they refer to the same historical intelligibility, their collective image participates in the same form of classification; in short, a vast identity comprehends the activities and the images; but between the two, there remain the (social) "roles," and the artist's and the scientist's are still quite different: here we have an opposition whose mythic force rests on a vital economy of our societies, the artist's function being to exorcise the irrational by fixing it within the limits of an institution ("art"), at once acknowledged and contained: formally, the artist is the separated man whose very separation is assimilated *as* separation, while the scientist (who may have had, in the course of our history, this same ambiguous status of acknowledged exclusion: the alchemists, for instance) is today an entirely progressive figure. However, it is quite possible that history will liberate or invent new projects, unknown choices, roles unsuspected by our society. Already certain frontiers are opening, if not between the artist and the scientist, at least between the artist and the intellectual. This is because two myths, though stubborn, are in the process if not of disappearing, at least of shifting: on the one hand a certain number of writers, filmmakers, musicians, painters are being intellectualized, knowledge is no longer plagued with an esthetic taboo; and on the other hand (but this is complementary) the human sciences are losing some of their positivist obsession: structuralism, psychoanalysis, even Marxism prevail by the coherence of their system rather than by the "proof" of their details: we are endeavoring to construct a science which includes itself within its object, and it is this infinite "reflexiveness" which constitutes, facing us, art itself: science and art both acknowledge an original relativity of object and inquiry. A new anthropology, with unsuspected watersheds of meaning, is perhaps being born; the map of human *praxis* is being redrawn, and the form of this enormous modificaton (but not, of course, its content) cannot fail to remind us of the Renaissance.

IX. *You have said:* "Every work is dogmatic," *and elsewhere:* "The writer is the opposite of dogmatic." *Can you explain this contradiction?*

The work is always dogmatic, because language is always assertive, even and essentially when it is surrounded by a cloud of oratorical precautions. A work can keep nothing of its author's "good faith": his silences, his regrets, his naïvetés, his scruples, his fears, everything that would make the work fraternal—none of this can pass into the written object; for once the author proceeds to *say* it, he merely parades what he wants us to believe, he does not emerge from a theatrical system which is always comminatory. Thus there is no such thing as generous language (generosity is behavior, not utterance), because generous language is nothing but language marked with the *signs* of generosity: the writer is someone to whom "authenticity" is denied; neither politeness nor torment, neither the humanity nor even the humor of a style can conquer the absolutely terrorist character of language (once again, this character derives from the systematic nature of language, which in order to be complete needs only to be valid, and not to be true).

But at the same time, to write (in the curiously intransitive sense of the term) is an act which transcends the work; to write is precisely to be willing to see the world transform into dogmatic discourse a language one has nevertheless chosen (if one is a writer) as the depositary of a meaning; to write is to permit others to conclude one's own discourse, and writing is only a *proposition* whose answer one never knows. One writes in order to be loved, one is read without being able to be loved, it is doubtless this distance which constitutes the writer.

1963

THIS BOOK was composed, printed, and bound by *Kingsport Press, Incorporated*, Kingsport, Tennessee. The text type font is ten-point linotype Electra, three points leaded. Display type is monotype Garamont, with Delphian Open Title initial letters. The paper used is Olde Style Laid, manufactured by the *S. D. Warren Company*. Binding materials include a matte tan fabric from *Arkwright-Interlaken, Incorporated*, and Kivar 5 Victoria (patterned pyroxlin coating over fiber base) by the *Plastic Coating Corporation*. This book was designed by *Elizabeth G. Stout*.